The Trading Edge
How to Trade Like A Winner

The Trading Edge
How to Trade Like A Winner

Rickey Cheung

WILEY

John Wiley & Sons (Asia) Pte Ltd

Copyright © 2006 John Wiley & Sons (Asia) Pte Ltd
Published in 2006 by John Wiley & sons (Asia) Pte Ltd
2 Clementi Loop, #02-10, Singapore 129809

This publication is designed to provide accurate and authoritative information with regard to the subject matter covered. It is sold with the understanding that the Publisher is not engaged in rendering professional services. If professional advice or other expert assistance is required, the services of a competent professional person should be sought.

Other Wiley Editorial Offices
John Wiley & Sons, Inc., 111 River Street, Hoboken, NJ 07030, USA
John Wiley & Sons Ltd, The Atrium, Southern Gate, Chichester PO19 BSQ, England
John Wiley & Sons (Canada) Ltd, 5353 Dundas Street West, Suite 400, Toronto, Ontario M9H 6HB, Canada.
John Wiley & Sons Australia Ltd, 42, Mc Dougall Street, Milton, Queensland 4064, Australia
Wiley-VCH, Boshstrasse 12, D-69469 Weinheim, Germany.

Library of Congress Cataloging-in-Publication Data:
ISBN-13 978-0-470-82216-6
ISBN-10 0-470-82216-3

Typeset in 11/13 points Garamond by Exceledit Services Private Limited
Printed in Singapore by Kyodo Printing Co (S'pore) Pte Ltd.
10 9 8 7 6 5 4 3 2 1

Contents

Preface

It is perhaps easier to describe what this book is not. It is not an academic tome on trading, with tonnes of theory. It is not a book sprinkled with quotes of wisdom from scholarly traders across the world. It is not a book meant to be a good read but of little practical value.

This book offers a peep into the mind of – if I may say so at the risk of being called immodest – a reasonably successful trader. It is borne out of my personal experience in trading. No theory. No bookish arguments. I simply want to share with you the secret of my success so that you may succeed too.

Is success in trading such a big deal? Yes, it is. It doesn't come easily. Consider this: despite the myriad of sophisticated technologies that aid traders today, and the easier and instant availability of knowledge, only 5% to 10% of traders are successful. Why? Because it takes years to figure out what works and what does not.

20 years ago, I plunged into trading without reading books. I failed many times. When I followed a trend, it would reverse and cost me. Then when I decided to follow the reverse trend, the market too would reverse, costing me even more. In other words, when I lost and wanted to make it back, I lost even more. I realized that it was easy to advise "follow the trend, cut your loss quickly and ride with profit" but it was very difficult to practice.

About eight years ago, I began reading a lot of books on trading in order to discover a way to cut my losses quickly. But the books didn't help much. That set me to think, learn and develop my own trading system which helped me find the "real" trend. With it came profit.

You must be able to observe the market through proven tools and strategies to be able to detect the "real" trend. That will help you discover your trading edge. This book will explain how to find it. Without it, you cannot trade successfully, no matter what else you do.

My RC systems and trading methods reflect my ideas. My approach is fairly simple: observe the market, collect data for hypothesis, and test it with the past and the present data before using it in real trading. If it works, then form a theory and continue to use it. If not, keep looking out for other strategies or trading methods that can be verified.

In 2004, I sent my system to John Hill (President, Futures Truth). Having seen thousands of systems, he was perhaps not sure if it was any different. But when he did have a look, he said: "The indicator used in your logic is unusual and I have not seen any system that uses similar indicators. I congratulate you on developing this excellent system."

Though this book deals mainly with Emini SP futures, it will also benefit traders in other markets. Reading about others' experiences in trading is always useful no matter which market you are in. Given the increasing linkages between the global equity markets, the new thinking might be relevant across market segments sooner rather than later. You may be into Nikkei, Hang Seng or FTSE futures or stocks, but understanding the Emini SP futures market in the US, the largest futures market in the world, would add to your strength. If there is a big fall or a run up in SP futures, you may use Emini SP futures as a hedge against your other equity stock portfolios or index futures.

Before we start on the journey to discovering success in trading, I would like to thank everyone who has been supportive of me and my trading career. My parents, Mr and Mrs Kam To Cheung, my wife Annie, my sister Rowena, and my brother Billy have been the principal drivers of my success. They are joined by Chelsia Chan Renee Tang, Cecilia Lim, TL Poon, Gordon Poon, Peter Poon, Naka, Kitty, Telmo Pinto, Dr. Brett

Steenbarger, John Hill, Mike the Traderman, Bill Gibbs, Pius Gal, Peter Aeiou, Ivy Tsang, Oded Rochman and Tiffany Chan. My thanks also go to all those who participated in the RC seminar and/or have used the RC systems.

I hope you will find the ideas in this book provocative and beneficial. However, don't take my ideas for granted. Think on your own – preferably, think outside the box – and discover the methods that will work for you.

Happy Trading!

Foreword

I've always thought of trading as one of the hardest ways to make an easy living. To the uninitiated, it all seems so simple. Buy low, sell high and all of that. However, once you become experienced, you realize that although it may seem simple, it is in fact very complicated. It requires not only hard work and discipline, but an ability to understand the inner workings of the market. This knowledge is what Rickey Cheung calls developing your trading edge. You must learn to see the market in a way that others do not. In other words, since trading is a zero sum game, you must know something that the individual on the other side of the trade does not know. More importantly, you have to be correct.

In this book, he demonstrates that to be a successful trader, you must hone the skills of your craft by constantly reviewing the data and your performance to find your edge. To assist you along this path, he explains a key discovery that allowed him to become one of the world's greatest traders. He not only explains what this edge is, and how to use it, but he also shows you how he discovered it. It is this latter point that I found most interesting.

Rickey explains that by keeping methodical notes, he was able to make his discoveries by continually reviewing what went right and what went wrong in his trading. By looking over his notes day after day, month after month, he was able to discover the patterns and indicators that were not seen by others. This is important because it is a step most traders do not perform. It is however, a crucial step. Only by honing your skills will you be able to develop your own edge and progress from a novice trader, to a serious trader, and finally to a consistent trader. Once you have become a consistent trader, you will be a successful trader.

William H. Gibbs
Former President, University of Phoenix

1

From School to the World of Trading

School Days in Hong Kong

To understand the way I trade, you need to understand *me*. So, here's the story of how I have been shaped into a trader.

I was born in Hong Kong in a low middle class family. My parents had enough money to buy a five bedroom flat, but we had to share it with others to make some extra money in rent. (This was common among lower middle class house-owners.) We occupied the two largest rooms and the other three rooms were sub-let to three families. We all shared a common kitchen and bathroom.

I was the eldest of the three children. Rowena was my sister and Billy, the youngest, was my brother. We had all the things that we needed for a decent lifestyle, such as new clothes, shoes and toys for the Chinese New Year. We could have even bought a television set but my parents thought it would distract us from our studies. So they didn't buy one. Sometimes we stood outside our neighbors' rooms and watched their TV. The place was small and obviously noisy, but we rarely had arguments. In general, there was more laughter and less woe at our house.

Between the age of three and five, I attended kindergarten for two years – Lower K & Higher K. When I was six, I went to primary school and studied from P.1 to P.6, and then moved to high school for five years from Form 1 to Form 5. Form 6 and Form 7 led to matriculation (which makes one eligible to attend universities in Hong Kong). "Munsang College" is the name of the school I attended from kindergarten to Form 6 for 14 years. Our school had a large playground, a rarity among Hong Kong schools.

1

I had a few friends in the school and knew them well. I still remember their names and faces vividly – after all, we grew up together for 14 years – but I have managed to keep in touch only with a few. Most were older than me, since I went to kindergarten at the age of three and graduated from high school when I was 16.

I had friends all right, but our situations were vastly different. They could afford to enjoy parties. I could have done that too, but I knew I had to work hard to get into university, an achievement in those days. So I kept to my work, most of the time. I was not among the toppers in the school but nor was I at the bottom. I was an average student but kept improving every year.

Munsang College is a Christian school. Every morning, we used to assemble in the hall or classroom. We would sing a hymn, pray, or the headmaster would make a short speech. He used to repeat an advice often: " *Do the right things at the right time* ". The profound advice applies to every life situation, including trading. (Perhaps one could rephrase it slightly for a trader – "*Trade the right trend at the right time!*".) The advice may sound simple but if you think about it, you would know that it is very difficult to practice.

School life was memorable. It offered a lot of extra-curricular activities, but my parents did not allow me to join because they cost money. The only activity I was allowed to attend with the support of my grandma was a weekly guitar class when I was in F.2. Actually, the course was free, but the guitar cost money! My grandma bought me one that was made in China. I was very happy and still feel grateful. This helped me make some money when I was in university at Houston. I taught guitar to a small class and made approximately US$50 per hour.

My father, a civil servant with the Hong Kong government, was in charge of public swimming pools and beaches. He was dedicated to his job and the family and when he came home from the office, he assisted us in our school work. He seldom took holidays except when we had school exams or fell sick. His position was not high, so he did not have a housing allowance like higher ranking officers. But after he retired, he was awarded a British Empire Medal (BEM) from the then governor of Hong Kong in honor of his dedicated service. He was probably the lowest ranking officer ever to get such an honor.

My mother worked as a kindergarten teacher till her retirement. Her hobby was to play "mahjong" once a week with her colleagues. My parents were both ordinary citizens doing their duties to serve the Hong Kong community consistently. They had no big ambitions, nor investments. Once, they were tempted to invest about US$3,000 in the Hong Kong stock market, perhaps when they saw that some relatives and friends made some money. Needless to say, they lost it.

University Days in the US

The first time that I traveled abroad was in 1974, when I went to the US to pursue a course in biochemistry at the University of Houston. I was 17 then. The campus presented a new environment, new friends and new challenges. One afternoon, just after I had arrived, a Chinese student asked me if I wanted to be a bus boy in a restaurant. I would get paid 90 cents per hour plus some tips. At that time, most of the international students would get a part-time job, mostly in restaurants. I worked four days a week from 6 pm to 12 midnight and also attended a full-time course at the university. Soon I was promoted as a waiter and got my driving license too. (I purchased a used car for US$500). I worked as a part-time waiter until my senior year when I got a job at the Student Center to look after the reading room. Nothing could be better. I watched others read, I could study too and got paid to do it! I also got another job as a part-time reporter with a local Chinese newspaper named *South West Chinese Journal*. Interviewing people, writing stories, editing, layout and artwork were also a good experience.

I studied hard throughout my college years, and worked hard to make money to pay for my education. I joined the Student Organization and became a student senator. I learned about the "Roberts Rule of Orders". Interacting with a number of intelligent associates, I developed my communication and speech skills. So much so, I even assisted in a congressman's campaigns.

Among the awards that came my way were the "Outstanding International Student Award" which recognized my contributions to all international students, "Mayor Award" which made me an honorary citizen of the city of Houston, and the "Chinese Professional Club Scholarship Award."

I attended the graduate school to study biochemistry. This is perhaps where the skills required for my trading years were sown – the ability to work alone at my own pace for long hours in a research environment. We used GCMS (gas chromatography and mass spectrometry) to identify chemicals. It still remains one of the best analytical tools in science.

One day my professor, Dr. Brian Middleditch, invited me to dinner with his family. He showed me his quote machine with charts in trading soy bean. He said there was a seasonal pattern. He tried to explain to me how to profit by trading in soy bean futures. I had no knowledge of the subject at all and was, in fact, shocked that an academic was trading in soy beans. But slowly, as we began to have more discussions, I was attracted to trading. We thought an MBA would suit my personality and would do well for my future. So I abandoned biochemistry and became an MBA student with the blessing of Dr. Middleditch, and completed the course in about a year and a half.

Before I got my degree, I wrote letters – like everybody did – to request job interviews. I still had 12 credits to complete in the summer semester before I could graduate. Just two weeks after I had sent my letter out, I got three calls for interviews: two in Houston and one in Chicago. The Chicago firm sent me air tickets for the interview. I got two offers but I still had my 12 credits left. They all wanted me to start training as soon as I could for a year, then I would be sent back to Asia to open a regional office. They were multinational companies but I did not know anything about their products. I picked the one in Houston that allowed me to work from 7 am to 12 noon for four months till I finished all my courses. The first four months on the job were in the factory, working with the assembly staff. I was trained in assembling the product.

To start work at 7 am, I had to wake up at 5:30 am and drive for an hour to the factory. After completing my work by noon, I would drive another hour back to the University of Houston. I studied from 2 to 6 pm. Then I rushed to get something to eat in a small Chinese restaurant. I could afford to eat out as I had a decent income. After a long day, I went back to the apartment to complete my course work. It was a tight schedule but I was happy. The ability to withstand long hours of hard work, which would come in handy in trading in my later years, was nurtured in those days.

I remember the day I took the final examination. After I completed my paper, I knew that I was going to become an MBA. I was elated beyond words, and never had that feeling again in my life till now, not even on the day when I made my first million at the age of 31.

The company put me through each department for a month, and then put me through a three-month training for the sales and marketing department. Then they said I was ready and sent me to Singapore where they had a sales office. The evening before I left Houston, I went back to the university alone and walked around slowly, looking at the different buildings where I attended classes. I greeted those I knew well at the University Center. But I did not tell anyone I was going to leave. I knew I would miss this place, the city and all the people that I interacted with. I knew I would not come back as many other places in the world beckoned me. I have not visited since but memories of the place are still fresh in my mind.

My Initiation into Trading

I was now an MBA in Finance, an expatriate with a nice job back in Asia. Life and work were both wonderful. I gained the respect of my customers and enjoyed traveling from country to country doing business as well as enjoying the food and culture of many Asian countries. I subscribed to the *Wall Street Journal* and read it everyday, a habit formed during my MBA years. One of my finance professors even spent an entire session teaching us how to read the *Wall Street Journal*. Besides the business news, I read the commodity pages, market comments and changes in commodity prices.

In less than a year after I was back in Asia, I opened my trading account and started to play with currency futures. "Play" is the right word to use since I was doing just that, without any research or clear understanding of the currency market. It was fun. The currency market was far more interesting than it is today since it was volatile and had more choices. Japanese Yen and the British Pound were my favorites. However, I lost money.

Novice: 1985 – 1990

In the early days, I was more like a gambler with little market knowledge. When I saw the market going up a little, I would follow the "trend" and sometimes profit too. Once I had a small profit, I would be content. Since I was afraid of losing the profit, I would take it and quit instead of going for something bigger. I did not know how to use a trailing stop or even a loss stop. Also, my brokerage firm in Hong Kong did not permit me to do that then. I also traded in currency futures and other commodities futures.

Tools, charts and market news were not available to me. Some tools were expensive. I had to do with a price quote which was available at a low cost of US$1,500 a year. But the price quote came with a delay of 40 seconds. My losing percentage was well over 80%. And month after month, the percentage was all losing but I continued trading. I never lost hope. I kept dreaming that one day I would be successful and make lots of money. Also, I told myself that if I can be successful then I do not have to retire and I can trade for a living till my last day. But for that, I had to acquire the required skills.

Learned Beginner: 1990 – 1995

I acquired more knowledge through lots of reading and some thinking. But I was still not taking trading seriously. It was fun, despite frequent losses. The only difference was that I was a bit more knowledgeable. But I still had no edge. When we don't have an edge, we are gambling. I was not able to detect the real trend or reverse trend to follow, and was not able to ride with profit and cut loss quickly.

However, with increasing knowledge, the results started improving too. I was able to win 30% of the time, but at other times, I lost. The 30% winning kept me going. However, with 70% loss, I was an overall loser. I would have perhaps given up. But the hope that I could make money some day prevented me from quitting.

As I got to know more, I became more aggressive. Sometimes I traded more than 20 times a day, taking small profits and suffering small losses. My broker was happy since I was paying a huge commission. I continued to experiment. Big losing days kept me awake at nights, as I was depressed about the losses. But within a day, I would recover and get back to trading again.

Serious Trader: 1996 – 2000

With years of continuous loss, the fun element was waning. The fact was that it was proving a negative-sum game after paying a high commission. But there were winners out there. One day, I began wondering why I could not be among them. The more I thought about it, the more serious I got about trading. I was not merely hoping to be a winner but was determined to be one.

But, how would I be a winner? I had no answer to this question as no one could provide it. From my own experience at school and at work, I knew I had to start working very hard in order to be successful.

I began studying and researching the market whenever I got time, even during holidays. I bought whatever trading books I could lay my hands on at bookshops and read them diligently, taking elaborate notes. I subscribed to all the data and charts that were available to me in Hong Kong at that time, to test whether the wisdom the books doled out was right. An important step I took was to start taking notes during the trading hours and writing down my views on why I lost and why I won. I reviewed my notes during weekends. I wanted to know what I was doing right and what was going wrong.

I tried not to get it wrong again and kept doing the right things repeatedly. More winnings came my way and my winning rate improved to 50%. However, I still lost more than I profited. Things that appeared simple now became more complicated. I learnt quite a bit about the market from the books, including terms and charts. But I was still not winning in a consistent manner.

I continued to face the same three problems that I used to face as a beginner. First, I could not identify the trend or reverse trend accurately. Secondly, I always knew only 50% for sure — it was like flipping a coin. Thirdly, sometimes I could cut loss quickly and ride with profit and felt like I was on the top of the world. But at other times, I rode with loss and cut profits quickly and felt like a loser.

I was debating several questions within myself. If I was losing due to lack of discipline, how could I be disciplined in other aspects of life, but not in trading? Why was winning in trading so difficult?

The first discovery I made was that my trading was better on Mondays and Tuesdays and then started to decline towards the end of the week. I thought that it was because I reviewed my notes of the previous week over weekends and was therefore more calm and assertive on Mondays and Tuesdays. The effect waned later and I began making mistakes.

Consistent Trader: 2000 onwards

I could not identify a trend, a reverse trend and choppy or tight range day. If only I could spot them with a high degree of accuracy, my winnings would improve to 70% or even 80%. The traditional, popular indicator that I had been using seemed not possible or probable. Also, I faced psychological challenges in cutting loss quickly and riding with profit more consistently.

I read more and took more detailed notes from the books that dealt with discipline, trading rules and money management. Each book offered a different solution. For example, some suggested finding a trading partner to make sure you are disciplined. Others suggested a few mental exercises. They all sounded logical, but in practice, they were not helping me.

Why? It was simple. Different traders have different mindsets and each has to overcome the problem in his own way. I had to think of a better way that suited *me*. I did not need to know what worked for others. I just needed a solution that worked for me.

I did not have TradeStation. I had not even heard about it then. I could not get historical data or a print-out for my record. I continued doing research using pen and notebooks, marking down the prices and all the other indicators a few times per minute. Tens of note books were used every week to copy the data.

It was not a waste of time. Continuous observation helped me spot the trend, reverse trend, choppy day or tight range day with accuracy of approximately 80%. I discovered my trading edge. I could win on consecutive days because I could detect the trend and follow it. The first obstacle was crossed.

Consistency still remained an issue. I could do wonders during some months but was trading terribly during the other months. Those who saw me trading really well thought I was a great trader. But I knew that something was still missing.

If I had my trading edge why was I still not a consistent winner? It was because I needed more practice to be a consistent winner. It is like participating in an international sport event like the Olympics. You need to practice, practice and practice. There was no other way to get better every day.

The formula I discovered was:

Trading Edge → Winning Strategies → Practice → Consistency

However, following a simple rule could often be the most arduous task. Month after month, my trading edge was proving to be effective, giving me more and more confidence, but some confusion over trading still remained in me. I had no one to consult or talk to. All the trading books I had read also did not tell me much. All I could do was to "think" and discover the solution myself.

When I look back, I realize it's the trading edge that worked, giving me the confidence in trading. It helped me overcome negative psychological factors such as greed, fear, anxiety, "frozen mindset", and inability to pull the trigger, which prevented me from cutting loss quickly and riding with profit.

The combination of trading edge and confidence enables one to see his indicator correctly. He can undoubtedly ride with profit. When one sees his market indicator going the other way, then one knows that he just needs to cut loss quickly. This becomes easier if you have a trading edge indicator.

I wanted to share my discovery. So I started teaching some friends about trading edge to see if they could also win. Also, I wanted fellow-traders to know about this and also learn from my experience. I e-mailed my ideas to some gurus. One said that I didn't stand a chance while others saw the results and wanted me to join their trading groups. One of them wanted to test it and I did well with a score of eight out of 10. He asked me to join his firm but it did not work out.

It was then I received a response e-mail from Dr. Brett Steenbarger. We had begun corresponding frequently through e-mails. Though we have not met yet, he remains a good advisor. He advised me to compose a trading system, so that I could verify my trading edge. It was almost three years ago. It was the first time I heard about a trading system and TradeStation. Even now, 95% of traders in Hong Kong have not heard about TradeStation or a trading system. So I hired an Easy Language specialist and a technician to assist me in programming my knowledge into the system.

It was a long and expensive process but through constant testing and verification, I became more and more confident of my logic and strategies. The strategies I used became simpler and more direct.

I have no knowledge of programming. When I think of an idea or new strategy, I have to go through each trading day for four to five years. I do this by hand. After testing one strategy by hand for one to two weeks I ask my technician to write out the ELD (Easy Language that is used in TradeStation). She would do it in 10 minutes flat and I could see how my work in the previous two weeks was no good.

I found that the simplest of strategies that gives the best historical performance is the most robust in actual trading. The fact that I do not know programming and do the test by hand is actually a blessing. If you simply run a program and test a new idea, there is no scope for any idea generation during the process of testing. When you constantly observe the market, review and practice, new ideas would be formed. Programming is no substitute to sound logic and actual trading experience.

This process went on for months till I had come up with my first trading system. After that, my confidence has grown substantially and many of my trading strategies have become very simple and direct. Research, back testing by hand and my lack of programming knowledge are what make my system good and what have turned me into a better trader.

From understanding to mastery, the only path is to think and practice because the systems cannot develop themselves. Also, systems have limitations. At the most, about 50% of your knowledge can be programmed into a system. That will leave out many strategies and experiences that cannot be programmed at all.

The simpler the system is, the better are the results it begets in real time trading. My strategies in trading have become very simple. The market is simple: it either goes up, down or sideways. So if the market is so simple, why deal with it using complicated strategies? It is simple, but not easy.

I teach my students all the strategies but some want even more. There is no end to this appetite. They must first practice on the ones I teach them, and master them before getting into more strategies. Once you master all that you know, you will do well. Then go on to think and learn new things one by one, continue practicing and absorb them into those you have mastered. This is the key to success.

Therefore, after teaching all the strategies, I also teach my students not to use strategies. It's a state of transition from being complex to being simple. Some are doing very well with it. It took me years to realize but for my students it will be faster because they have a teacher.

In the case of my search for a trading edge, the answer for your questions too should be right around the corner. Mastery is a process of evolution from a state of no knowledge and simplicity through acquisition of knowledge to the final stage of complete knowledge combined with simplicity.

Experience in trading doesn't diminish the need for hard work. I still work very hard, continue to do research and review my notes, and occasionally, when new ideas come up, they keep me busy in testing and evaluating results. I still prefer to do research with a pen and a notebook.

I still lose sometimes. There is no foolproof formula for success in trading. There is just a high probability trade and you will have to spot it. There is no certainty in trading; we just have to work hard, research hard and practice hard in order to excel.

If one has a trading system or a method that has a profit percentage of 70% and a profit factor over 2.00, in the long run, it is certain it will come out winning. But there will be times when the profit percentage will fall to a loss of 30%. If this situation lasts longer than your capital, you will lose everything, even if you have a profit percentage of 70% and a profit factor over 2.00 in your trading system or method.

After you get your trading edge, you have to use your money management skills to preserve your capital during the system drawdown period or your losing days. In the long run, your trading edge will take you to profit.

Even when you become a consistent trader, you still have to continue to take notes, review your notes, do your own thinking and continue to research, learn from the market and then practice what you have learnt, when you have the time. A trader is like an athlete. If you don't practice constantly, you will fail.

As in any other profession, hard work pays off in trading too. Sure, some traders are more talented than others. But in the long run, it doesn't matter if you are not endowed with great talent. I am not a gifted trader. I merely work hard, even during weekends. So be prepared to work hard if you want to take on the trading challenge. Remember, nobody in the world has ever died of hard work.

2

Learning from Mistakes

Making mistakes is inevitable in trading. Even a master trader makes mistakes occasionally. But one has to learn from one's mistakes among other things, not to repeat the mistakes. In this chapter we will look at some common trading errors and how to handle them.

Economic Data Release

Earlier, I used to be obsessed with the economic data that are released one hour before the US markets open, or during the time the markets are open. I would check with the broker to ensure the time and the expectation number, so that I could interpret the actual outcome and see if the market was bullish or bearish in the light of the figures as well as the expectations. I thought these figures and expectations moved the market most of the time. I also believed that other traders thought so too. This was a source of needless tension, till I realized that I was wrong.

The economic data release is surely important. But it is not for a trader to interpret the data. That onerous task is best performed, on the one hand, by experts and professionals and, on the other, by the market itself. And between the two, it is the market that is a lot better and faster and, almost as a rule, it is always right. Even as the experts and the professionals grapple with the data and attempt to explain and interpret them, the market begins to price the data within seconds, and after 10 minutes the pricing becomes clearer.

When I was only a beginner in trading, on a particular occasion, the CPI data release was higher than expected. The market immediately went down eight points in ES, as traders were worried about inflation. I called the broker and shorted the ES. Before the broker came back with my entry price, the market rose eight points again. Since the market always weighted the core data much heavier, once the brokerage price came back, I had already lost eight points or more.

So here is the rule: *don't hold any position 10 minutes before AND after the economic data is released.* The rule applies to Federal Open Market Committee (FOMC) announcements and other economic data releases.

It is very stressful and time-consuming to guess about the impending data and take a position before the data is released. First, this is gambling and not trading. Secondly, it is even worse if you have guessed it right and earned a profit from it, as it will make you want to guess more, and therefore gamble again. It would appear to be an easy way to make quick money. This kind of guessing blunts the trading edge and leads to bad trading habits, which would eventually lead to a loss.

Important Economic Data that will Affect the Market

1. Productivity
2. Unit Labor Costs
3. Red Book
4. Factory Orders
5. Durable Goods (Ex-Transportation)
6. Challenger Layoffs
7. Consumer Credit
8. Initial Claims (Four-week average)
9. Continuing Claims
10. University of Michigan Sentiment Survey
11. Wholesale Inventory
12. Non-farm Payroll (Thou)
13. Avg Hourly Earning (PCT)
14. Consumer Price (PCT)
15. CPI (Ex-Food / Energy)
16. Producer Price (PCT)
17. PPI (Ex-Food / Energy)
18. GDP (PCT)
19. GDP Deflator

20. Retail Sales (PCT)
21. International Trade (BLN)
22. Employment Cost
23. Industrial Production
24. Capacity Utilization
25. Jobless Claims
26. Federal Budget (BLN)
27. Leading Indices (PCT)
28. Personal Income (PCT)
29. Personal Spend (PCT)
30. FOMC Announcement
31. Minutes of FOMC Announcement

This is only a partial list. Any trader who has been in this profession for a while would know what it represents. However, don't fall into the trap of trying to "guess" about the economic data before they are released, or "interpret" their effect on the market. That is a perfectly avoidable waste of time and effort. Have patience and wait for the market to tell you.

Technical Analysis

Many books have been written on technical analysis. The field is replete with jargon. You might find traders communicating with each other in terms such as "stars", "upside gap two cows", "three black crows", "head and shoulder" and "double bottom" while talking about charting.

Should you bother to remember these terms? Not really. These terms are for communicating with others, so that they would be able to understand what pattern in charting you are talking about. If you do not want to talk to others, there is no need to remember these terms. Just observe the chart (if you want to know about charting) and you will be able to discover a few high-probability patterns on your own.

This process of discovering patterns for oneself is much better than trying to recognize some patterns in others' trading books. As you discover them through your own observation, the chances are higher that you would remember and apply them to real situations. You can name the patterns yourself, the simpler the better – like everything else in trading. Just simplify the pattern that you can recognize as an "up trend", "down trend" or "turn around". If you can see the chart and can tell whether it is moving up, moving down or turning around, you will be a good trader with your own chart patterns.

Use charting only if it makes sense to you and makes you feel comfortable. As far as trading is concerned, do not believe in others. Try out something for yourself. You have to be responsible for your own success or failure.

Ride with Loss and Cut Profit Quickly

While we all know we should ride with profit and cut loss quickly, often we indulge in the opposite. This is a process that every trader has to go through, especially in the learning stage. I have had my share of making this mistake many times. The tendency to "average down" aggravates it. To average down besides riding with loss means the trader will add more contracts when they are losing with the hope to even it out. When I was losing, I used to think that I would ride with the loss and give it a few more points and see if the market would turn. I had hoped to reverse all the losses. This is a typical loser's thinking process.

Here's where trading edge makes a difference. The trader with a trading edge and confidence would be able to tell when his trades are not going well so he can get out immediately. He can even reverse his position when he sees the trend confirming his indicators, so as to ride with the correct trend immediately.

When I started to think, I found that my notes told me that averaging down and riding with the loss often led to much bigger losses. I learnt my lesson. When the market was moving in the opposite direction to my position and my indicator showed that the market was right, I would reverse my losing position immediately and give the new trade a few more points, a higher probability trade than the one I just got out of. It risked the same "few more points". However, there was a big difference: one followed the trend, with the confirmation from one's indicators.

This strategy reversed the initial losing position and turned it into a winning position.

There is no reason why one should not reverse the position in such a scenario. Following the trend helps stop the bleeding and puts the trader back on the winning track. Even if a trader's indicators do not reveal that he has been on the wrong side of the trade, if the trader reasons out with himself, takes a close look at his note book, and figures out it is logical to reverse the wrong position, then he should cut his losses quickly and take a step towards success.

Switching from the habit of riding with loss to that of riding with profit is not easy. I used to force myself to switch off the computer price quote and go to sleep with a stop in order to cut loss. Once you experience how to make a profit, you will immediately move your stop to the point of entry, and then enjoy watching the trade. Then you would not have to force yourself to learn to ride with profit by turning off your quote machine. If you lose the four or five point profit on hand, it's fine. From this position, you cannot lose more. But you can make a huge profit.

Pick Tops or Bottoms

Every trader has tried to pick tops and bottoms. I used to do this very often before I discovered my trading edge. Most of the time, it was when I found the markets moving up or down significantly, especially after the US market opened. (It would be already up or down in Globex session for five or six points or even as high as 10 points.) I used to feel anxious since I was not in the trade yet and it would be too late to follow the trend. My anxiety would overcome reason and I would pick tops or bottoms in order to get ahead.

Sure, it made me feel good once I entered the trade. But later, when the market continued to go up or down, my anxieties would return and pretty soon I would find myself at the losing position. This developed into a self-destructive pattern, till I found my trading edge.

The discovery of my trading edge enabled me to tell with a great degree of accuracy whether it was really a top or bottom. If there was a high probability that it was reaching top or bottom, then I would pick the top or bottom and trade countertrend with loss stop. (Remember, you should enter a stop immediately after you enter a trade.) If I saw that it's not the top or bottom even with 10 points up or down, I would not pick tops or bottoms, but just follow the trend with a loss stop.

Herein lies a lesson. If you have not yet found your trading edge, don't trade. You would feel uncomfortable if you are long after the market is up 10 points thinking that it might be the top. It's difficult for you to take a long at that moment. It may not be the top. The best option is NOT to trade.

After reading the contents on RC 5 Seminar in this book, you would realize that you have a choice. If you study the indicator and the whole seminar, you would be able to research your own SP. In Chapter 11 (RC Trading Edge) you would see how my program is a method that can pick tops or bottoms with a high degree of accuracy. In fact, some of my biggest trading victories are a result of picking tops or bottoms.

To sum up, the trick is not to trade when the market "gaps" is up or down unless you find a trading edge that will help you to pick tops or bottoms with a high degree of accuracy. When the market moves up or down with many points and you still have no position, take a day off. Don't trade till you find a trading edge so that you can trade with confidence and a high profit percentage.

How to Handle Consecutive Winning Days?

Initially, when I won for three or four days consecutively, I used to feel elated. However, as I continued to win further, I used to become more anxious and worried for no reason at all. Only a small loss one day would relieve me of my anxieties and I would feel that I could start winning again. The uncomfortable feeling of winning many consecutive days subsided only with experience.

How to Handle Consecutive Losing Days?

I am sure all traders have experienced this, though the length of the losing streak would vary. Some may have experienced it for a few more consecutive days than others. I too have had my share of losing experience and have learnt from it.

What should you do? Some would suggest that taking a break will do some good. I disagree completely. A trader needs to be with the market everyday. He may not have to trade, but it is not good to take a few weeks or a few months off without paying attention to the market. He has to take notes, review them, practice and figure out the ways to improve. Remember, you don't trade the whole day. You trade only for eight hours, a third of a day. During the remaining 16 hours, you can afford to relax or unwind. That should be effective. Even if you take a vacation, you can still spend one to two hours watching the market, preferably during the opening and closing hours.

I would re-examine the consecutive days that I lost, find out why I lost and what I should do differently if I had the chance to do it again. I would look at my strategies and see if there is a 30% chance that it would not work in those losing days. I would continue to observe the market. Once I determine a better way to trade, then I would ask my technician to try to back test and see if the strategies would work in the past to confirm that they are good strategies. If it would work in the past, I know how to deal with a similar situation when it arises in the future. I work even harder on consecutive losing days.

The lesson: consecutive losing days are laden with lessons on how to trade better in the future. Don't miss them.

How to Trade with a Bigger Contract Size?

Bigger size than what you are used to could rattle you a bit. When you begin trading in bigger sizes, through discretionary or system trades, you could tighten your stop. For example, if you use a 10 point stop, you could tighten it to eight points so that you would feel more comfortable. After one to two weeks' adjustment, you can go back to your normal protective stop. Through experience and practice, you will soon be trading 10, 50 or 100 ES the same way you dealt with 1 ES. The point is that your strategies (and loss stop too) should not change just because the size has changed.

How to Handle a Loss in the Early Session?

When a trader starts with a loss in the early session, it is likely that he will lose more and lose big because instinctively he would want to even out as soon as he can. Even confident and experienced traders fall into the trap, if only occasionally.

When you become a good trader, you will be able to make it back on the same day as long as you have the patience to wait for your indicator to give you another high probability trade. If it does not give you this chance on the same day, you don't have to feel frustrated. You know it will come either the next day or the day after. The point is you should not act impulsively.

Remember, trading goes on every day. But you don't have to count your profit and loss daily and eventually lose big. Even an experienced trader, after winning many consecutive days, might give it all back on another day. He might average down and lose big.

So what should you do to turn the early session loss into profit? Take a short break and forget about the loss. Then take a clear look at the market and your indicator. Treat it as a new day. After all, the small loss is nothing compared to the many winning days you have had in the past and will have in the future.

More important, do not reverse your position and follow the trend immediately, as it may be heading to a reverse trend. Look at it afresh with no position, and then wait for your indicator to confirm the trend, and then trade with the same contract size as you had lost. You have a great chance to make a comeback or even turn it to a profitable day. It just takes confidence and patience to do that.

Psychological Factors

Trading is part of life and therefore the psychological forces and emotions that affect our lives affect trading too. It is not a bad idea to consult a psychiatrist if you feel there is a problem that affects your performance. Rooting out overwhelming and disruptive negative emotions quickly is essential for a good trader.

If you cannot do it through auto-suggestions, you should take expert help. Allow your confidence to overcome disruptive emotions such as greed, fear and anxiety.

It is important not to spend too much time purposelessly brooding over your negative emotions. It would not help you trade better. If you find it difficult to deal with negative emotions directly and quickly, divert your attention to research and practicing trading. Confidence will rise and positive feelings will take over.

You know that your trading strategy is based on sound logic and has worked well in the past. Then why not trade with confidence and peace of mind? If you are assertive, you can trade with ease. It is fine to lose because you know your system or method and have a high profit percentage. If you are confident, even if you experience consecutive losses, you know that you will win.

Two Interesting E-mails and Replies

These two instances can teach valuable lessons on how to avoid costly mistakes:

1) I got an e-mail from a trader whom I would call "Mount" narrating his problem. He was devoted to trading but he focused on the wrong goal.

He told me he has been trading for over 10 years on day trade Emini SP. He has learnt personally from many gurus listed in *The Market Wizards* book on a one-on-one basis. He once hired three PhDs to work with him on the system. He attended over 10 seminars in the US. He kept learning and searching, but he was still not successful and was about to lose his family and his house because he lost so much.

He asked me if I could teach him to make four points per ES a day. That was his goal for trading. Four points means $200 per ES per day. It's $4,000 per ES per month. If he traded only 10ES, he would have $4,000 per month. I told him he should focus on trading to make a profit on a consistent basis and not bother about how many points he should win per day. Fixing a profit target every day is bad for a trader's mental health. A trader just needs to do the right thing on a consistent basis, then how many points he gets per day depends on the market, his own knowledge and skill, or how powerful his trading edge is. If he was obsessed with four points profit a day, he would miss a lot of other things in the market.

A year later, he e-mailed to say that he had read my system somewhere. I called him since I knew he was still struggling. He had not changed a bit and asked me the same question: whether my system could deliver four points per day. I told him frankly my system could not do it on a consistent basis but it is the longer period that truly mattered.

2) Another trader, let's call him "Frank", said he had $30K as trading capital. He wanted to make $1K per day on trading and asked if I could help. I told him to do a bit of arithmetic: $1K per day is 20 points profit per day. If he trades 3ES ($10K per ES), it means that he is aiming at approximately seven points profit per ES per day consistently. If he succeeded, he would make $20K per month ($1K per day). In one year, he would get $240K (without even compounding); that is, he will have turned $30K into $240K in a year. *It is NOT impossible but it is not probable for "Frank" to do.* Afterwards, he e-mailed me, saying that he would set a more realistic goal for himself.

As in life, goal setting is important in trading . It must be realistic and must not add unnecessary tension during trading. Just do your best; the profit will come. Before you know, you may be making more profit than you set out to make. I have repeated these words many times but they are worth repeating: observe, think and practice. By the time you are through with this book, I hope to have these words planted in your mind.

3

Let Your Notes Coach You

Can you be Your own Coach?

Are you having trouble finding a good coach? Not to worry. There are few capable *and* available coaches in this business. The reason is not hard to see: coaching is time-consuming and is apparently not rewarding. A trader is likely to think that he should use the time to trade rather than coach others. But you still need guidance. What is the solution?

The solution is to be your own coach. I didn't have any coach. I simply observed the market, took notes, reviewed them on a daily and weekly basis and continuously learnt and profited from my mistakes. I became my own coach.

Write down what you observe and how you react to events and spell out the reasons for your entry and exit. Reflect on your notes. That should help you become your own coach.

Talk to yourself, as I do.

"Let's see what happens to the market.",

"Take it easy."

"Have patience."

"Now it's up, so you cannot short, unless you see your indicator is acting reversely or maybe with price confirmation."

"There was no major economic data today. The market will probably move in the normal range."

Being your own coach will make you more objective. Don't exchange opinions with others on MSN, ICQ, etc. Once you express a view, you may be unwilling to review it since your ego would get in the way. Instead, stay focused. If you have to give a new reason to terminate an old position in the market, you have to explain it. After that, the trade goes on and there is nothing for you to short or long.

Therefore, in order to trade well, do it alone. Learn by thinking through any situation. Friendship is fine, perhaps essential, but it should be confined to post-market hours. During the market hours, devote all your time and attention to experiencing the market.

I have stopped giving opinions on the market. Even when I coach students, I do not give them my views on the market. I tell them to think, make their own decisions and analyze if they work or do not work and learn from their mistakes. Later, I give them feedback on the situations and perhaps provide even an insight, which is a function of experience that they lack. But when they trade, they are on their own, as they should be. That is the only way they would become good traders.

My friends often ask me what I think of the market. I tell them honestly and repeatedly that I don't know because it would be bad for both of us to know *my* views. It's an avoidable, lose–lose situation. In trading, all of us face difficulties sometime or another which lead to losses. The causes for these losses may not be known, and even if they are, it takes time for traders to make corrections. My solution to this trading problem is simple: be your own coach.

How to do it?

Simple. Observe the market, take notes, and review them on a daily and weekly basis.

It may be simple but it takes determination. My students who practiced this advice usually traded better than those who didn't. As for myself, there was a period when I consistently made profit in the early session, only to give it all back in the late session of the day. It was easy to detect from my own notes and from the broker's statement. I could not fix this problem instantly but I kept thinking and reviewing my notes. After detailed reviewing, I figured that my entries in the late session were not of high probability – some were even unreasonable. It was different from my successful trades in early sessions. I thought that perhaps I had not seen the indicators well enough. So I tried to focus more but that didn't help. The results did not improve. This made me wonder, almost illogically, if my skill only worked in the morning and not in the afternoon session! But I knew that this could not be the case.

The question remained unanswered: why did I trade well in the morning but could not trade as well in the afternoon?

The Importance of Taking a Break

One day, I had to attend a celebration dinner in the evening (morning for the US market). I rushed back after the dinner and started trading. That day, I won easily (it was the afternoon session of the US market). My way of trading remained the same. It was obvious that the break had helped in some way. The next day, I traded during the morning session and after making a profit, went out for a walk, took a shower and returned to trading after an hour. Needless to say, I won.

The reason is not as important as the result of trading. You may have the best reason, but may still lose. In my case, it was clear that physical and mental exhaustion after the morning session was taking a toll in the afternoon session. Though I continued to be fully absorbed in trading, and my skills were intact, fatigue had set in and was leading to mistakes and losses. More effort to focus in the afternoon session meant higher stress and inability to trade well as fatigue took over at about 3:00 am Hong Kong time.

The solution: taking a break for an hour from trading. It should be a complete break. You shouldn't look at the screen at all. I still practice this since there is always slow movement in the US market during lunch. The last two hours are always full of action. My rejuvenated mind, without fatigue, helps me trade better. If it works for me, I am sure it will work for you too.

The Importance of Taking and Reviewing Notes

Taking notes during the trading session is a must. If we coin a phrase like *"Show me a person with good daily notes, and I will show you a good trader"* it will not be entirely out of place.

Whenever we commit mistakes, we tell ourselves that we'll

never let them happen again. Yet, mistakes happen repeatedly. There could be only two reasons for this. Either we are pathologically addicted to making mistakes despite being aware of them or we forget the situations that led to mistakes so they are repeated.

Solution to the former lies in approaching a psychiatrist for help. Solution to the latter lies in taking notes.

In fact, when you repeat mistakes, focus more on changing the habit rather than analyzing the root cause of the problem. That could take a lot of time and there is no guarantee that the result will improve your trading. However, in trading, the end justifies the means. You can find out the problem from your notes and figure out a solution to solve it. Think of a solution, and then move forward. You do not need to find out the root or cause of the problem.

The solution to the problem of making mistakes repeatedly is to practice harder and consistently. After changes are made, review notes daily and weekly. Do this until it becomes a habit. Your mistakes then become learning opportunities and you will become a better trader.

Each time you review your notes is a practice session. Through continuous practice, all gains and changes will be consolidated and you will trade better each passing day. Believe me, even now, after years of trading, when I look at some of my old notes, I find valuable new lessons in them. This is an undeniable truth: traders who write notes, review and practice always trade better than those who do not.

I use my notes to find out my problem and *think* of a solution to deal with it. After reviewing and practicing the solution to get rid of my trading problem, I am a better trader. So the set pattern is:

Take notes → THINK → Practice.

Here is a chart that should help you internalize the importance of taking notes:

Simple and Lack of Knowledge (unsuccessful)

↓

Education (gathering information)

↓

Thinking and Absorbing (internalizing)

↓

Simple with Knowledge (successful)

If you are new to trading, here are some suggestions:

- Practice is the most important thing you can do.
- Practice paper trade. For novice traders, paper trade can save lots of money. If you cannot profit from paper trade, why start trading with real money? I highly recommend paper trade until you can "honestly" make a profit. Only then should you start trading in real money. There is no argument about this.
- After a hectic week of five trading days, use the weekend to review the notes and get organized and to *think*. I used to spend 10 hours a day over weekends reviewing and organizing the notes and thinking of better ways to trade. You can then practice and review the previous five trading days, so you will imbibe valuable lessons and trade better than those who do not take or review their notes.

4

Should you Cut Loss Quickly or Ride with Profit?

Which is more important? Cutting loss quickly or riding with profit? How can you do it? If you know the answers, you have already crossed quite some distance on your way to success in trading.

Undoubtedly, cutting loss quickly should be your priority. If you don't, you will lose large amounts of your trading capital, if not all. You would then be out of the game. If you do not ride with profit, you will not make lots of money but the result will not be as fatal, but the result would not be any better either: you will still lose a large amount of your trading capital.

That is why I do not have any profit stop in my system or my trading. I ride with as much profit as the market is willing to give me. I am often asked: what is your profit target in each trade? I cannot and do not set a profit target. If the market has no target, why should I have one? It's not logical. When the indicator shows that the market is not going my way or is showing reverse signals, I take the profit before it evaporates.

In fact, what makes sense is not a profit target but a loss target (stop). Ideally, how much capital you commit in each trade should be based on your historical profit factor and profit percentage, how much capital you have as well as your own risk tolerance. You gain control once you place a stop loss.

Let me cite an example. One of my students trades 10ES per signal but his risk tolerance is only four points. So he sets a four-point stop since he feels comfortable with it. His stop always gets hit and then the market reverses his way. This makes him lose often and he cannot win big. I told him to change to a 10-point stop instead and watch the indicator to see if an earlier stop would do. But he cannot do it. He feels more comfortable losing with a four-point stop, instead of paying attention to the market with a 10-point stop that has higher probability of winning in the long term.

Should he see a psychologist? I don't know. All I know is that there are solutions if you trade right and you don't have to go to a psychologist. There is a simple alternative if he has a problem in using a 10-point protective stop: he will trade 5ES instead of 10ES and use an eight-point stop instead of a four-point stop. After this, his trade's stop does not get hit easily with bigger and more frequent winning days. He can trade at ease. With a protective stop that he is comfortable with, he can even take a short break or have lunch during trading, as there is a protective stop in his comfort zone.

The rules I teach my students are only pointers to solutions. They have to think and figure out what suits them most.

Rule 1: With even contract size (2ES, 4ES, 40ES, 100ES......) each entry, a 10-point protective stop should be placed immediately to avoid any sudden and fast movement in the market.

Rule 2: If there is four points profit, take the profit for half contract sizes. (If you trade 10ES, then take 5ES profit and leave 5ES to continue.)

Rule 3: Move the stop to point of entry of the balance ES contract and ride with the profit. Then watch the indicator carefully: if the flow is good, continue till the market closes; if the indicator shows reverse trend, then close it any time with a profit; if the stop gets hit, it will be a breakeven, but it is still a good profitable day because you have taken a four point profit earlier.

This practice will allow you to cultivate the habit of cutting loss quickly and riding with profit. Since you know that you already have a profit in your pocket, you can ride the balance contracts in a much easier way. The more you practice this, the more it will be ingrained in you as a habit. You would not even be conscious of it.

With a four - point profit, take half contract sizes of the profit. If you trade 40ES, then you take 20ES and move the stop to the point of entry. This will ensure a winning day and the balance contracts will ride with the profit till market closes.

This helps you trade with a relaxed mindset. I used to do this and switch off the computer and take a nap. This works well for me as my trading time is Hong Kong time, approximately 10:30 pm to 5:00 am (US central time 8:30 am to 3:00 pm). If I have already gained a profit and if my contracts are still gaining, I can hit the pillow without worries at 3 am instead of waiting till 5 am (HK time) for the market to close.

In short, this set of rules is effective in enabling you to have a protective stop while at the same time taking a profit. If you practice this as a student, your confidence will steadily soar with more frequent winning days. In trading, as in life, confidence is key.

Also, when you make it a habit, it becomes effortless. There is no strain on your mind. It is better than remaining disciplined, since discipline requires rigorous efforts and therefore adds to the stress. Making the right practice a habit helps in gaining a better mental frame for trading.

It's just like playing American Football. The ability to cut loss quickly is like having a great defense team. But that is not enough. The team with the best defense but little else cannot make it to the Super Bowl. You need to score goals too (make profit) to win. Ride with the profit is the offensive team. The trading arena isn't much different.

The 10-point stop is for protective use. If you see the indicator reversing, you should cut loss immediately (be it of four points or six points), so the 10-point stop rarely gets hit. But once you have a four-point profit, then you take the half contract sizes profit and ride with the balance with a stop at the point of entry.

Some experts talk about trading in the "zone". Now, the word "zone" has different meanings for different people. Some of you may have experienced "zone" in meditation. But to imply a similar experience in trading is a bit of an exaggeration. All I can say is this: find the trading edge and trade with confidence; you will succeed, with or without the "zone" effect.

I tell my advanced students to focus more on riding with profit. I advise them that it is not necessary to trade with even size contracts or take the four-point profit. When there is a four-point profit, I advise them to move the stop of all contracts to the point of entry, and follow it up with the observation of the market and indicators. If the indicator shows more strength, then add more contracts and watch it with focus. Calculate the point of breakeven of all contract sizes, as a few new ones have been added with different prices, and move all stops to the breakeven point. If it is hit, there would be no loss. If not, there would be a much bigger gain as more contracts are added with good flow.

However, this applies to a friendly situation. Do it only once for day trading as normally there is an average range. At the time of writing this book, the average range of the high and low in Emini SP futures is approximately 15 points. Of course, on volatile days, the range would be a lot more than normal, and on tighter days, a lot less.

Under normal circumstances, adding contracts once is good enough, as there is not enough time (intra-day) or room to add more for the second or third time. We will push to the limit but not go beyond it. Some of my novice students feel quite attached to the first rule because they have been using it for a long time: take half profit and ride half contracts. It's fine; they may do what they are comfortable with.

Advanced traders, however, are expected to use both methods wisely. In a choppy market day, they should use the first rule. (Take half profit and ride the other half.) In a trendy day or reverse trend day, they should use the second rule: add more contracts when the flow is good.

How can you determine a choppy or trendy market day? It's not easy. Many realize it only at the end of the trading session. I have a simple and effective way to determine it at 9:10 US central time, or even earlier. Read the contents of RC 5 seminars and see if you can spot the answer. I am sure you can.

5

The Agony and Ecstasy of Developing a System

S ince the introduction of RC systems, many traders have been surprised at its efficacy. So was I. I had approached the issue as scientifically as I could, and was focusing on developing my own trading edge. Finally, in June 2002, I succeeded. To check its effectiveness, I e-mailed my signals to some well-known traders. The feedback was exceptionally good.

However, I was still not totally convinced. My friend Dr. Brett Steenbarger told me to write down my trading strategies in a mechanical and systematic manner in order to verify whether I indeed had a trading edge. It would also help in explaining my system to others. I had little interest in computers then; writing down suited me fine. So with Dr. Brett's encouragement, I set out to develop my system.

I had no knowledge of programming with *Easy Language* (a programming language) or *TradeStation,* which were needed to develop the system. At that time, few in Hong Kong knew anything about these. I managed to hire an Easy Language specialist and a computer programming student. Ivy Tsang helped me program my trading methodology, and after she graduated, Tiffany Chan joined me and has remained with me till now.

It was like one blind person leading another. My strategies were unique and could not be found in TradeStation functions. So my specialist friend had a hard time understanding what I wanted to do while the student was trying to figure out trading. Despite their best efforts, it was a tedious and expensive process – I would have spent not less than US$50,000 in developing my system – with a lot of bugs and misunderstanding, but all the same, we were determined to make the project a success.

Upon Dr. Brett's advice to back test the system as far back as possible, I purchased data back to 1998. We back tested and perfected the code. Throughout the process, Dr. Brett analyzed the system performance report and made comments. So did some other experts I had contacted. All of them were of the opinion that while the system was good, better systems were available in the market. We would then go back to the drawing board to make it even better.

The most popular S&P day trading systems then got profits of $350 per trade. After eight months of writing, my system was getting a hypothetical profit factor of 2.5 with a profit percentage of 70%, but the profit per trade was only $120. In order to get more profit per trade, my system had to trade less and very conservatively.

Months of hard and dedicated work was not taking me anywhere close to the magic figure of $350. I was extremely discouraged but never thought of giving up for two reasons. First, I knew my trading edge was the best. The challenge was in programming it. Secondly, I had an enormous amount of time and money invested in the project and I just couldn't walk away from it empty handed. Nonetheless, my resources were fast getting depleted and I was racing against time to perfect the system before my savings ran out. Worse, since I was working more than 12 or more hours a day in developing the system, I had no time to trade and make money.

I attempted to program more of my trading strategies into the system but many of them simply could not be systematically defined. I was not sure if I could not communicate it well to the programmers or if they couldn't get my ideas right. In any case, only about 50% to 60% of my personal trading strategies could be incorporated into the electronic trading system that is fully automated. Suffice it to say that this was the darkest phase I have had after I discovered the secret of trading profitability with the trading edge.

One day, when I was examining the performance results that a trading expert had sent me, I suddenly realized a crucial difference in my system. My system was based on the eMini SP which has a dollar value five times less than the big S&P system that the experts were using. In other words, all these days, we were comparing apples and oranges. The results were obviously flawed. Even Dr. Brett had overlooked this, so he continued to push me to do better because it appeared that the results from my system were still far behind others available in the market.

All I had to do now was to reprogram my system workspace using the big S&P. Making the correction took less than three minutes and the result was an exceptional trading system that generated an average of $600 profit per trade – one that trades infrequently with the highest profits per trade – RC Success.

Upon the request of my students, I started developing another system, RC Miracles, which traded more aggressively (RC Success traded only once in three days at an average). By March 2004, I had sent my systems to *Futures Truth* for a four-month incubation period. They were released in October 2004 with RC Miracles at rank No. 1 and RC Success at rank No. 2. (*Futures Truth* tracks hypothetical results of most systems). (Note: Past performance is no indication of future results.)

Commented John Hill, President of *Futures Truth*:

"*Futures Truth* has looked at your model for trading the SP's. TradeStation performance showed excellent returns during the test period of around three years. Profitable trades were 66.9%, net profit of $39,062, and max drawdown, only $2,100. This is by trading one mini SP per signal. The indicator used in your logic is unusual and I have not seen any systems that use similar indicators. I congratulate you on developing an excellent system."

The lesson from my experience is this: good and robust systems are developed with a trading edge and not with programming, technical analysis or mathematics. In fact, RC Success demonstrates that a good system can be developed even without programming knowledge. The single most important ingredient of a good system is sound logic with good strategies. This is what sets the RC systems apart from others.

It was not serendipity or luck. I had to work very hard for the success of my systems. Now I find great pleasure in teaching others to trade the Emini successfully using my strategies that I painstakingly learned over the years, and in licensing my systems for other traders to use as a trading tool to assist them.

My first system (RC Success 1) took me almost a year to complete. Later, this incubation time had shortened. When I develop a system, I do so with a new idea or new set of strategies. Sure, there are bound to be about 10% or 20% similarities, but I don't add a few strategies to an existing system with the aim of packaging it in a new name. Beyond RC Success and RC Miracles, I have developed new systems such as RC Winners, RC Stars, RC Chance, and so on. They all use different strategies and different indicators for different market conditions because they serve different purposes.

After my systems RC Success and RC Miracles were ranked No. 1 and No. 2 by *Futures Truth*, I got many subscribers. The number of e-mails I received kept growing. Brokerage firms were after me to market them more. But it only takes two months drawdown and the developer would lose one-third to one-half of the customers.

When Others Lose Confidence in Your System

Traders experience consecutive winning or losing days. So would systems. At times, even those close to you, including your students, would lose confidence in you and your system. What should you do?

In such a situation, I would keep quiet, do more research and testing, and work on finding an answer to why the system has consecutive losing days that it never has had before. Is it because the trading edge no longer exists? (It could not be because it has been built with sound logic.) If it turns out that the same set of strategies have a profit percentage of 70% but they now have 30% loss consecutively, rather than randomly, I would not lose sleep over it and continue to carry on trading when I see the indicator showing high probability, taking notes, reviewing my system and my strategies.

In fact, when everyone loses faith in you is the time to prove your mettle, time to prove that you have developed a great system.

Every system developer will experience disheartening moments at some point of time. Facing the adversity with confidence and perseverance will further develop the trader or system developer to be more successful. When you face consecutive losing days, which I am sure you will, please continue to research and work hard. You are the only one who can pull yourself out and be a winner again.

Joys and agonies happen in all professions, but in trading they happen with certain acuteness. If you want to become a system developer, do not optimize the system to get a smooth equity curve, and then fret over the scorn heaped on you when the system's performance is bad. You don't have to defend your system against every single criticism. If it's robust, it will defend itself. You just make sure the users understand the risk of trading the system.

System users, like traders, have to be responsible for their own buying or selling decisions and consequently for their successes and failures. Some may not do so, but there are many honorable users who know that they should take responsibility for their trades. They will not blame the system when it loses. They know what trading is, what the risk is and the trade-off between the risk and the return.

Do you want to become a system developer? I would strongly urge you to do so. Developing a system is a vital process for becoming a successful trader. It will inject tremendous confidence in you. You could develop it for your own use or for others. But the process of doing it is valuable to both new and experienced traders.

I am sure that everyone reading this book is a better programmer than I am. Your programming skills are a bonus to your trading edge. But remember not to mistake this to be a substitute for your trading edge and ability to work hard.

6

Develop a System and
Evolve into a Better Trader

Dr. Brett offered perhaps the most unforgettable piece of advice in my entire trading career: "*Write the system and see if you really have an edge.*"

Developing a system makes you think in a structured way, which then becomes a habit. Why do some strategies work and others don't? Why do some strategies work only for specific market conditions? Why is the profit factor low? Why is the profit per trade low? When you think on these issues, you would perhaps realize some of the mistakes you made. You might change your views and may develop the habit of using only verified and tested strategies in trading.

This thinking and verification process will add to your confidence. When you use only a verified strategy in trading, you are more relaxed and at ease. This will help you evolve into a more consistent trader, even if your trading strategies remain the same. Success cannot be far away when you are both confident and consistent.

In this process, you would make amazing discoveries in trading. Like, I discovered that trading many times a day with a trading edge is still not as good as trading only once or twice a day. This is verifiable by back testing TradeStation's historical data. If someone had told me earlier that it would be better if I traded only twice or thrice a day, I might not have agreed. When I verify the data and the results show that it is true, there is no dispute. I have to agree.

The process also helps finding out the strength and weakness of my trading edge. There are days of tight range when it is not worth trading at all. Oversold and overbought market situations could also be difficult to trade. An oversold situation may lead to more oversold situations, or the market may bounce back quickly. Ditto an overbought situation. When I realize that in a certain market condition I cannot win at all, I stop trading. Back testing and verifying the data may help in identifying such situations as they arise.

When I don't find a trading edge, I will avoid trading until my continual research leads me to an edge. Then I will trade. I strongly believe that difficult market conditions help you improve skills and systems. By avoiding low probability trades and by trading only when you have a definite edge, your profitability improves. Doing so consistently is the surest way to becoming a better trader.

If you have a good trading method, put it to test. First, determine if it is good. Secondly, find out how good it is. Finally, figure out a way to make it a better trading method. You can do this with the help of programming, or by hand like I did. I believe that doing it by hand is a relatively better way to learn.

The learning curve or experience is irreplaceable. You begin by simply recording your trading methods into the system. Over time, through the development process, you will make changes in the original version of your trading system to improve it. This happens because you are constantly thinking and researching. When your trading system improves, so will you, as a trader.

Do you now get the importance of Dr. Brett's advice? It does not matter if your trading rule is simple. Just write it down, back test it – by hand, if you can. Within a short time, you would find your trading methods improving.

Remember, even after finding your trading edge, you have to continue to practice and research to keep improving. This is especially true when you face conditions in which you don't have a trading edge at present and cannot win. You cannot afford to ignore these conditions. Continue to research till you find an edge. It is the lack of this attitude to continual research that has pulled down many great traders. Be relentless in research. The more conditions you research, the higher the chances of your success in the future.

I did not trade well in two market conditions. One was when the market gap was down on opening. My success rate was low. The other one was "tight range but choppy" condition. I tried to avoid trading in these conditions but continued to research them. I developed many strategies but they all failed. Finally, after two and a half years of continual thinking and researching, I got it right. Now I can trade with confidence in both market conditions as I have discovered the trading edge with 80% profit percentage and high profit factor.

After you write your system, continue to improve its strategies by verification. You become a better trader every time you discover a new strategy that passes the back test and the verification process.

Here are some common mindsets of traders which could pose problems. All of them can be taken care of by writing your own system or your own set of rules.

Trigger Shy

Some traders simply cannot pull the trigger. They would be afraid of entering an order even if the market conditions meet their trading criteria. This is mainly due to lack of confidence, perhaps aggravated by a few losing experiences in the past. If you have developed your system, you will enter the trade when the market meets your expectations, without any irrational fear. Your experience would tell you that you have a good winning probability.

Impulsive

It is common to find traders jumping into trading impulsively. When the market is up, they are afraid of missing the tide; and when it is down, they are afraid of losing more. A good system will calm an overactive trader and inject a lot of patience into his brain. When you develop your own system, if your entry conditions are met, you enter the market. Otherwise, you don't. Period. You will also become more patient as you will be watching your system signals rather than the quote machine prices.

Being impulsive is the best way to ensure averaging down in a losing trade. Since the entry is not of high probability, chances are that the market will turn the other way after the impulsive trader's entry. He will keep adding contracts to the losing trade in the hope that when the market turns, he would make a huge profit. But the market might continue its direction and not reverse. The trader will lose big because he is averaging down on a losing trade.

With your own system, you are less likely to trade prematurely, so your chances of averaging down will be reduced. Since you will be confident, even when the trade is losing, you will not average down. You will let it stop by itself as a stop has been built into the system. You know that your system will perform the next day and bring you profits. Some traders make brilliant profits but lose it all in one careless trade. Your trading edge system is the solution to this problem.

Overtrading

Some traders enter a position, become nervous, don't pay attention to the market and eventually make huge losses. After developing your system, you know the statistical edge is on your side. You know your max drawdown of the particular trade and the probability of the trade. You will remain relaxed and take the trade when it comes since you have simulated the experience while writing the system. You have an in-built stop in your system and probably use a trailing stop to ride with profit. You have done it mechanically and verified it many times. It is a habit now.

Conclusion

Start writing your system now. Then, continually monitor it, research it and refine it. The time you spend on the system is like practicing real trading, like a simulation game. Believe me, immense benefits that you have not thought of before will follow.

7

How to Evaluate a Good Trading System

A good system can be defined by three characteristics:
1) A sound logic.
2) Ability to convert this logic into a program with a trading edge, which includes a trading signal and stops.
3) Robust and forward-looking characteristics including a trading indicator that is logical and sustainable in the future.

A Sound Logic is the Foundation of the System.

The word *sound* is crucial. Everything else rests on sound logic. If that is lacking, then great discoveries by the trader about correlations among various factors are useless. A statistical edge without sound logic is meaningless. Only when it combines with sound logic does it become a trading edge. How effective the system is depends on how sound the logic is.

Ability to Convert this Logic into a Program with a Trading Edge

An architect may have a blueprint for a great building. It is on the drawing board. When he meets the structural engineers, he may find that some of the plans cannot be put into practice. So he may have to compromise and find other solutions for the construction project. When the project is completed, it will differ from what was set on the drawing board.

This happens often in trading. Consider, for example, the speed of price movements of indicators. I see the changes every second in the quote machine, but to convert that into strategies and program is impossible. So I have to find ways of doing it to arrive at the same result, perhaps by using indirect measurements.

Robust and Forward Looking Characteristics

Among the platforms for trading, perhaps the most popular is TradeStation. It provides historical data, all kinds of indicators, and uses "Easy Language" to write programs. This single-window service has enabled traders to create reality-simulating programs. Professional "Easy Language" specialists charge about US$100 to US$200 per hour. Normally, writing a program takes about 15 hours, and fine-tuning may take another 15. You have to be careful here since a programmer may not really understand how you want to trade and may misinterpret your ideas.

People often ask me why I didn't develop trading systems for other stock index futures or currency futures. The reason is obvious. You can trade or develop trading systems only when you have a trading edge. I have my trading edge in SP futures, so I just write systems for this market.

When I look at *Futures Truth* magazine, I do not find any system that can be ranked as the best across markets. This confirms my view that each market needs different skills and trading edges. Some argue that if a system is good, then it must apply to a variety of markets. This is NOT true. It may only be valid when one uses popular market indicators and analytical tools like MACD and RSI. But that's about it. Would you ask a cardiologist to prescribe medicines to you for a knee ailment? You won't. That logic applies here too.

Hypothetical Performance Report of RC Success

Here is a hypothetical performance report of RC Success 1 for your reference. It will show you how to interpret a hypothetical performance report of a day trade ES system. This is a quick interpretation guide for new users. A quick look at the following five items will give you a general picture of the trading system:

a) **Profit factor**: Most systems average from 1.5 to 2.5 – 1.5, means for $1 invested, it gives $1.50 return. The higher the better. If the value goes too high, the system must have fewer trades, or look for high-probability trades only. There is risk that the high probability trade occurs too infrequently.

b) **Percentage profitable:** The usual range is 45% to 75%. The higher the better but it has to match the average trade net profit and the profit factor. If the system wins 80% with only $20 profit per trade, but the losing trade costs $90 per trade, then it's like writing options. You would win for 10 months, but lose it all in two months.

c) **Average trade net profit:** $40 to $120 after commission and slippage. If the system reports do not include commission and slippage, the user has to make deductions himself and check. (Commission ranges from $2.50 to $30 per ES r/t or higher.) The user has to do his calculations.

d) **Max. trade drawdown**: This is how much maximum loss per trade for the system in historical hypothetical performance. Please note that it is *historical*, future drawdowns may be more. Remember, the worst drawdown has yet to come.

e) **Equity curve:** Just a quick look to see if the equity curve is smooth, so the system performance will be more consistent if it generates a smooth 45 degree equity curve.

You may do more detailed analysis with the trade list and other money management software to see if it fits your need. Ask for the actual trading result. If the actual trading result is close to the past hypothetical report, then you have got a system that you can trade on. The majority of trading systems available will have worse performances compared to the hypothetical ones. If you find one that gives out close or better actual trading performance, compare it with the hypothetical one. Take a closer look at it. It may be worth it if the developer agrees to lease or sell to you.

The key is the actual trading figures besides the hypothetical back test. Usually, system developers do not provide this, perhaps because they don't have them. If the actual trading figures match the hypothetical back test and can profit in real time trading, then you may consider that system for trading. An alternative is to get a hypothetical ranking report from *Futures Truth*. It may cost you

$20 or so. Given that you are likely to invest thousands of dollars, it is worth it. If the system has been tracked by *Futures Truth*, the longer the better. Then it is as close to actual trading results as you can get. As *Futures Truth* tracks the hypothetical performance of the system for months or years, it is better than any report that your developer may send.

When you look at the figures closely, you will discover more valuable information that suits your immediate need. Also, the smoother the equity curve, the better it is. Some fund managers use data such as the Sharpe ratio, number of trades, percentage win, K ratio, and the correlations between different systems if they are running a portfolio. You may read a lot of these but always remind yourself that *"past performance is no indication of future results"*.

Here is a story of my friend who seemed to have got everything right but actually got it all wrong. Nine months ago, he came across an *apparently* good day trade ES system. It seemed to have all the five key indications of a good system. It had a profit factor above 5.0; its percentage profitable was above 70%; its average trade net profit was $120; max trade drawdown was very low; and it had a beautiful smooth equity curve. And it traded a few times a day, and did not have a single losing month in the past five years. Obviously, my friend was excited and paid the developer $25,000 and got a copy of the system to trade.

What followed was a debacle. The system had six consecutive losing months, and my friend was lucky to get out after the third losing month. So he lost capital and the $25,000 he paid.

What went wrong? Because for a day trade system that traded a few times a day, to have a profit factor of 5.0 was improbable. In fact, if such a system worked, the developer would have sold it for $250K or more and not $25K, because someone could make millions by trading for hedge funds with this system. My friend did not ask for actual trading results. If there were no actual trading reports, he should have asked for a *Futures Truth* ranking report. The developer probably did not have it either. If you meet such developers, just run away. Your capital is at stake.

Moral of the story: please be careful before committing capital to lease or trade a system.

Hypothetical Performance Report of RC Success
(No commission and slippage included)
Net profit: $78,775.00
Profit factor: 2.04
Percent profitable: 61.22%
Average trade net profit: $89.31

Commission - This is the total amount of commission your broker will charge you for all trades during the specified period.

Slippage - This is used as a safety cushion for historically simulating the difference in price from when you place an order to when the order is actually filled, for all trades during the specified period of this trading strategy

Net Profit - This value is the net profit or loss during the specified period. Net Profit = Gross Profit + Gross Loss

Profit factor - This value is calculated by dividing Gross Profit by Gross Loss. By definition, a value greater than 1 means the trade have a positive net profit.

Percent profitable - This is the percentage of the completed trades that were profitable, during the specified period. Percent Profitable = Winning Trades divided by Total Number of Trades.

Average trade net profit - Average Trade Net Profit = Total Net Profit divided by Total Number of Trades.

TradeStation Performance Summary			Collapse ≈
	All Trades	**Long Trades**	**Short Trades**
Total Net Profit	$78,775.00	$38,337.50	$40,437.50
Gross Profit	$154,500.00	$82,350.00	$72,150.00
Gross Loss	($75,725.00)	($44,012.50)	($31,712.50)
Profit Factor	2.04	1.87	2.28
Open Position P/L	$0.00	$0.00	$0.00
Select Total Net Profit	$61,812.50	$30,425.00	$31,387.50
Select Gross Profit	$137,537.50	$74,437.50	$63,100.00
Select Gross Loss	($75,725.00)	($44,012.50)	($31,712.50)
Select Profit Factor	1.82	1.69	1.99
Adjusted Total Net Profit	$67,818.53	$30,355.52	$32,919.25
Adjusted Gross Profit	$147,851.38	$77,657.67	$67,413.12
Adjusted Gross Loss	($80,032.84)	($47,302.15)	($34,493.87)
Adjusted Profit Factor	1.85	1.64	1.95
Total Number of Trades	882	512	370
Percent Profitable	61.22%	60.16%	62.70%
Winning Trades	540	308	232
Losing Trades	309	179	130
Even Trades	33	25	8
Avg. Trade Net Profit	$89.31	$74.88	$109.29
Avg. Winning Trade	$286.11	$267.37	$310.99
Avg. Losing Trade	($245.06)	($245.88)	($243.94)
Ratio Avg. Win:Avg. Loss	1.17	1.09	1.27
Largest Winning Trade	$1,887.50	$1,887.50	$1,825.00
Largest Losing Trade	($600.00)	($600.00)	($537.50)
Largest Winner as % of Gross Profit	1.22%	2.29%	2.53%
Largest Loser as % of Gross Loss	0.79%	1.36%	1.69%
Net Profit as % of Largest Loss	13129.17%	6389.58%	7523.26%
Select Net Profit as % of Largest Loss	10302.08%	5070.83%	5839.53%
Adjusted Net Profit as % of Largest Loss	11303.09%	5059.25%	6124.51%
Max. Consecutive Winning Trades	11	9	11
Max. Consecutive Losing Trades	6	4	4
Avg. Bars in Total Trades	50.47	50.62	50.27
Avg. Bars in Winning Trades	54.02	54.57	53.30
Avg. Bars in Losing Trades	45.57	45.98	45.00
Avg. Bars in Even Trades	38.30	35.16	48.13

Table 7.1 Hypothetical Performance Report of RC Success

Continue from page 48

Max. Shares/Contracts Held	1	1	1
Total Shares/Contracts Held	882	512	370
Account Size Required	$4,087.50	$3,300.00	$3,287.50
Total Slippage	$0.00	$0.00	$0.00
Total Commission	$0.00	$0.00	$0.00
Return on Initial Capital	78.77%		
Annual Rate of Return	11.09%		
Buy & Hold Return	(2.74%)		
Return on Account	1927.22%		
Avg. Monthly Return	$920.00		
Std. Deviation of Monthly Return	$1,196.97		
Return Retracement Ratio	0.30		
RINA Index	3591.88		
Sharpe Ratio	0.61		
K-Ratio	n/a		
Trading Period	5 Yrs, 2 Mths, 25 Dys, 2 Hrs, 30 Mins		
Percent of Time in the Market	9.21%		
Time in the Market	5 Mths, 23 Dys, 5 Hrs, 10 Mins		
Longest Flat Period	11 Dys, 18 Hrs, 25 Mins		
Max. Equity Run-up	$80,987.50		
Date of Max. Equity Run-up	05/19/06 10:15		
Max. Equity Run-up as % of Initial Capital	80.99%		
Max. Drawdown (Intra-day Peak to Valley)			
Value	($5,062.50)	($3,462.50)	($4,275.00)
Date	09/19/02 13:30		
as % of Initial Capital	5.06%	3.46%	4.28%
Net Profit as % of Drawdown	1556.05%	1107.22%	945.91%
Select Net Profit as % of Drawdown	1220.99%	878.70%	734.21%
Adjusted Net Profit as % of Drawdown	1339.63%	876.69%	770.04%
Max. Drawdown (Trade Close to Trade Close)			
Value	($4,087.50)	($3,300.00)	($3,287.50)
Date	09/18/02 10:35		
as % of Initial Capital	4.09%	3.30%	3.29%
Net Profit as % of Drawdown	1927.22%	1161.74%	1230.04%
Select Net Profit as % of Drawdown	1512.23%	921.97%	954.75%
Adjusted Net Profit as % of Drawdown	1659.17%	919.86%	1001.35%
Max. Trade Drawdown	($837.50)	($837.50)	($787.50)

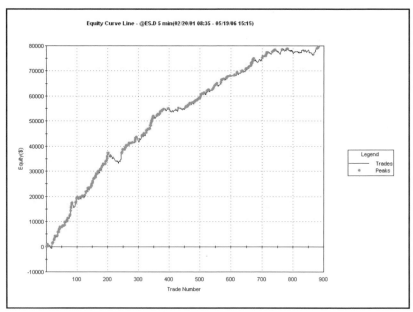

Figure 7.1 Performance graph - Equity Curve Line

Source: Created by TradeStation

Figure 7.1 is a performance graph (equity curve) that tally a strategy's individual trades to present in a time-line of trade-by-trade results. The graph examine the same basic monthly, annual or rolling period information as in the annual, monthly, weekly, and daily tabs, but in a graphic format.

8

Should a Trader Outsmart
His System?

I f the trading system is mechanical, then all you have to do is to follow its rules. If not, you should apply your own entry and exit rules. If you are following someone else's system without knowing the logic, you have to follow a set of rules consistently to know the system's efficacy.

Some rules apply, irrespective of the system you follow:

- Add contracts only when the system is having a run-up or you have higher equity.
- Never add contracts when the system is having a drawdown. Any system will have drawdown.
- Make your own rules to manage your capital based on your corpus size, your needs and risk tolerance. You might feel comfortable in trading one ES contract with $10,000. It's fine. But if you lose by trading one ES on the run-up but two/three ES when the system is having a drawdown, then don't blame the system. The system is not responsible for the loss you incurred because of your desperation to recoup the losses immediately.
- Remember the golden maxim: *Past performance is no indication of future results.*

If you are using someone else's system, even if you know its logic, don't try to tinker with it and outsmart the system. Merely knowing the system's logic doesn't make you its developer. If you have decided to use a system, follow the rules consistently with contract sizes that make sense given your situation.

A developer takes a long time in creating a system. It may not be possible for him to program every possible situation into his system, even if he wants to. I can only program 50% of my trading strategies into my system, regardless of how hard I try to explain the details to my technicians. Certain things just cannot be expressed in Easy Language.

The three stages through which traders can outsmart a system are as follows:

1) Initially, they follow the system's entry signals, and then monitor the process. They know the logic, the indicator, and why they have entered. If the indicator moves the other way, or if the reason for the entry no longer exists, they get out before the set stop loss is hit. If the system is doing well, they keep checking if the indicator and the reason for entry remain valid. They may add more contracts to ride with more profit. By doing so, they trade better than the system.

2) After some practice, they will practice by *not* following the system entry. When the system is long, they wait till the indicator confirms more before any action takes place. If there is no further confirmation, they don't long but they do not short either. They can get the benefit of the system and avoid a losing trade. But they also do not trade against the system. This will let them end up with higher profit percentage than the system.

3) At the advanced level, they do not need the system anymore, as they understand as perfectly as the developer. All the entries will be automatic, without any need to remember the strategies. Trading becomes easier and simple.

Outsmarting the system is not easy and should not be attempted when you don't know the logic of the system. It is possible and should be attempted only when you have internalized the system's logic.

Some of my students know my system thoroughly and have practiced with me for months. But even they will have to modify or re-write it to suit their needs. It is just that about 80% of their logic and strategies will still follow mine because they are comfortable with the entry level, the stop point and the frequency of trade.

9

The World's Most Expensive Trading Seminar

S everal people have complained that I charge exorbitantly for my seminars. Well, my answer has always been that I charge what I think my services are worth. They offer value for money spent on them. Those who think the seminars are overpriced are free not to join.

I also tell anyone who has a query that they don't *have* to trade since trading is very risky. They have to think through the risks before taking a plunge. There is no guarantee that they will be successful. I can only do my best to coach them, which is usually in real time trading for months. This is very demanding on me and my time, which is why I charge an appropriate fee for the course. It's not a $3,000 course with common content meant for a group of 20 to 50 students. It's on a one-on-one basis. I would make more money if I did it in a group, charging a lower price. But that is not how students will learn trading effectively. It is not possible to coach a group of 30 to be successful within days. At least I cannot do it.

Another criticism is that my seminar is for wealthy traders. I certainly don't intend it to be so. If anyone is keen to attend the seminar, but has financial difficulties, I look into the details and take a fair decision, perhaps by offering a discount to those who are keen but have financial difficulties. This book's price is affordable for any trader. RC 5 Seminar, meant to provoke the reader to think and be his coach, comes free with it. It saves traders money and time in learning how to trade.

I also sometimes face this question: why would you want to teach others if you have something unique? It's funny but I always thought the other way round – if I do not teach, then where will anyone learn from? Self-learning is terrific but is difficult and takes a lot of time and money. I wish I had got a teacher like myself years ago. It would have shortened my learning curve by years. Think about it: if everyone who knew something special kept it to himself, then the human race would not have made any progress.

Honestly speaking, almost every time I teach someone, I learn something new and unique, or something that makes me come up with a new idea or better strategies. The more challenges the student presents, the more I learn. I have benefited immensely from my own seminars in terms of learning.

RC Trading Basics

1) You should not listen to any market-impacting information from any source and act on it impulsively. What is important for us is the time when the economic news is released. Do not trade 10 minutes before and after the data is released. You do not need to know the data. All kinds of experts will give their opinions immediately after the release of the data and the market will react to it. Now, we care about that – how the market chooses to interpret the experts' views. There is nothing inherently good or bad in any news. It is how the market interprets it that holds the key to your fortunes.

2) Some try to predict what may happen in the market that day, before the trading begins. I think any opinion before the market action is of little significance. Of course, to predict market movement is not entirely wrong and if it adds to your comfort feeling, please go ahead. If not, save your energies for the market. In any case, any planning based on what you predict will happen in the market could prove futile as the market's behavior may be completely different from what you thought it would be.

3) Should you tune up your body and mind before the trading begins? Keep fit anyway, whether you are trading or not. But it doesn't really matter if you exercise before or after the trading session. All you need to succeed in trading are lots of confidence in yourself and a good trading method. And confidence will come only when you know you can win and win consistently. When you know that you have a terrific trading edge that will take you to success, your confidence will be immeasurable.

How do I Prepare for Trading?

I don't plan my day before the trading begins. Nor do I fix a target for profits for the day. As long as the market goes my way with the confirmation of my indicator, I will ride with the profit. However, I do have a loss stop. I will cut loss quickly when the market moves against my position and my indicator.

I do not prepare for the trading. I just switch on my computers and check when the last economic report will be announced. I have no expectations towards the economic data since any expectation will create bias in me, affecting the evaluation of the market's reaction. I don't want to know what the data is about. I only want to know the time that an economic report is released, so I will not trade 10 minutes before and after the release. I will trade only 10 minutes <u>after</u> the <u>last</u> economic report of the day. So before the trading begins, I relax, take a nap or reply to e-mails.

During trading, I observe the market intermittently but closely. No one should look at the price quote non-stop for the whole day. I look at the market movements once in a while. If you are too geared up for the whole day, you will get exhausted, and when an opportunity comes you may not be alert to be able to react. Being relaxed and at ease enables me to spot a trading opportunity when it arises. At the same time, there *is* such a thing called over-alertness. If you are too alert, you tend to become too sensitive and overreact when the opportunity arises.

Be comfortable with what you do. Make sure you are in a relaxed mood and not too tense before the trading begins. If you are tense before the market opens, your anxiety and tension will increase as trading progresses. That will take a toll on your profits.

Is it a Choppy Market Day or a Trend Day or a Reverse Trend Day?

If you read the chapter on the RC 5 Seminar, you may be able to find a way to identify whether the market is choppy, trend or reverse trend. Try and find out your edge. And consider the market to be a cycle. If the past week was choppy, then you should treat the present market as choppy and take profit. If you spot a trend or a reverse trend, then you can add more contracts to follow the trend and use the second rule, as market conditions will take some time to change (of course, there are always exceptions).

How Different are RC 5, RC 7, RC 8 and RC 9?

RC 7 deals with more strategies to tackle various market situations. RC 8 teaches more indicators that can lead ES or are led by ES faster and more accurately than just the use of NQ. RC 9 is a secret and may not remain so for long. All I can say now is that RC Magic is developed using RC 9 strategy.

I have offered RC 7 and RC 8 Seminars earlier, but not RC 5, which is the foundation of RC Logic and RC system. It introduces Nasdaq (NQ) as a leading indicator to trade ES, when it will lead ES and when it will lag behind (details shown in Chapter 13 of this book). With this as a base, I am sure you will be able to research more systems and new indicators to trade successfully.

RC 5 Seminar and System are offered in this book at *zero additional cost*. In my opinion, the RC 5 System alone is worth thousands of dollars (including the source code) going by what an equivalent system commands in the market.

So why am I doing this? Some even objected to my doing this. I want to do this so that more traders can share and can research ES using new ways and new indicators. I would also like to see more winning traders, maybe 10% or even 50%. There are too many traders who have a great passion for trading, and against all odds they want to trade for a living. This book is an attempt to convert that passion for trading into being good at it.

Many have asked me for a hypothetical report of RC Magic. I thought it would be useful to put it up here as a reference:

Hypothetical Performance Report of RC Magic
(No commission and slippage included)
Net profit: $95,087.50
Profit factor: 4.54
Percent profitable: 77.81%
Average trade net profit: $138.81

TradeStation Performance Summary			Collapse ⌃
	All Trades	**Long Trades**	**Short Trades**
Total Net Profit	$95,087.50	$56,762.50	$38,325.00
Gross Profit	$121,912.50	$69,300.00	$52,612.50
Gross Loss	($26,825.00)	($12,537.50)	($14,287.50)
Profit Factor	4.54	5.53	3.68
Open Position P/L	$0.00	$0.00	$0.00
Select Total Net Profit	$79,362.50	$48,737.50	$30,625.00
Select Gross Profit	$106,187.50	$61,275.00	$44,912.50
Select Gross Loss	($26,825.00)	($12,537.50)	($14,287.50)
Select Profit Factor	3.96	4.89	3.14
Adjusted Total Net Profit	$87,539.76	$51,394.17	$33,002.99
Adjusted Gross Profit	$116,631.88	$65,351.27	$49,105.00
Adjusted Gross Loss	($29,092.13)	($13,957.09)	($16,102.01)
Adjusted Profit Factor	4.01	4.68	3.05
Total Number of Trades	685	393	292
Percent Profitable	77.81%	78.37%	77.05%
Winning Trades	533	308	225
Losing Trades	140	78	62
Even Trades	12	7	5
Avg. Trade Net Profit	$138.81	$144.43	$131.25
Avg. Winning Trade	$228.73	$225.00	$233.83
Avg. Losing Trade	($191.61)	($160.74)	($230.44)
Ratio Avg. Win:Avg. Loss	1.19	1.40	1.01
Largest Winning Trade	$1,987.50	$1,775.00	$1,987.50
Largest Losing Trade	($500.00)	($500.00)	($500.00)
Largest Winner as % of Gross Profit	1.63%	2.56%	3.78%
Largest Loser as % of Gross Loss	1.86%	3.99%	3.50%
Net Profit as % of Largest Loss	19017.50%	11352.50%	7665.00%
Select Net Profit as % of Largest Loss	15872.50%	9747.50%	6125.00%
Adjusted Net Profit as % of Largest Loss	17507.95%	10278.83%	6600.60%
Max. Consecutive Winning Trades	22	20	18
Max. Consecutive Losing Trades	3	3	3
Avg. Bars in Total Trades	37.77	38.18	37.22
Avg. Bars in Winning Trades	38.02	38.45	37.43
Avg. Bars in Losing Trades	37.14	37.94	36.13
Avg. Bars in Even Trades	34.25	29.14	41.40

Table 9.1 Hypothetical Performance report of RC Magic

Continue from page 57

Max. Shares/Contracts Held	1	1	1
Total Shares/Contracts Held	685	393	292
Account Size Required	$1,250.00	$925.00	$1,575.00
Total Slippage	$0.00	$0.00	$0.00
Total Commission	$0.00	$0.00	$0.00
Return on Initial Capital	95.09%		
Annual Rate of Return	13.40%		
Buy & Hold Return	7.57%		
Return on Account	7607.00%		
Avg. Monthly Return	$1,297.19		
Std. Deviation of Monthly Return	$792.39		
Return Retracement Ratio	0.37		
RINA Index	12082.02		
Sharpe Ratio	1.02		
K-Ratio	n/a		
Trading Period	4 Yrs, 11 Mths, 25 Dys, 2 Hrs, 30 Mins		
Percent of Time in the Market	4.82%		
Time in the Market	2 Mths, 26 Dys, 17 Hrs, 45 Mins		
Longest Flat Period	13 Dys, 21 Hrs, 10 Mins		
Max. Equity Run-up	$95,162.50		
Date of Max. Equity Run-up	03/21/06 14:40		
Max. Equity Run-up as % of Initial Capital	95.16%		
Max. Drawdown (Intra-day Peak to Valley)			
Value	($1,887.50)	($1,700.00)	($2,587.50)
Date	06/14/02 11:50		
as % of Initial Capital	1.89%	1.70%	2.59%
Net Profit as % of Drawdown	5037.75%	3338.97%	1481.16%
Select Net Profit as % of Drawdown	4204.64%	2866.91%	1183.57%
Adjusted Net Profit as % of Drawdown	4637.87%	3023.19%	1275.48%
Max. Drawdown (Trade Close to Trade Close)			
Value	($1,250.00)	($925.00)	($1,575.00)
Date	02/22/02 13:40		
as % of Initial Capital	1.25%	0.93%	1.58%
Net Profit as % of Drawdown	7607.00%	6136.49%	2433.33%
Select Net Profit as % of Drawdown	6349.00%	5268.92%	1944.44%
Adjusted Net Profit as % of Drawdown	7003.18%	5556.13%	2095.43%
Max. Trade Drawdown	($500.00)	($500.00)	($500.00)

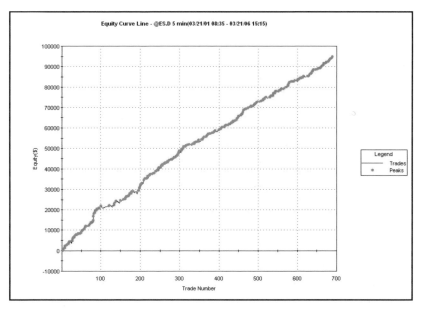

Figure 9.1 - Performance Graphs - Equity Curve Line

Source: Created by TradeStation

10

Three Steps to Becoming a Winner

Do you really want to trade for a living? Be sure about the answer before aspiring to become a trader.

If you think that trading is little work and lots of money, perish the thought. Trading is not a short route to riches. In fact, it is extremely demanding and if you want to trade for a living, you should consider the enormous amount of hard work involved before taking the plunge.

Statistics tell us that only 5% to 10% of those that trade, win. The rest, a good 90%, lose.

The market does not take the loser's money. It is the better trader who takes it. It is a negative-sum game, if the broker's commission is included. You have to be better than your competitor to win in this game.

Always remember the objective of trading: to make money by winning over other traders. It is hard to become a successful trader if your objective is not clear enough.

Follow three simple rules:
1) Have a trading edge.
2) Convert the edge into a trading system.
3) Practice a lot.

Edge >> Strategies >> Practice >> Success

With these steps, the profit will come sooner or later.

1. Find a Trading Edge

The most basic and important task is to find the winning edge. In order to do this, you should be prepared to observe and learn a lot. Some discover their edge in a few months, while others may take a few years. Some may never find it. If you don't have this edge, you can't possibly win in this negative-sum game. This is why only 5% to 10% of people can win consistently. This has nothing to do with your intelligence, education level, experience or age. It's the edge that matters.

You can find your trading edge by learning and thinking continuously. For example, you may discover that a particular pattern or certain market sentiment brings profit. These patterns may appear once a day, or once in a few weeks. A good trader will be patient and will trade when the patterns or market sentiment appear. Such practice could also constitute an edge. The more frequently the patterns or market sentiment appears, the higher the winning ratio.

2. Convert the Edge to a Trading System

After finding the edge, the next step would be to convert it into a trading system. Then try it in real time until you achieve a winning ratio of 70% or more. Work to improve the system. If it is complicated, make it simple. The simpler it is, the better it is. Do not add more and more complicated strategies in the guise of improvement. Add more simple strategies from your real experience. A good system is simply a system that is usable and profitable. It need not be complicated at all.

Don't expect to never fail. Your learning curve will have to pass through failures, but over time, you will win much more than you lose. Practicing consistently will also make you highly disciplined.

Some traders may take years to find their edges and strategies. If you find a mentor, you may be able to shorten the learning time span. However, it is not easy to find a successful trader to be your mentor. If you cannot find a good trading coach, be your own coach (Refer to Chapter 3).

You may have the best money management skills but to put them to use, your system has to generate profits for you. The best money management skills cannot substitute a winning edge and good strategies.

3. Practice

Several experts and traders help their students and readers find a trend or a reverse trend of the market. But that doesn't constitute an edge by itself. What is more important is to understand a trend or a reverse trend *faster* than others. Hence, even if everyone else knows about technical analysis and market indicators as much as you do, by being quick in spotting the trend or reverse trend, you increase your chances of winning.

You need to spend time and effort to observe and find the edge. If you can be faster than others at finding the market direction, using indicators or technical analysis that others have (but take longer to identify) or don't have, then you have created a trading edge.

Thus, to become a successful trader, to belong to the small 5% or 10% of the trading community that is successful, you should learn, observe, think and find a trading edge. You should be able to identify a trend or a reverse trend faster than others. And then practice and practice to perfect your skills.

To do all this you cannot rely on memory. Would you remember what the Dow Jones Index was 30 days ago? Unlikely, isn't it? However, you need to analyze details so that you can improve. The only option is to take elaborate, detailed notes of your trading activity. Taking notes helps refresh your memory and improve your trading.

I used to spend about four hours a day writing notes on my daily trading activities, writing down everything that happened in the market and what I had observed. Over the weekends, I would use another five hours to organize the notes of the previous five days. In sum, I used to spend 25 hours a week making notes and constantly revising, reviewing and improving them. I still take notes, but not as heavily as I once did.

I still spend over 30 hours a week, including over weekends, researching the market. As with everything in life, you have to be demanding and hardworking to be a successful trader. Keep learning, demanding, observing, reading and improving. If you do these consistently, you will trade well and success will follow.

11

RC Trading Edge

How do we define the trading edge? If you are looking for a formula, it is this: (Probability of Winning x Winning Amount) + (Probability of Losing x Losing Amount). An example in trading ES (miniSP) is as follows: if a system or a trader has a winning ratio of 50% and a profit factor of 2:1, the edge of the system or the trader (historically) is (0.5 x 2) + (0.5 x -1) = 1 + (-0.5) = 0.5. This means that for every dollar the system or the trader trades, it will get $0.50 in return, so for $1,000 each time it trades, the return will be $500. The edge of the system or the trader is 0.5. The higher this number is, the higher is the edge. So when a trader or a system has a high probability of winning and a high winning factor, a high trading edge results.

Trading is a game of probability. Many will agree that a trading edge is a statistical edge. I also do, but would like to clarify that only a part of the trading edge is a statistical edge. To have a statistical edge is to be able to find the historical patterns. However, it has no logic to explain any particular pattern or its present or future efficacy. But a real trading edge must have a sound logic to explain why the past statistical edge (through back testing) had occurred and the logic will be good in future trading too; that is to say, there is, or should be, a reason for the recurrence of the statistical edge. This enhances the present and future efficacy of the trading edge. A sound logic is the key, as it can help in formulating high-probability winning strategies, essential for forming the trading edge. If the trading edge continues to perform, it is naturally more reassuring for the trader.

I came up with the concept of RC Trading Edge in 2002. I began writing the RC Success System in 2003 and completed it in 2004. I sent it to John Hill, President of *Futures Truth*, for a review. The system has remained in *Futures Truth* top 10 SP day trade systems (after the mandatory four months incubation period) as the No. 1 S&P Day Trading System for over a year till January 10, 2006.

How to Develop Your Own Trading Edge

1) You need only two things: a notebook and a pen since all you have to do is to observe, think and jot down.

2) Write down *why* you entered the trade, *why* you got out, *why you think* you made a profit or a loss (this also implies *why do you think* your indicator worked or did not work). If you write down all the data with your observations, you will probably find some specific and recurring patterns. Out of these may emerge some consistent winning strategies. Be patient and keep noting down your observations for some length of time.

3) Review the notes over the weekends, with a calm and open mind. Your process of discovery would accelerate.

Some of my students have told me that they also observed this before, but its usefulness had not struck them.

You have to collect more data after your observation and form a strategy to test and verify it. Why does it work? Is there logic to it? You can analyze the responses scientifically. Observation should be followed by verification of data and creation of consistent strategies. Remember, for centuries, many people would have surely wondered why apples were falling from the trees. But only Isaac Newton pursued his observation to its logical end – the discovery of the Law of Gravity.

So observation is just the first step. It has to be followed up with:

a → analysis of lots of data

b → forming a hypothesis after thinking of the logic underlying the data

c → testing it backward and applying it to actual trading

d → consistent results

e → formulating trading edges and strategies

a→ back to analysis…

The cycle, from a → e → a → e → a, must go on without a break. It should be a perpetual cycle in your mind.

Can You Win Without a Trading Edge?

Can you ride with profit without being able to identify the trend? You may cut your losses quickly but that will not necessarily make you a winner. To identify the trend is difficult enough; to identify the reverse trend is even more so (top or bottom). This is exactly where trading edge comes in.

The lack of trading edge is the reason why many traders lose, despite working hard and having the right attitude towards trading. Once you determine a trend or a reverse trend with 60% to 70% accuracy, verify the edge by back testing it. If it works in the present as well as in the past, then you have a good shot in the future.

Using market indicators is no protection against loss. If market indicators such as moving averages cannot detect a trend or a reverse trend correctly, the traders using them would fail. This may be the reason why a large number of traders fail; they use popular indicators, which may not be leading indicators.

To find or discover a leading and a highly accurate indicator for detecting the trend (or reverse trend) is the solution to the main problem faced by most traders. In Chapter 13, the RC 5 Seminar will give you a trading edge with simple strategies that any trader can learn in a couple of hours. If this could turn a trader into a consistent winner, maybe there will be 20% or 30% or more winning traders in this zero sum game in comparison to the present 5% to 10% winners.

We see that Nasdaq moves faster than the ES and the Dow Index most of the time. The most interesting fact, however, is that when both are in positive territories, if and when Nasdaq (NQ) suddenly turns negative, the ES follows the NQ into the negative territory in a short while (approximately in about two to 10 minutes).

If it is so simple, it means that the NQ leads the ES and we have enough time (one to two minutes or more sometimes) to trade ES using NQ as a leading indicator. Why? There could be a number of reasons, such as the heavy weighted NQ stock being highly volatile and in both indexes. Also, usually, a tech stock is traded heavily and will move faster than the ES stock. If so, just following the NQ to trade the ES would be a simple and powerful strategy, especially during the reverse trend; that is, NQ turns a few minutes faster than ES does. And NQ will continue to be a forward-looking indicator to trade ES as long as we are in the technology era, perhaps for another two decades.

Of course, you have to research and find out under what conditions the NQ will not lead the ES, so that you may still trade to profit. Some traders know this. About 10% of the students also observe this correlation. But the obvious is often overlooked by most traders. Also, the other difficulty exists, namely that on many days the NQ doesn't lead the ES. Following the NQ to trade the ES on such days would result in loss.

I have found ways to trade ES irrespective of whether NQ is leading or lagging. I identify different situations and use NQ to trade ES to make a profit. This could be a potential "trading edge" for those who want to research. In a sense, it seems obvious, like gravity. But it needs someone to quantify so that it can be applied to trading.

Understanding how NQ Leads ES by Observation Using Simple RC Logic

Example (1) Date: 2005 / 9 / 14

	ES	NQ
0910	-0.5	-4.5

```
  1050914   835  ES=   2.25  NQ=   1.00
  1050914   840  ES=   2.00  NQ=  -3.00
  1050914   845  ES=   1.00  NQ=  -3.50
  1050914   850  ES=   0.75  NQ=  -6.00
  1050914   855  ES=   0.75  NQ=  -4.00
  1050914   900  ES=  -0.50  NQ=  -6.00
  1050914   905  ES=   0.50  NQ=  -3.50
* 1050914   910  ES=  -0.50  NQ=  -4.50
  1050914   915  ES=   0.50  NQ=  -3.50
  1050914   920  ES=  -0.25  NQ=  -5.00
  1050914   925  ES=  -0.50  NQ=  -5.50
  1050914   930  ES=  -1.75  NQ=  -6.50
  1050914   935  ES=  -1.00  NQ=  -6.50
  1050914   940  ES=  -1.00  NQ=  -6.00
  1050914   945  ES=   0.00  NQ=  -5.00
  1050914   950  ES=  -0.25  NQ=  -5.50
  1050914   955  ES=   0.25  NQ=  -5.00
  1050914  1000  ES=  -0.75  NQ=  -6.00
  1050914  1005  ES=  -0.25  NQ=  -6.00
  1050914  1010  ES=   0.25  NQ=  -4.00
  1050914  1015  ES=   0.75  NQ=  -4.00
  1050914  1020  ES=   0.00  NQ=  -5.00
  1050914  1025  ES=   0.25  NQ=  -4.50
  1050914  1030  ES=   0.75  NQ=  -4.00
  1050914  1035  ES=   0.50  NQ=  -4.00
  1050914  1040  ES=   1.75  NQ=  -2.00
  1050914  1045  ES=   1.25  NQ=  -3.00
  1050914  1050  ES=   1.25  NQ=  -3.00
```

Remarks:

*   Price is compared to yesterday's closing. We use 5 min bar, that is 5 min time interval to observe.

*1050914 stands for year 2005, September 14. 910 = US central time, 09.10 a.m. ES = -0.50, NQ = -4.50 means ES value is down 0.5 point, NQ value is down 4.5 point compared to yesterday's

ES and NQ closing value. (closing value is calculated when US
market close at 3 p.m. or 1500 US time)
* **1050914 910   ES=-0.50   NQ= -4.50,** we highlight this line
because we will start looking at market at 09.10 a.m. as most data
are released at US central time 09.00 a.m. We start observing the
market 10 minutes after release of data.

```
1050914 1055  ES=  0.75  NQ= -3.50
1050914 1100  ES=  1.00  NQ= -4.00
1050914 1105  ES=  0.75  NQ= -4.00
1050914 1110  ES=  1.00  NQ= -3.00
1050914 1115  ES=  1.50  NQ= -2.50
1050914 1120  ES=  1.00  NQ= -3.00
1050914 1125  ES=  0.75  NQ= -3.50
1050914 1130  ES=  0.75  NQ= -4.00
1050914 1135  ES=  0.50  NQ= -5.00
1050914 1140  ES=  0.00  NQ= -6.00
1050914 1145  ES=  0.50  NQ= -5.00
1050914 1150  ES=  0.25  NQ= -5.50
1050914 1155  ES=  0.75  NQ= -6.00
1050914 1200  ES=  1.25  NQ= -5.00
1050914 1205  ES=  1.25  NQ= -5.00
1050914 1210  ES=  1.75  NQ= -4.50
1050914 1215  ES=  1.00  NQ= -5.00
1050914 1220  ES=  1.25  NQ= -4.50
1050914 1225  ES=  0.75  NQ= -5.00
1050914 1230  ES=  1.00  NQ= -5.00
1050914 1235  ES=  0.75  NQ= -5.50
```

1050914 1240 ES= 0.00 NQ= -6.00
```
1050914 1245  ES= -0.50  NQ= -6.50
```
1050914 1250 ES= -1.00 NQ= -8.00
```
1050914 1255  ES= -1.25  NQ=-10.00
1050914 1300  ES= -0.75  NQ= -9.50
1050914 1305  ES= -0.25  NQ= -9.50
1050914 1310  ES= -0.75  NQ= -9.50
```
1050914 1315 ES= -1.50 NQ=-11.00

1050914 1320 ES= -4.50 NQ=-15.00
1050914 1325 ES= -4.00 NQ=-15.00
1050914 1330 ES= -3.50 NQ=-13.50
1050914 1335 ES= -3.50 NQ=-13.50
1050914 1340 ES= -3.25 NQ=-13.50
1050914 1345 ES= -4.00 NQ=-14.00
1050914 1350 ES= -3.75 NQ=-15.00
1050914 1355 ES= -4.00 NQ=-15.00
1050914 1400 ES= -4.00 NQ=-15.00
1050914 1405 ES= -5.75 NQ=-19.50
1050914 1410 ES= -5.25 NQ=-19.00
1050914 1415 ES= -5.75 NQ=-18.50
1050914 1420 ES= -6.00 NQ=-19.00
1050914 1425 ES= -5.75 NQ=-18.00
1050914 1430 ES= -5.25 NQ=-18.00
1050914 1435 ES= -5.00 NQ=-17.00
1050914 1440 ES= -5.00 NQ=-17.00
1050914 1445 ES= -4.25 NQ=-15.50
1050914 1450 ES= -4.25 NQ=-16.00
1050914 1455 ES= -5.25 NQ=-18.00
1050914 1500 ES= -4.75 NQ=-19.00
1050914 1505 ES= -4.75 NQ=-19.50
1050914 1510 ES= -4.50 NQ=-19.00
1050914 1515 ES= -4.25 NQ=-19.00

Interpretations:

i)   At 09:10, ES is down 0.5 points and NQ is down 4.5 points compared to the previous day's closing; normal and nothing unusual.

ii) At 10:10, ES turns up +ve (+0.25) but NQ is still down -ve (-4.00), NQ is still down and remains -ve. RC traders understand they will not long ES because NQ is not leading ES up.

iii) At 10:40, ES continues to go up (+1.75) but NQ is still down 2 points; no confirmation.

iv)   At 12:40, ES is unchanged but NQ is down 6 points, more than at 10:40, and becomes more -ve, even more bearish than at 09:10 (which NQ is -4.5 only). RC traders may get ready to short.

v)   At 12:50, ES is -1 and NQ is -8; now RC traders can short as NQ is leading ES down; other traders may still be waiting as they see ES only down 1 point. They may even think today is a tight range day as ES range is only +1.75 to -1. But RC traders using NQ as indicator know the market is bearish from 09:10 till 12:50. Just waiting for confirmation to short ES as NQ may have high probability to lead ES to go down.

vi)   At 13:15, ES is -1.5 and NQ is -11; it's confirmed; RC traders will short with stop with confidence.

vii)   At 13:20, ES is -4.5 and NQ is -15; this time RC traders are happy and move stop to the point of entry while the price is at 13:15. Then they can relax. Other traders are probably still thinking if they should short now as the market "seems" to go down. They will be undecided on whether they should follow the trend or pass it. What if the ES is up again?

viii) At 15:00, RC traders profit; other traders lose or breakeven.

Example (2) Date: 2005 / 9 / 29

1050929	835	ES=	-2.25	NQ=	-3.00
1050929	840	ES=	-3.00	NQ=	-5.00
1050929	845	ES=	-3.25	NQ=	-4.00
1050929	850	ES=	-4.25	NQ=	-6.00
1050929	855	ES=	-3.00	NQ=	-4.00
1050929	900	ES=	-4.50	NQ=	-8.00
1050929	905	ES=	-4.00	NQ=	-8.00
1050929	**910**	**ES=**	**-3.25**	**NQ=**	**-4.50**
1050929	915	ES=	-3.25	NQ=	-5.00
1050929	**920**	**ES=**	**-2.75**	**NQ=**	**-2.50**
1050929	925	ES=	-2.25	NQ=	-3.00
1050929	**930**	**ES=**	**-0.75**	**NQ=**	**1.00**

```
1050929   935  ES=  -1.00  NQ=   0.00
1050929   940  ES=  -1.00  NQ=   2.00
1050929   945  ES=  -1.75  NQ=   1.50
1050929   950  ES=  -2.75  NQ=  -0.50
1050929   955  ES=  -3.00  NQ=   0.00
1050929  1000  ES=  -4.25  NQ=  -3.00
```
1050929 1005 ES= -3.75 NQ= -0.50
```
1050929  1010  ES=  -5.75  NQ=  -4.50
1050929  1015  ES=  -4.75  NQ=  -2.50
1050929  1020  ES=  -4.00  NQ=  -1.50
1050929  1025  ES=  -3.00  NQ=  -0.50
1050929  1030  ES=  -4.00  NQ=  -1.50
1050929  1035  ES=  -4.25  NQ=  -0.50
1050929  1040  ES=  -3.50  NQ=   0.50
1050929  1045  ES=  -2.50  NQ=   1.00
```
1050929 1050 ES= -1.00 NQ= 4.00
1050929 1055 ES=   2.25 NQ= 8.50
```
1050929  1100  ES=   2.00  NQ=   8.00
1050929  1105  ES=   2.00  NQ=   9.50
1050929  1110  ES=   1.00  NQ=   9.00
1050929  1115  ES=   1.00  NQ=   8.00
1050929  1120  ES=   1.50  NQ=   8.50
1050929  1125  ES=   0.75  NQ=   7.00
1050929  1130  ES=   1.25  NQ=   7.50
1050929  1135  ES=   0.25  NQ=   6.50
1050929  1140  ES=   0.75  NQ=   7.00
1050929  1145  ES=   0.75  NQ=   7.00
1050929  1150  ES=   0.75  NQ=   7.00
1050929  1155  ES=   1.00  NQ=   7.50
1050929  1200  ES=   1.50  NQ=   8.00
1050929  1205  ES=   3.00  NQ=   9.50
1050929  1210  ES=   2.00  NQ=   9.00
```
1050929 1215 ES=   3.50 NQ= 13.00
```
1050929  1220  ES=   5.25  NQ=  16.00
1050929  1225  ES=   6.00  NQ=  16.50
```

```
1050929 1230  ES=   5.50  NQ= 16.00
1050929 1235  ES=   6.50  NQ= 18.00
1050929 1240  ES=   5.50  NQ= 16.50
1050929 1245  ES=   5.75  NQ= 16.00
1050929 1250  ES=   6.25  NQ= 15.50
1050929 1255  ES=   6.00  NQ= 15.00
1050929 1300  ES=   5.50  NQ= 15.00
1050929 1305  ES=   8.50  NQ= 19.00
1050929 1310  ES=   9.00  NQ= 19.00
1050929 1315  ES=   8.25  NQ= 17.50
1050929 1320  ES=   8.25  NQ= 17.00
1050929 1325  ES=   8.50  NQ= 17.50
1050929 1330  ES=   9.00  NQ= 17.00
1050929 1335  ES=   8.75  NQ= 16.00
1050929 1340  ES=   8.50  NQ= 16.00
1050929 1345  ES=   8.75  NQ= 15.50
1050929 1350  ES=   7.75  NQ= 13.50
1050929 1355  ES=   8.25  NQ= 13.00
1050929 1400  ES=   8.50  NQ= 16.00
1050929 1405  ES=   8.50  NQ= 15.50
1050929 1410  ES=   9.50  NQ= 17.50
1050929 1415  ES=   9.00  NQ= 17.50
1050929 1420  ES= 10.50  NQ= 21.00
1050929 1425  ES= 11.00  NQ= 21.50
1050929 1430  ES= 11.25  NQ= 21.50
1050929 1435  ES= 10.25  NQ= 20.00
1050929 1440  ES= 10.25  NQ= 19.50
1050929 1445  ES=   9.75  NQ= 18.50
1050929 1450  ES=   9.75  NQ= 18.50
1050929 1455  ES= 10.50  NQ= 20.50
```

<u>1050929 1500 ES= 11.00 NQ=22.00</u>

```
1050929 1505  ES= 10.50  NQ= 20.00
1050929 1510  ES= 10.25  NQ= 20.00
1050929 1515  ES=   9.50  NQ= 20.50
```

Interpretations:

i)   At 09:10, ES is -3.25 and NQ is -4.5; the market seems normal, RC traders watch NQ to see if NQ will lead ES down or up.

ii)   At 09:20, ES is -2.75 and NQ is -2.5; NQ is no longer leading ES down. In fact, NQ is less –ve than ES, this means NQ may go up and lead ES up. RC traders are aware of this discrepancy in the market and will not short ES. They await more confirmation of NQ leading ES up.

iii)   At 09:30, ES is -0.75 and NQ is +1; aggressive RC traders will long with 10-point protective stop and continue to observe NQ. Conservative RC traders will wait till NQ turns +ve and leads ES to +ve, and then they will long with a stop.

iv)   At 10:05, ES is –3.75 and NQ is -0.5; it seems NQ cannot lead ES up. But it is still OK because ES is -3.75 and NQ is -0.5. Aggressive RC traders will not worry and hold the long position, while conservative RC traders would wait. If ES is -4 and NQ is -6, RC 5 traders will short. But now that ES is -3.75 and NQ is -0.5, RC traders will NOT short and will wait for an opportunity to long.

v)   At 10:50, ES is -1.00 and NQ is +4. Now RC traders who had taken long positions relax again. Conservative RC traders will long since NQ is up after some tests to low. At 09:10, NQ was -4.5, and now at 10:50, NQ is +4. NQ is moving up.

vi)   At 10:55, ES is +2.25 and NQ +8.5. NQ has led ES up. Both aggressive and conservative RC traders know that the up trend is established. The most aggressive ones will add more contracts to long with stop. When NQ is leading ES, it's a high probability trade.

vii)   At 12:15, ES is +3.50 and NQ is +13; at this NQ level, there is a high probability that ES will be up.

viii)   At 15:00, ES is +11.00 and NQ is +22. It's a profitable day for RC traders. RC 6, 7, 8 and 9 traders will also be able to profit with different indicators to confirm.

Example (3) Date: 2006 / 5 / 23

```
1060523  835  ES= 11.25  NQ= 17.25
1060523  840  ES= 11.75  NQ= 17.50
1060523  845  ES= 11.25  NQ= 17.25
1060523  850  ES= 10.25  NQ= 15.25
1060523  855  ES= 10.50  NQ= 15.50
1060523  900  ES= 10.50  NQ= 15.75
1060523  905  ES= 10.25  NQ= 13.75
1060523  910  ES= 12.75  NQ= 17.50
1060523  915  ES= 13.00  NQ= 19.75
1060523  920  ES= 12.25  NQ= 17.25
1060523  925  ES= 13.00  NQ= 19.00
1060523  930  ES= 12.50  NQ= 18.00
1060523  935  ES= 13.75  NQ= 19.50
1060523  940  ES= 13.50  NQ= 19.50
1060523  945  ES= 13.00  NQ= 19.50
1060523  950  ES= 12.00  NQ= 18.75
1060523  955  ES= 12.25  NQ= 19.25
1060523 1000  ES= 12.00  NQ= 19.50
1060523 1005  ES= 12.00  NQ= 19.50
1060523 1010  ES=  9.50  NQ= 14.25
1060523 1015  ES= 11.25  NQ= 16.25
1060523 1020  ES= 11.75  NQ= 17.75
1060523 1025  ES= 10.50  NQ= 15.50
1060523 1030  ES= 10.75  NQ= 15.75
1060523 1035  ES= 11.25  NQ= 17.25
1060523 1040  ES= 12.00  NQ= 18.75
1060523 1045  ES= 11.75  NQ= 18.25
1060523 1050  ES= 12.00  NQ= 18.50
1060523 1055  ES= 10.75  NQ= 17.00
1060523 1100  ES= 10.00  NQ= 16.00
1060523 1105  ES=  9.00  NQ= 14.75
1060523 1110  ES= 10.00  NQ= 16.50
1060523 1115  ES= 10.50  NQ= 17.50
1060523 1120  ES= 10.50  NQ= 17.50
```

1060523 1125 ES= 8.50 NQ= 15.50
1060523 1130 ES= 9.00 NQ= 16.00
1060523 1135 ES= 8.00 NQ= 14.50
1060523 1140 ES= 9.75 NQ= 15.75
1060523 1145 ES= 10.00 NQ= 15.75
1060523 1150 ES= 9.25 NQ= 15.50
1060523 1155 ES= 9.00 NQ= 14.50
1060523 1200 ES= 9.00 NQ= 13.50
1060523 1205 ES= 9.50 NQ= 13.75
1060523 1210 ES= 9.75 NQ= 14.00
1060523 1215 ES= 10.00 NQ= 16.00
1060523 1220 ES= 10.75 NQ= 16.25
1060523 1225 ES= 10.50 NQ= 16.00
1060523 1230 ES= 11.00 NQ= 16.50
1060523 1235 ES= 12.00 NQ= 17.50
1060523 1240 ES= 11.50 NQ= 17.50
1060523 1245 ES= 12.25 NQ= 18.00
1060523 1250 ES= 11.75 NQ= 17.25
1060523 1255 ES= 11.25 NQ= 16.25
1060523 1300 ES= 10.25 NQ= 14.75
1060523 1305 ES= 11.00 NQ= 15.75
1060523 1310 ES= 9.25 NQ= 13.25
1060523 1315 ES= 10.25 NQ= 14.50
1060523 1320 ES= 9.50 NQ= 13.25
1060523 1325 ES= 9.75 NQ= 12.25
1060523 1330 ES= 9.50 NQ= 12.25
1060523 1335 ES= 10.25 NQ= 13.25
1060523 1340 ES= 8.75 NQ= 11.25
1060523 1345 ES= 9.00 NQ= 10.75
1060523 1350 ES= 7.00 NQ= 6.50
1060523 1355 ES= 6.00 NQ= 5.75
1060523 1400 ES= 6.50 NQ= 5.75
1060523 1405 ES= 5.75 NQ= 4.00
1060523 1410 ES= 6.25 NQ= 4.00
1060523 1415 ES= 8.00 NQ= 6.50

```
1060523 1420  ES=   8.75  NQ=   8.50
1060523 1425  ES=   7.25  NQ=   6.50
1060523 1430  ES=   6.25  NQ=   3.00
1060523 1435  ES=   5.75  NQ=   2.00
1060523 1440  ES=   5.00  NQ=   1.00
1060523 1445  ES=   1.50  NQ= -4.00
1060523 1450  ES=   0.75  NQ= -4.00
1060523 1455  ES=  -2.75  NQ=-10.50
1060523 1500  ES=  -3.00  NQ=-12.50
1060523 1505  ES=  -4.25  NQ=-17.25
1060523 1510  ES=  -7.25  NQ=-18.75
1060523 1515  ES= -10.00  NQ=-20.50
```

Interpretations:

i)   At 09:10, ES is up 12.75 points and NQ is up 17.5 points. The market looks bullish.

ii)   At 10:10, ES is up 9.5 points and NQ is up 14.25 points. Although the market seems bullish, traders don't see ES breaking new high. Even NQ cannot break a new high. RC traders wait and watch.

iii) At 13:10, another three hours later, both ES and NQ are up, but not much change. RC traders don't take any position.

iv)   At 13:50, ES is down by a few points to +7. NQ is down a lot to +6.5, compared to the position at 09:10. ES was +12.75 and NQ was +17.5. RC traders see NQ leading ES, so it's normal. Now we see ES and NQ are both positive, but NQ is lagging behind. We see NQ may lead ES down. Aggressive traders will short at this point. Conservative traders will wait till 14:45 when ES is +1.5 and NQ is -4 to confirm NS position to short. Both will profit if trade closes at 15:00. You can see clearly how NQ leads ES down; we follow, short and profit. If one looks only at ES, he will not be able to short at 13:50 when ES is +7 points.

NQ Indicator can also be Used to Trade Dow, Mid-cap and e-Russell Futures

When I began a few years ago, I used to simply think and work hard. During the process I developed more indicators besides NQ, with more leading characteristics to trade ES successfully. In 2004, RC Success mechanical system was written and I let John Hill, President of *Futures Truth*, see my system. He said "Rickey, I have seen thousand of systems in my career, and you are the first one to use 'NQ' as an indicator with a sound logic. Congratulations!"

After the four months mandatory incubation period, RC Success started at rank No. 8 in the Top Ten SP day trade table. Then it moved up to No. 2 in the next issue (this means six months after we sent the system to *Futures Truth*). Over the next two months, RC Success was ranked No. 1 and remained in No. 1 for over 12 months till now (January 10, 2006).

So I have back tested RC Success using NQ and some other indicators. It has worked well in real time hypothetical tracking by *Futures Truth* for over 22 months from March 2004 till now. The system continues to perform well which indicates that my logic and strategies are working fine. I expect it to continue to work in the future. Please remember past performance is no guarantee of future results.

Examples of RC Trading Edge for Advanced Courses

Examples below emphasize that trading edge strategies can be verified by back testing. With a trading edge, traders can long to profit when the market is down and short to profit when the market is up.

Strategy (1) Priority 1c-L1: We long when ES is down and (-ve). Many traders may short since the market is down.

Strategy (2) Priority 6-S1: We short when ES is up and (+ve). Many traders may long since the market is up.

Strategy (3) Priority 3L: We long when ES is up and (+ve).
We follow the real trend to long. Many traders may want to long since the market is up. They have to be sure that it is the top of the market. It is difficult for someone without Trading Edge to see the trend or countertrend with a high degree of accuracy.

Strategy (4) Priority 1b-Sg: We short when ES is down and (-ve) and follow the real trend to short. Many traders may follow and short.

(P/N: Down or -ve means ES is down from yesterday's close price. Up or +ve means ES is up from yesterday's close. For example, if ES is up five points, it means ES today is up five points from yesterday's closing price.)

Capture the trend and the countertrend with a high probability of winning. Below is the RC trading edge that allows the RC system user or RC students to trade and verify with *Easy Language* back testing. The reader can check all the dates and results. We use TradeStation to verify the result. We have picked two days with image shots for easy visualization.

Strategy (1) Priority 1c-L1

This strategy starts at 09:10 (US central time) while ES is negative. We long with stop while ES is negative (compared to yesterday's closing price) as shown in Table 11.1. Most traders will probably follow trend and short while some may still be waiting. We'll long with confidence and with high profit percentage.

Table 11.1 below shows all the long (buy) entries at 09:10 on different days, the profit per one ES signal. You will see how this strategy has worked well from 2001 till now.

Type	Date/Time		Signal	Price	Net Profit - Cum Net Profit
Buy	7/2/2001	9:10	Priority 1c-L1	US$1,263.75	US$525.00
Buy	08/20/01	09:10	Priority 1c-L1	US$1,192.00	US$625.00
Buy	12/3/2001	9:10	Priority 1c-L1	US$1,156.25	US$12.50
Buy	04/25/02	09:10	Priority 1c-L1	US$1,109.75	US$12.50
Buy	8/2/2002	9:10	Priority 1c-L1	US$899.75	(US$500.00)
Buy	12/11/2002	9:10	Priority 1c-L1	US$918.00	US$225.00
Buy	01/27/03	09:10	Priority 1c-L1	US$879.75	(US$500.00)
Buy	02/13/03	09:10	Priority 1c-L1	US$832.75	US$300.00
Buy	4/8/2003	9:10	Priority 1c-L1	US$897.75	US$12.50
Buy	05/13/03	09:10	Priority 1c-L1	US$964.00	US$12.50
Buy	6/9/2003	9:10	Priority 1c-L1	US$1,004.00	(US$500.00)
Buy	08/28/03	09:10	Priority 1c-L1	US$1,017.00	US$375.00
Buy	9/5/2003	9:10	Priority 1c-L1	US$1,047.25	US$12.50
Buy	12/19/03	09:10	Priority 1c-L1	US$1,112.75	(US$62.50)
Buy	1/7/2004	9:10	Priority 1c-L1	US$1,141.25	US$500.00
Buy	1/9/2004	9:10	Priority 1c-L1	US$1,151.00	US$12.50
Buy	01/29/04	09:10	Priority 1c-L1	US$1,153.00	US$175.00
Buy	02/20/04	09:10	Priority 1c-L1	US$1,172.00	(US$137.50)
Buy	02/26/04	09:10	Priority 1c-L1	US$1,164.25	US$250.00
Buy	3/3/2004	9:10	Priority 1c-L1	US$1,172.25	US$150.00
Buy	3/5/2004	9:10	Priority 1c-L1	US$1,179.00	US$12.50
Buy	04/13/04	09:10	Priority 1c-L1	US$1,167.50	(US$500.00)
Buy	6/8/2004	9:10	Priority 1c-L1	US$1,162.75	US$262.50
Buy	7/2/2004	9:10	Priority 1c-L1	US$1,152.25	US$12.50
Buy	8/3/2004	9:10	Priority 1c-L1	US$1,130.25	(US$325.00)
Buy	08/25/04	09:10	Priority 1c-L1	US$1,120.50	US$562.50
Buy	10/5/2004	9:10	Priority 1c-L1	US$1,160.25	US$12.50
Buy	11/18/04	09:10	Priority 1c-L1	US$1,207.75	US$12.50
Buy	12/6/2004	9:10	Priority 1c-L1	US$1,212.75	US$125.00
Buy	2/3/2005	9:10	Priority 1c-L1	US$1,213.50	US$50.00
Buy	2/11/2005	9:10	Priority 1c-L1	US$1,218.25	US$625.00
Buy	02/16/05	09:10	Priority 1c-L1	US$1,231.25	US$187.50
Buy	3/2/2005	9:10	Priority 1c-L1	US$1,230.25	US$212.50
Buy	03/18/05	09:10	Priority 1c-L1	US$1,213.00	(US$125.00)

Buy	03/31/05	09:10	Priority 1c-L1	US$1,204.25	(US$75.00)
Buy	05/20/05	09:10	Priority 1c-L1	US$1,209.00	US$25.00
Buy	05/24/05	09:10	Priority 1c-L1	US$1,210.50	US$12.50
Buy	7/12/2005	9:10	Priority 1c-L1	US$1,236.00	US$212.50
Buy	07/15/05	09:10	Priority 1c-L1	US$1,243.00	US$125.00
Buy	07/18/05	09:10	Priority 1c-L1	US$1,240.75	(US$25.00)
Buy	8/3/2005	9:10	Priority 1c-L1	US$1,258.25	US$12.50
Buy	8/4/2005	9:10	Priority 1c-L1	US$1,256.50	(US$225.00)
Buy	08/30/05	09:10	Priority 1c-L1	US$1,222.25	US$50.00
Buy	08/31/05	09:10	Priority 1c-L1	US$1,219.50	US$850.00
Buy	9/7/2005	9:10	Priority 1c-L1	US$1,246.00	US$250.00
Buy	09/19/05	09:10	Priority 1c-L1	US$1,246.50	(US$100.00)
Buy	09/27/05	09:10	Priority 1c-L1	US$1,227.00	US$125.00
Buy	09/29/05	09:10	Priority 1c-L1	US$1,227.25	US$675.00
Buy	10/25/05	09:10	Priority 1c-L1	US$1,207.50	US$12.50
Buy	11/10/2005	9:10	Priority 1c-L1	US$1,229.50	US$587.50
Buy	11/28/05	09:10	Priority 1c-L1	US$1,274.25	(US$312.50)
Buy	12/5/2005	9:10	Priority 1c-L1	US$1,269.75	US$87.50
					US$4,912.50

Table 11.1 TradeStation Trade list
Hypothetical Performance Report of RC Magic
For analysis of Table data, please refer Figure 11.1 in the next page.

Figure 11.1 shows a TradeStation screen shot of a selected trade from Table 11.1 trade list. This is a graphic illustration for easy reference. We have made one screen shot, so that readers can see the movement of ES after we long at 09:10 with stop.

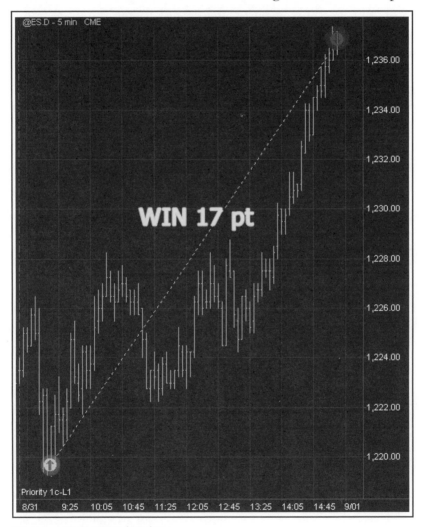

Figure 11.1 2005/08/31
Performance Graphs - Equity Curve Line
Source: Created by TradeStation

Strategy (2) Priority 6-S1

Using this strategy we short at 09:10 when ES is up (compared to yesterday's closing price). Most traders will be buying or waiting for more momentum to long, or will be waiting for more upside to short. But we short at 09:10. We do not follow the price trend, which is up. Our indicator told us that the market is weaker, so we short to profit at the earliest possible stage.

Table 11.2 below shows all short entries at 09:10 from 2001 till now, the profit per one ES signal.

Type	Date/Time	Signal	Price	Net Profit - Cum Net Profit
Sell Short	11/14/0 09:10	Priority 6-S1	US$1,168.50	US$387.50
Sell Short	02/20/02 09:10	Priority 6-S1	US$1,110.75	US$125.00
Sell Short	02/27/02 09:10	Priority 6-S1	US$1,137.50	US$375.00
Sell Short	4/10/2002 9:10	Priority 6-S1	US$1,145.00	US$87.50
Sell Short	05/31/02 09:10	Priority 6-S1	US$1,094.75	US$262.50
Sell Short	07/26/02 09:10	Priority 6-S1	US$862.75	US$12.50
Sell Short	9/4/2002 9:10	Priority 6-S1	US$903.50	US$275.00
Sell Short	09/25/02 09:10	Priority 6-S1	US$845.75	US$387.50
Sell Short	11/8/2002 9:10	Priority 6-S1	US$928.00	US$325.00
Sell Short	11/20/02 09:10	Priority 6-S1	US$921.00	(US$500.00)
Sell Short	11/25/02 09:10	Priority 6-S1	US$953.50	US$525.00
Sell Short	01/13/03 09:10	Priority 6-S1	US$953.75	US$312.50
Sell Short	3/11/2003 9:10	Priority 6-S1	US$834.25	US$437.50
Sell Short	03/21/03 09:10	Priority 6-S1	US$903.75	US$12.50
Sell Short	04/14/03 09:10	Priority 6-S1	US$892.00	(US$500.00)
Sell Short	5/5/2003 9:10	Priority 6-S1	US$950.50	US$12.50
Sell Short	5/6/2003 9:10	Priority 6-S1	US$953.25	US$12.50
Sell Short	05/20/03 09:10	Priority 6-S1	US$946.75	US$12.50
Sell Short	05/22/03 09:10	Priority 6-S1	US$949.50	(US$187.50)
Sell Short	6/10/2003 9:10	Priority 6-S1	US$1,003.75	US$12.50
Sell Short	06/19/03 09:10	Priority 6-S1	US$1,031.50	US$387.50
Sell Short	06/24/03 09:10	Priority 6-S1	US$1,005.25	US$137.50
Sell Short	07/22/03 09:10	Priority 6-S1	US$1,002.75	US$12.50
Sell Short	8/11/2003 9:10	Priority 6-S1	US$1,002.50	US$12.50
Sell Short	9/11/2003 9:10	Priority 6-S1	US$1,040.00	US$212.50
Sell Short	09/23/03 09:10	Priority 6-S1	US$1,047.00	(US$187.50)
Sell Short	09/29/03 09:10	Priority 6-S1	US$1,022.50	US$75.00
Sell Short	10/2/2003 9:10	Priority 6-S1	US$1,042.25	US$125.00
Sell Short	10/20/03 09:10	Priority 6-S1	US$1,063.50	US$100.00

Sell Short	11/21/03 09:10	Priority 6-S1	US$1,058.25	US$137.50
Sell Short	01/16/04 09:10	Priority 6-S1	US$1,159.75	(US$200.00)
Sell Short	01/20/04 09:10	Priority 6-S1	US$1,166.75	US$337.50
Sell Short	2/5/2004 9:10	Priority 6-S1	US$1,150.75	US$87.50
Sell Short	02/13/04 09:10	Priority 6-S1	US$1,180.50	US$200.00
Sell Short	02/19/04 09:10	Priority 6-S1	US$1,180.50	US$0.00
Sell Short	02/25/04 09:10	Priority 6-S1	US$1,167.25	US$162.50
Sell Short	02/27/04 09:10	Priority 6-S1	US$1,175.75	US$175.00
Sell Short	3/8/2004 9:10	Priority 6-S1	US$1,183.25	US$112.50
Sell Short	4/8/2004 9:10	Priority 6-S1	US$1,171.00	US$312.50
Sell Short	05/21/04 09:10	Priority 6-S1	US$1,118.25	(US$87.50)
Sell Short	06/25/04 09:10	Priority 6-S1	US$1,169.50	US$262.50
Sell Short	7/7/2004 9:10	Priority 6-S1	US$1,146.00	US$175.00
Sell Short	7/9/2004 9:10	Priority 6-S1	US$1,140.00	US$37.50
Sell Short	07/13/04 09:10	Priority 6-S1	US$1,142.00	US$125.00
Sell Short	09/21/04 09:10	Priority 6-S1	US$1,150.75	(US$262.50)
Sell Short	09/24/04 09:10	Priority 6-S1	US$1,136.75	US$12.50
Sell Short	11/2/2004 9:10	Priority 6-S1	US$1,162.50	US$125.00
Sell Short	11/24/04 09:10	Priority 6-S1	US$1,206.50	US$50.00
Sell Short	11/26/04 09:10	Priority 6-S1	US$1,211.00	(US$37.50)
Sell Short	12/13/04 09:10	Priority 6-S1	US$1,219.50	US$100.00
Sell Short	12/15/04 09:10	Priority 6-S1	US$1,231.75	US$212.50
Sell Short	01/14/05 09:10	Priority 6-S1	US$1,203.50	(US$287.50)
Sell Short	02/18/05 09:10	Priority 6-S1	US$1,226.75	US$187.50
Sell Short	03/22/05 09:10	Priority 6-S1	US$1,209.50	US$212.50
Sell Short	03/28/05 09:10	Priority 6-S1	US$1,199.50	US$12.50
Sell Short	4/5/2005 9:10	Priority 6-S1	US$1,204.75	US$62.50
Sell Short	5/2/2005 9:10	Priority 6-S1	US$1,183.25	US$162.50
Sell Short	5/6/2005 9:10	Priority 6-S1	US$1,196.25	US$87.50
Sell Short	05/19/05 09:10	Priority 6-S1	US$1,209.25	US$50.00
Sell Short	05/23/05 09:10	Priority 6-S1	US$1,213.00	US$125.00
Sell Short	6/8/2005 9:10	Priority 6-S1	US$1,221.00	US$112.50
Sell Short	07/14/05 09:10	Priority 6-S1	US$1,247.00	US$75.00
Sell Short	8/2/2005 9:10	Priority 6-S1	US$1,258.75	(US$100.00)
Sell Short	8/9/2005 9:10	Priority 6-S1	US$1,246.00	US$25.00
Sell Short	08/19/05 09:10	Priority 6-S1	US$1,240.50	US$212.50
Sell Short	09/20/05 09:10	Priority 6-S1	US$1,247.75	US$200.00
Sell Short	09/26/05 09:10	Priority 6-S1	US$1,232.25	US$262.50
Sell Short	10/7/2005 9:10	Priority 6-S1	US$1,207.50	US$12.50
Sell Short	12/6/2005 9:10	Priority 6-S1	US$1,275.00	US$112.50
				US$6,825.00

Table 11.2 TradeStation Trade list
Hypothetical Performance Report of RC Magic

Figure 11.2 below shows a TradeStation screen shot of a selected trade from Table 11.2 trade list. This is a graphic illustration for easy reference.

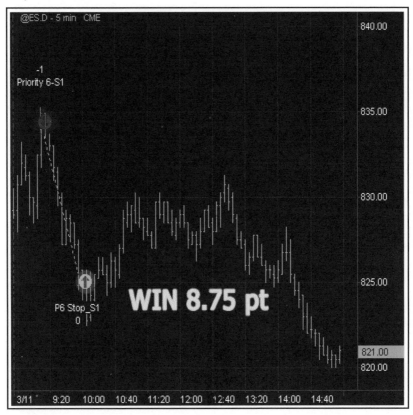

Figure 11.2 2003/03/11
Performance Graphs - Equity Curve Line
Source: Created by TradeStation

Strategy (3) Priority 3L

At 09:10 ES is up and positive. We can detect that the market is bullish and we long. In strategy 2, we detect weakness in the market and therefore despite ES being positive and up from yesterday's closing, we short.

Table 11.3 below shows long entries at 09:10 when ES is up. Profit per one ES signal.

Type	Date/Time	Signal	Price	Net Profit - Cum Net Profit
Buy	4/5/2001 9:10	Priority 3L	US$1,180.75	US$637.50
Buy	4/10/2001 9:10	Priority 3L	US$1,208.50	US$137.50
Buy	4/11/2001 9:10	Priority 3L	US$1,214.00	US$12.50
Buy	04/18/01 09:10	Priority 3L	US$1,253.50	US$12.50
Buy	05/17/01 09:10	Priority 3L	US$1,334.75	(US$500.00)
Buy	06/28/01 09:10	Priority 3L	US$1,263.00	US$12.50
Buy	07/19/01 09:10	Priority 3L	US$1,257.50	(US$500.00)
Buy	09/24/01 09:10	Priority 3L	US$1,020.25	US$537.50
Buy	10/10/2001 9:10	Priority 3L	US$1,094.25	US$700.00
Buy	10/11/2001 9:10	Priority 3L	US$1,121.75	US$12.50
Buy	12/5/2001 9:10	Priority 3L	US$1,185.50	US$425.00
Buy	1/3/2002 9:10	Priority 3L	US$1,183.50	US$350.00
Buy	3/8/2002 9:10	Priority 3L	US$1,195.00	(US$500.00)
Buy	5/8/2002 9:10	Priority 3L	US$1,093.00	US$762.50
Buy	06/17/02 09:10	Priority 3L	US$1,041.25	US$787.50
Buy	07/17/02 09:10	Priority 3L	US$944.00	(US$500.00)
Buy	07/29/02 09:10	Priority 3L	US$897.25	US$12.50
Buy	8/6/2002 9:10	Priority 3L	US$879.50	US$12.50
Buy	9/6/2002 9:10	Priority 3L	US$911.00	US$12.50
Buy	10/11/2002 9:10	Priority 3L	US$847.00	US$12.50
Buy	10/15/02 09:10	Priority 3L	US$890.50	US$550.00
Buy	10/17/02 09:10	Priority 3L	US$898.25	US$12.50
Buy	11/14/02 09:10	Priority 3L	US$918.00	US$12.50
Buy	11/27/02 09:10	Priority 3L	US$949.25	US$450.00
Buy	1/9/2003 9:10	Priority 3L	US$942.75	US$12.50
Buy	4/2/2003 9:10	Priority 3L	US$897.75	US$162.50
Buy	5/2/2003 9:10	Priority 3L	US$941.25	US$412.50
Buy	05/15/03 09:10	Priority 3L	US$968.00	(US$37.50)
Buy	05/29/03 09:10	Priority 3L	US$980.25	(US$500.00)
Buy	05/30/03 09:10	Priority 3L	US$981.25	US$12.50
Buy	6/4/2003 9:10	Priority 3L	US$998.00	US$475.00
Buy	6/6/2003 9:10	Priority 3L	US$1,027.75	(US$500.00)

Buy	7/2/2003	9:10	Priority 3L	US$1,008.50	US$12.50
Buy	7/7/2003	9:10	Priority 3L	US$1,022.50	US$12.50
Buy	07/14/03	09:10	Priority 3L	US$1,032.00	US$12.50
Buy	07/24/03	09:10	Priority 3L	US$1,018.00	(US$500.00)
Buy	08/21/03	09:10	Priority 3L	US$1,030.75	(US$500.00)
Buy	9/8/2003	9:10	Priority 3L	US$1,050.25	US$12.50
Buy	09/16/03	09:10	Priority 3L	US$1,042.75	US$437.50
Buy	10/1/2003	9:10	Priority 3L	US$1,027.00	US$637.50
Buy	10/3/2003	9:10	Priority 3L	US$1,056.25	US$12.50
Buy	10/28/03	09:10	Priority 3L	US$1,059.75	US$500.00
Buy	11/3/2003	9:10	Priority 3L	US$1,082.25	(US$87.50)
Buy	11/12/2003	9:10	Priority 3L	US$1,072.25	US$450.00
Buy	11/18/03	09:10	Priority 3L	US$1,069.75	(US$500.00)
Buy	12/1/2003	9:10	Priority 3L	US$1,089.00	US$225.00
Buy	12/11/2003	9:10	Priority 3L	US$1,088.00	US$400.00
Buy	12/29/03	09:10	Priority 3L	US$1,126.00	US$425.00
Buy	1/2/2004	9:10	Priority 3L	US$1,142.00	(US$500.00)
Buy	1/5/2004	9:10	Priority 3L	US$1,140.75	US$287.50
Buy	3/12/2004	9:10	Priority 3L	US$1,139.50	US$12.50
Buy	03/16/04	09:10	Priority 3L	US$1,137.00	(US$25.00)
Buy	03/23/04	09:10	Priority 3L	US$1,123.50	(US$275.00)
Buy	03/25/04	09:10	Priority 3L	US$1,122.25	US$537.50
Buy	03/29/04	09:10	Priority 3L	US$1,145.75	US$12.50
Buy	4/2/2004	9:10	Priority 3L	US$1,164.75	US$125.00
Buy	4/12/2004	9:10	Priority 3L	US$1,171.25	US$0.00
Buy	04/20/04	09:10	Priority 3L	US$1,163.50	(US$500.00)
Buy	5/11/2004	9:10	Priority 3L	US$1,117.75	US$12.50
Buy	05/18/04	09:10	Priority 3L	US$1,117.00	US$50.00
Buy	05/24/04	09:10	Priority 3L	US$1,123.25	(US$150.00)
Buy	05/27/04	09:10	Priority 3L	US$1,149.50	(US$75.00)
Buy	6/7/2004	9:10	Priority 3L	US$1,157.00	US$500.00
Buy	06/29/04	09:10	Priority 3L	US$1,161.50	US$50.00
Buy	07/27/04	09:10	Priority 3L	US$1,115.50	US$212.50
Buy	08/16/04	09:10	Priority 3L	US$1,100.25	US$250.00
Buy	08/24/04	09:10	Priority 3L	US$1,127.50	(US$212.50)
Buy	9/7/2004	9:10	Priority 3L	US$1,146.25	US$12.50
Buy	09/16/04	09:10	Priority 3L	US$1,150.75	US$12.50
Buy	10/1/2004	9:10	Priority 3L	US$1,152.75	US$312.50
Buy	10/4/2004	9:10	Priority 3L	US$1,166.25	(US$212.50)
Buy	11/3/2004	9:10	Priority 3L	US$1,169.75	US$12.50
Buy	12/1/2004	9:10	Priority 3L	US$1,208.00	US$500.00
Buy	12/28/04	09:10	Priority 3L	US$1,237.50	US$125.00
Buy	01/25/05	09:10	Priority 3L	US$1,197.25	(US$175.00)

Buy	01/26/05	09:10	Priority 3L	US$1,199.25	(US$62.50)
Buy	3/4/2005	9:10	Priority 3L	US$1,244.50	US$175.00
Buy	03/24/05	09:10	Priority 3L	US$1,200.75	(US$312.50)
Buy	03/30/05	09:10	Priority 3L	US$1,195.00	US$500.00
Buy	4/6/2005	9:10	Priority 3L	US$1,207.25	US$12.50
Buy	04/19/05	09:10	Priority 3L	US$1,173.25	US$87.50
Buy	04/21/05	09:10	Priority 3L	US$1,168.00	US$725.00
Buy	04/25/05	09:10	Priority 3L	US$1,182.75	US$50.00
Buy	05/18/05	09:10	Priority 3L	US$1,201.00	US$287.50
Buy	05/26/05	09:10	Priority 3L	US$1,215.50	US$87.50
Buy	6/1/2005	9:10	Priority 3L	US$1,220.25	US$12.50
Buy	6/7/2005	9:10	Priority 3L	US$1,226.50	(US$412.50)
Buy	06/28/05	09:10	Priority 3L	US$1,216.75	US$237.50
Buy	10/21/05	09:10	Priority 3L	US$1,192.25	US$12.50
Buy	10/24/05	09:10	Priority 3L	US$1,200.25	US$525.00
Buy	10/31/05	09:10	Priority 3L	US$1,217.00	US$12.50
Buy	11/18/05	09:10	Priority 3L	US$1,259.25	(US$37.50)
Buy	12/1/2005	9:10	Priority 3L	US$1,269.00	US$225.00
					US$8,075.00

Table 11.3 TradeStation Trade list
Hypothetical Performance Report of RC Magic

Figure 11.3 below has a TradeStation screen shot of one selected trade from Table 11.3 trade list. This is a graphic illustration for easy reference.

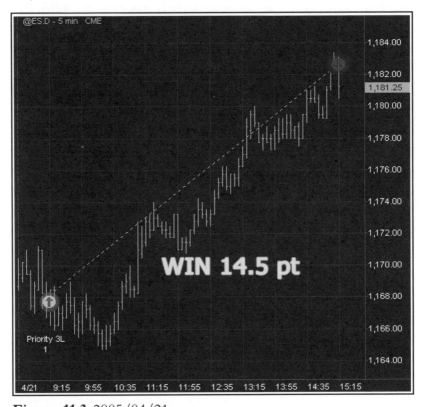

Figure 11.3 2005/04/21
Performance Graphs - Equity Curve Line
Source: Created by TradeStation

Strategy (4) Priority 1b-Sg

ES is negative (down) from yesterday's close. We detect continued weakness and short at the "right time" with profit. Alternatively, we detect strength and do not follow price trend and long "immediately" with profit.

Table 11.4 below shows short positions at various time on different days when the conditions were weak.

Type	Date/Time	Signal	Price	Net Profit - Cum Net Profit
Sell Short	05/30/02 11:55	Priority 1b-Sg	US$1,079.50	US$12.50
Sell Short	07/19/02 09:50	Priority 1b-Sg	US$885.25	US$1,062.50
Sell Short	07/30/02 10:45	Priority 1b-Sg	US$908.75	(US$400.00)
Sell Short	8/5/2002 10:15	Priority 1b-Sg	US$868.75	US$12.50
Sell Short	10/4/2002 10:30	Priority 1b-Sg	US$822.75	US$12.50
Sell Short	10/7/2002 10:00	Priority 1b-Sg	US$816.50	US$12.50
Sell Short	12/27/02 10:10	Priority 1b-Sg	US$901.50	US$362.50
Sell Short	01/21/03 13:05	Priority 1b-Sg	US$914.50	US$362.50
Sell Short	2/6/2003 14:40	Priority 1b-Sg	US$853.00	(US$250.00)
Sell Short	02/24/03 11:10	Priority 1b-Sg	US$855.00	US$137.50
Sell Short	02/26/03 12:50	Priority 1b-Sg	US$852.00	US$250.00
Sell Short	3/4/2003 13:40	Priority 1b-Sg	US$843.50	US$50.00
Sell Short	3/6/2003 11:10	Priority 1b-Sg	US$842.50	US$12.50
Sell Short	4/7/2004 9:55	Priority 1b-Sg	US$1,163.75	(US$150.00)
Sell Short	3/8/2005 12:55	Priority 1b-Sg	US$1,245.00	US$100.00
Sell Short	3/9/2005 11:55	Priority 1b-Sg	US$1,236.25	US$262.50
Sell Short	04/28/05 10:40	Priority 1b-Sg	US$1,171.00	US$375.00
Sell Short	5/10/2005 10:50	Priority 1b-Sg	US$1,189.25	US$162.50
Sell Short	8/5/2005 10:30	Priority 1b-Sg	US$1,243.75	US$50.00
Sell Short	09/13/05 09:50	Priority 1b-Sg	US$1,248.75	US$137.50
Sell Short	10/10/2005 14:15	Priority 1b-Sg	US$1,200.25	US$25.00
Sell Short	10/18/05 12:35	Priority 1b-Sg	US$1,193.50	US$187.50
Sell Short	11/15/05 13:00	Priority 1b-Sg	US$1,243.00	US$162.50
				US$2,950.00

Table 11.4 TradeStation Trade list
Hypothetical Performance Report of RC Magic

Figure 11.4 below shows TradeStation screen shots of a select trade from Table 11.4 trade list. This is a graphic illustration for easy reference.

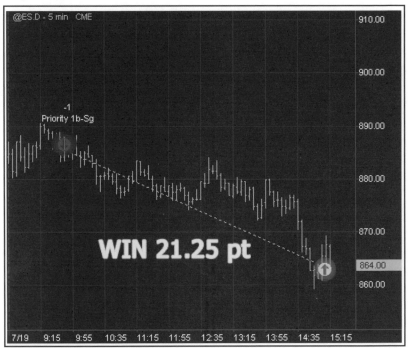

Figure 11.4 2002/07/19
Performance Graphs - Equity Curve Line
Source: Created by TradeStation

12

RC 5 Seminar: Strategies and Application

Now I will show you a simple and basic RC logic with strategies, namely RC 5. It is less sophisticated than RC 6, 7 and 8 indicators and strategies. But even RC 5 will shorten the learning curve of many traders. They may even be stimulated to think differently on how they should trade in Emini SP Futures, Dow Futures, e-Russell Futures, Mid-Cap Futures, etc.

You don't need to understand technical analysis to make sense of this chapter. Nor is any programming knowledge required. Even a beginner can master this within hours. This can be a starting point for further research and advancement. I hope you will find RC 5 a good, no non-sense system.

Please note that RC 5 is a trading method that assists you to think more and research more in trading the ES Futures or US equities or futures market. It is not intended to be an autotrade system. If you follow RC 5 strategies to trade, you are doing so at your own risk. Remember the dictum *past performance is no guarantee for future results* (this applies to all trading systems and methods.)

RC 5 is original. If you want to be successful in trading or development of a system, your system should be original with sound logic. RC 5 also provides scope for developing your own system to trade.

What is NQ? NQ stands for Nasdaq 100 Futures Index. Since we discovered that NQ moves faster than ES most of the time, we use NQ as an indicator to trade ES or Dow or e-Russell futures. (Please refer to Chapter 11 for details.)

RC 5 is a set of rules for traders to test and verify. To learn RC Logic is a lively experience. A few things like speed of NQ movements are not included in this book because these cannot be programmed into a mechanical system or written down as rules for traders to follow.

RC 5 Seminar

Before we start with the strategies, the rules to apply are:

A)   Once a long or short entry starts, put a 10 point stop immediately.

B)   When there is a four-point profit, move the stop to point of entry plus 0.25 pt. (0.25 pt is just to cover the commission.) So if the market falls back, then the trade will be even. It's not good psychologically for the trader to have profit turning into a loss. Breakeven is acceptable. This method has profit percentage over 60%.

C)   We use 5 minutes bars; that means we take data with 5 minutes intervals. You may do it by hand with any quote machine or use TradeStation print log to generate it. Do not use 15 minutes bars or longer. If the market moves fast, and you will miss the trade.

D)   As most economic data mentioned in Chapter 4 will be out by 09:00 (US central time), we start trading 10 minutes after the last data is released in a normal situation, i.e. 09:10.

E)   If the stop is not hit, we will close all positions at 15:00 (US central time)

Notations:

* S means single digits, i.e. 0 to 9.75.
* D means double digits, i.e. 10 , 15, 27, etc.
* +ve means Up from yesterday's market close.
* -ve means Down from yesterday's market close.

(If we say ES + 5, means ES this is up 5 points from yesterday's close. If we say NQ -10 means NQ is down 10 points from yesterday's close). These ups and downs will be available in any quote machine.

1) @ 0910 ES -ve S, NQ +ve S and absvalue(NQ) >= absvalue(ES) then Short immediately ("Short 1a")
(At 09:10 US central time, when you see ES is down and NQ is up compared to yesterday's closing of ES and NQ, ES is down single digit and NQ is up single digit, the absolute value of NQ is greater than or equal to the absolute value* of ES, then you Short ES immediately.)

ES	NQ
-ve S	+ve S
|ES| <=	|NQ|

* Absolute value of a real number is its numerical value without regard to its sign. Example: NQ = -8 is greater than ES = +6 in absolute term. Example: NQ = +10 or -10 is greater than ES = +7 or -7 in absolute term.

We start at 09:10 which is 40 minutes after market opens at 08:30 (US central time). We call this Opposite Day 1, since ES and NQ are in opposite direction at 09:10.

Explanation of rule 1: Opposite Day 1:
ES and NQ are in opposite direction, ES -ve single, NQ +ve single, so if NQ +ve cannot lead ES to +ve, then there is high probability that ES is leading NQ to -ve rather than vice versa. So, we Short with a 10-point stop. Advance RC traders who understand the NQ more can wait for more confirmation.

Please refer to the table explanation on page 100.

Example:

i) 2004 / 3 / 11

1040311	835	ES=	-1.25	NQ=	-2.00
1040311	840	ES=	-3.00	NQ=	-2.00
1040311	845	ES=	-3.75	NQ=	-4.50
1040311	850	ES=	-2.50	NQ=	-1.50
1040311	855	ES=	0.00	NQ=	5.00
1040311	900	ES=	0.75	NQ=	3.50
1040311	905	ES=	-2.25	NQ=	1.00
1040311	**910**	**ES=**	**-0.50**	**NQ=**	**6.00** ← **SHORT**

(OPPOSITE DAY 1)

```
1040311  915  ES=   2.25  NQ= 10.00
1040311  920  ES=   0.50  NQ=  7.50
1040311  925  ES=   2.00  NQ= 11.00
1040311  930  ES=   2.75  NQ= 11.50
1040311  935  ES=   1.75  NQ=  8.50
1040311  940  ES=   0.50  NQ=  6.50
1040311  945  ES=  -1.00  NQ=  2.50
1040311  950  ES=  -0.25  NQ=  4.50
1040311  955  ES=  -0.25  NQ=  3.50
1040311 1000  ES=  -0.75  NQ=  2.50
1040311 1005  ES=  -1.75  NQ= -1.50
1040311 1010  ES=  -1.75  NQ= -0.50
1040311 1015  ES=  -2.00  NQ= -1.00
1040311 1020  ES=  -3.25  NQ= -2.50
1040311 1025  ES=  -1.75  NQ=  1.50
1040311 1030  ES=  -1.25  NQ=  2.00
1040311 1035  ES=  -0.25  NQ=  2.50
1040311 1040  ES=   1.00  NQ=  4.50
1040311 1045  ES=   0.00  NQ=  3.00
1040311 1050  ES=  -0.75  NQ=  1.50
1040311 1055  ES=  -0.50  NQ=  2.50
1040311 1100  ES=   0.25  NQ=  5.50
1040311 1105  ES=   1.00  NQ=  5.00
1040311 1110  ES=   1.00  NQ=  5.00
1040311 1115  ES=   2.75  NQ=  7.50
1040311 1120  ES=   3.75  NQ= 10.00
1040311 1125  ES=   2.50  NQ=  9.50
1040311 1130  ES=   2.50  NQ=  9.50
1040311 1135  ES=   3.00  NQ= 10.00
1040311 1140  ES=   3.00  NQ=  9.50
1040311 1145  ES=   3.25  NQ= 10.00
1040311 1150  ES=   5.00  NQ= 12.50
1040311 1155  ES=   4.75  NQ= 11.00
1040311 1200  ES=   5.75  NQ= 13.50
1040311 1205  ES=   5.25  NQ= 12.50
```

```
1040311 1210  ES=   4.75  NQ= 11.00
1040311 1215  ES=   5.75  NQ= 12.50
1040311 1220  ES=   5.00  NQ= 12.50
1040311 1225  ES=   4.75  NQ= 10.00
1040311 1230  ES=   4.75  NQ= 11.00
1040311 1235  ES=   3.25  NQ=  9.00
1040311 1240  ES=   2.25  NQ=  7.50
1040311 1245  ES=   2.50  NQ=  6.50
1040311 1250  ES=   3.25  NQ=  8.50
1040311 1255  ES=   2.25  NQ=  7.00
1040311 1300  ES=   2.00  NQ=  7.50
1040311 1305  ES=   1.00  NQ=  4.50
1040311 1310  ES=   2.00  NQ=  7.00
1040311 1315  ES=   4.00  NQ= 11.50
1040311 1320  ES=   4.00  NQ= 10.50
1040311 1325  ES=   4.50  NQ= 12.00
1040311 1330  ES=   3.00  NQ= 10.50
1040311 1335  ES=   1.75  NQ=  8.50
1040311 1340  ES=  -0.25  NQ=  6.00
1040311 1345  ES=   0.50  NQ=  9.00
1040311 1350  ES=  -1.50  NQ=  6.00
1040311 1355  ES=  -2.50  NQ=  4.00
1040311 1400  ES=  -2.00  NQ=  5.00
1040311 1405  ES=   0.00  NQ=  7.50
1040311 1410  ES=  -1.50  NQ=  4.50
1040311 1415  ES=  -2.75  NQ=  4.00
1040311 1420  ES=  -8.00  NQ= -3.00
1040311 1425  ES=  -7.00  NQ= -3.00
1040311 1430  ES=  -8.00  NQ= -4.00
1040311 1435  ES=  -7.25  NQ= -3.50
1040311 1440  ES=  -6.50  NQ= -1.50
1040311 1445  ES=-10.25  NQ= -6.00
1040311 1450  ES=-10.75  NQ= -7.50
1040311 1455  ES=-13.75  NQ=-11.50
```
1040311 1500 ES= -12.75 NQ=-12.50 • ← STOP

```
1040311 1505  ES= -14.75  NQ=-14.00
1040311 1510  ES= -14.00  NQ=-11.00
1040311 1515  ES= -14.50  NQ=-11.50
```

ii) 2005 / 4 / 20

```
1050420   835  ES=  -1.50  NQ=   7.00
1050420   840  ES=  -3.00  NQ=   5.00
1050420   845  ES=  -4.75  NQ=   2.50
1050420   850  ES=  -4.25  NQ=   4.00
1050420   855  ES=  -4.50  NQ=   4.00
1050420   900  ES=  -6.00  NQ=  -0.50
1050420   905  ES=  -5.25  NQ=   1.50
```
1050420   910 ES= -3.25 NQ=   4.50 ← **SHORT**
                                              (OPPOSITE DAY 1)
```
1050420   915  ES=  -3.25  NQ=   5.50
1050420   920  ES=  -2.50  NQ=   7.50
1050420   925  ES=  -3.00  NQ=   6.00
1050420   930  ES=  -1.25  NQ=   8.00
1050420   935  ES=  -2.50  NQ=   6.00
1050420   940  ES=  -2.50  NQ=   6.00
1050420   945  ES=  -4.50  NQ=   1.50
1050420   950  ES=  -5.25  NQ=   2.50
1050420   955  ES=  -3.50  NQ=   5.00
1050420 1000  ES=  -1.25  NQ=   9.00
1050420 1005  ES=   1.25  NQ=  10.50
1050420 1010  ES=   0.25  NQ=   8.00
1050420 1015  ES=  -0.50  NQ=   7.00
1050420 1020  ES=  -0.75  NQ=   5.50
1050420 1025  ES=  -2.00  NQ=   4.00
1050420 1030  ES=  -2.75  NQ=   4.50
1050420 1035  ES=  -2.00  NQ=   5.00
1050420 1040  ES=  -2.75  NQ=   5.50
1050420 1045  ES=  -2.00  NQ=   5.50
1050420 1050  ES=  -2.50  NQ=   6.00
1050420 1055  ES=  -2.25  NQ=   7.00
```

```
1050420 1100  ES=   -1.50  NQ=    7.50
1050420 1105  ES=   -2.75  NQ=    6.00
1050420 1110  ES=   -2.75  NQ=    6.00
1050420 1115  ES=   -3.00  NQ=    5.00
1050420 1120  ES=   -4.00  NQ=    4.00
1050420 1125  ES=   -2.75  NQ=    5.50
1050420 1130  ES=   -3.50  NQ=    5.00
1050420 1135  ES=   -3.50  NQ=    5.00
1050420 1140  ES=   -5.25  NQ=    1.00
1050420 1145  ES=   -4.75  NQ=    2.00
1050420 1150  ES=   -5.75  NQ=    1.00
1050420 1155  ES=   -7.50  NQ=   -1.50
1050420 1200  ES=   -8.50  NQ=   -4.00
1050420 1205  ES=   -7.75  NQ=   -3.00
1050420 1210  ES=   -7.50  NQ=   -2.50
1050420 1215  ES=   -8.25  NQ=   -4.00
1050420 1220  ES=   -8.00  NQ=   -4.00
1050420 1225  ES=   -7.75  NQ=   -3.00
1050420 1230  ES=   -9.25  NQ=   -5.50
1050420 1235  ES= -10.00  NQ=   -8.00
1050420 1240  ES=   -9.25  NQ=   -6.00
1050420 1245  ES=   -9.25  NQ=   -5.00
1050420 1250  ES=   -8.50  NQ=   -4.50
1050420 1255  ES=   -7.75  NQ=   -4.00
1050420 1300  ES=   -8.00  NQ=   -4.50
1050420 1305  ES= -10.00  NQ=   -6.50
1050420 1310  ES= -11.25  NQ=   -7.50
1050420 1315  ES= -10.50  NQ=   -6.00
1050420 1320  ES= -11.00  NQ=   -7.00
1050420 1325  ES= -11.50  NQ=   -8.50
1050420 1330  ES= -12.75  NQ= -10.00
1050420 1335  ES= -12.25  NQ=   -8.50
1050420 1340  ES= -11.50  NQ=   -8.00
1050420 1345  ES= -11.50  NQ=   -7.50
1050420 1350  ES= -11.50  NQ=   -7.50
```

```
1050420 1355  ES= -11.50  NQ=  -7.50
1050420 1400  ES= -10.25  NQ=  -4.50
1050420 1405  ES= -11.00  NQ=  -6.00
1050420 1410  ES= -11.75  NQ=  -6.00
1050420 1415  ES= -14.00  NQ= -10.50
1050420 1420  ES= -14.75  NQ= -10.50
1050420 1425  ES= -15.50  NQ= -11.50
1050420 1430  ES= -14.50  NQ= -11.50
1050420 1435  ES= -14.50  NQ= -11.00
1050420 1440  ES= -16.00  NQ= -13.50
1050420 1445  ES= -17.25  NQ= -15.00
1050420 1450  ES= -16.50  NQ= -14.50
1050420 1455  ES= -16.25  NQ= -13.50
```
1050420 1500 ES= -16.50 NQ= -13.00 ← STOP
```
1050420 1505  ES= -18.25  NQ= -15.50
1050420 1510  ES= -18.00  NQ= -14.00
1050420 1515  ES= -16.00  NQ= -11.00
```

**2) @ 0910 ES -ve S, NQ +ve S and absvalue(ES) >
absvalue(NQ) then Short immediately ("Short 1b").**
This is called **Opposite Day 2 to distinguish it from
Opposite Day 1.**
**(At 09:10 US central time, when you see ES is down single
digit, and NQ is up single digit compared to yesterday's
closing, and the absolute value of ES is greater then absolute
value of NQ, then Short ES.)**

ES	NQ
–ve S	+ve S
|ES| >	|NQ|

Explanation to rule 2: Opposite Day 2:
Reason is ditto item (a); we make this item (b) while the absolute
value of ES is greater than absolute value of NQ. Item (a) is just
vice versa. The way to trade is the same for RC 5 Seminar. For
RC 7, 8 traders, it's significant for them to have different strategies
to trade items (a) or (b), not just Short immediately. This is also a

good exercise for readers to do some research and think of a better way to trade item (a) and (b) conditions, based on the movement of NQ.

Example:

i) 2005 / 1 / 13

1050113	835	ES=	-0.25	NQ=	3.00
1050113	840	ES=	-1.00	NQ=	2.00
1050113	845	ES=	-0.75	NQ=	2.00
1050113	850	ES=	-2.00	NQ=	-1.50
1050113	855	ES=	-1.50	NQ=	0.50
1050113	900	ES=	-0.50	NQ=	1.50
1050113	905	ES=	0.25	NQ=	3.50
1050113	**910**	**ES=**	**-1.00**	**NQ=**	**0.50** ← **SHORT**

(OPPOSITE DAY 2)

1050113	915	ES=	-0.25	NQ=	3.00
1050113	920	ES=	0.00	NQ=	3.50
1050113	925	ES=	-0.75	NQ=	3.00
1050113	930	ES=	0.00	NQ=	3.50
1050113	935	ES=	0.50	NQ=	4.00
1050113	940	ES=	-0.50	NQ=	3.00
1050113	945	ES=	-1.00	NQ=	2.00
1050113	950	ES=	-1.00	NQ=	1.50
1050113	955	ES=	-1.75	NQ=	-1.50
1050113	1000	ES=	-1.75	NQ=	-1.50
1050113	1005	ES=	-1.00	NQ=	-0.50
1050113	1010	ES=	-0.25	NQ=	0.00
1050113	1015	ES=	-1.00	NQ=	-2.00
1050113	1020	ES=	-0.75	NQ=	-1.00
1050113	1025	ES=	-0.50	NQ=	-0.50
1050113	1030	ES=	-0.50	NQ=	0.00
1050113	1035	ES=	-1.00	NQ=	-0.50
1050113	1040	ES=	-1.50	NQ=	-1.50
1050113	1045	ES=	-2.75	NQ=	-3.50
1050113	1050	ES=	-2.75	NQ=	-4.00
1050113	1055	ES=	-2.00	NQ=	-3.00

```
1050113 1100  ES=  -2.75   NQ=  -3.50
1050113 1105  ES=  -2.50   NQ=  -3.50
1050113 1110  ES=  -2.50   NQ=  -3.50
1050113 1115  ES=  -2.50   NQ=  -3.00
1050113 1120  ES=  -2.00   NQ=  -2.00
1050113 1125  ES=  -2.50   NQ=  -3.00
1050113 1130  ES=  -2.00   NQ=  -2.50
1050113 1135  ES=  -1.75   NQ=  -1.50
1050113 1140  ES=  -2.25   NQ=  -1.50
1050113 1145  ES=  -1.50   NQ=  -1.00
1050113 1150  ES=  -2.00   NQ=  -1.50
1050113 1155  ES=  -1.75   NQ=  -1.50
1050113 1200  ES=  -1.50   NQ=  -1.00
1050113 1205  ES=  -1.25   NQ=  -1.00
1050113 1210  ES=  -1.25   NQ=  -1.00
1050113 1215  ES=  -0.75   NQ=   0.00
1050113 1220  ES=  -1.00   NQ=   0.00
1050113 1225  ES=  -1.25   NQ=  -1.50
1050113 1230  ES=  -1.75   NQ=  -3.50
1050113 1235  ES=  -1.75   NQ=  -2.50
1050113 1240  ES=  -1.50   NQ=  -1.50
1050113 1245  ES=  -1.50   NQ=  -1.50
1050113 1250  ES=  -1.00   NQ=  -0.50
1050113 1255  ES=  -0.50   NQ=   0.00
1050113 1300  ES=   0.25   NQ=   1.50
1050113 1305  ES=  -0.25   NQ=   1.00
1050113 1310  ES=  -0.75   NQ=   0.50
1050113 1315  ES=  -0.50   NQ=   1.00
1050113 1320  ES=   0.00   NQ=   1.50
1050113 1325  ES=  -0.25   NQ=   1.50
1050113 1330  ES=   0.25   NQ=   2.00
1050113 1335  ES=  -0.25   NQ=   0.50
1050113 1340  ES=  -0.50   NQ=   1.50
1050113 1345  ES=  -1.00   NQ=  -1.00
1050113 1350  ES=  -1.25   NQ=  -1.00
```

```
1050113 1355  ES=  -2.25  NQ=  -3.00
1050113 1400  ES=  -2.00  NQ=  -2.50
1050113 1405  ES=  -2.25  NQ=  -3.00
1050113 1410  ES=  -2.50  NQ=  -2.50
1050113 1415  ES=  -2.75  NQ=  -3.50
1050113 1420  ES=  -4.25  NQ=  -6.00
1050113 1425  ES=  -6.25  NQ=  -9.00
1050113 1430  ES=  -7.75  NQ= -12.00
1050113 1435  ES=  -8.50  NQ= -14.50
1050113 1440  ES=  -8.50  NQ= -15.00
1050113 1445  ES= -10.75  NQ= -18.00
1050113 1450  ES= -10.00  NQ= -15.50
1050113 1455  ES= -10.25  NQ= -16.00
```

1050113 1500 ES= -9.25 NQ= -17.00 ← **STOP**

```
1050113 1505  ES=  -9.75  NQ= -18.00
1050113 1510  ES= -10.00  NQ= -17.50
1050113 1515  ES=  -9.75  NQ= -17.00
```

ii) 2005 / 6 / 23

```
1050623  835  ES=  -3.00  NQ=  -2.50
1050623  840  ES=  -3.50  NQ=  -2.50
1050623  845  ES=  -3.50  NQ=  -0.50
1050623  850  ES=  -2.75  NQ=   5.00
1050623  855  ES=  -4.00  NQ=   2.50
1050623  900  ES=  -3.50  NQ=   2.50
1050623  905  ES=  -4.75  NQ=  -1.00
```

1050623   910 ES= -4.50 NQ=   0.00 ← **SHORT**
(OPPOSITE DAY 2)

```
1050623  915  ES=  -5.25  NQ=  -1.50
1050623  920  ES=  -5.25  NQ=  -4.00
1050623  925  ES=  -4.25  NQ=  -2.00
1050623  930  ES=  -4.75  NQ=  -3.00
1050623  935  ES=  -4.75  NQ=  -4.50
1050623  940  ES=  -4.25  NQ=  -4.50
1050623  945  ES=  -4.75  NQ=  -4.00
```

```
1050623  950   ES=  -5.25  NQ=  -5.50
1050623  955   ES=  -5.75  NQ=  -5.50
1050623 1000   ES=  -4.50  NQ=  -4.00
1050623 1005   ES=  -4.75  NQ=  -3.50
1050623 1010   ES=  -3.25  NQ=  -1.50
1050623 1015   ES=  -4.00  NQ=  -1.50
1050623 1020   ES=  -3.00  NQ=   1.50
1050623 1025   ES=  -1.75  NQ=   5.00
1050623 1030   ES=  -2.50  NQ=   3.50
1050623 1035   ES=  -2.75  NQ=   4.50
1050623 1040   ES=  -1.50  NQ=   7.50
1050623 1045   ES=  -1.50  NQ=   7.50
1050623 1050   ES=  -0.50  NQ=  11.00
1050623 1055   ES=  -2.00  NQ=   8.50
1050623 1100   ES=  -2.00  NQ=   9.00
1050623 1105   ES=  -3.00  NQ=   8.00
1050623 1110   ES=  -3.00  NQ=   6.50
1050623 1115   ES=  -2.00  NQ=   8.00
1050623 1120   ES=  -2.50  NQ=   8.00
1050623 1125   ES=  -2.25  NQ=   8.00
1050623 1130   ES=  -2.75  NQ=   6.50
1050623 1135   ES=  -2.75  NQ=   5.50
1050623 1140   ES=  -2.25  NQ=   7.00
1050623 1145   ES=  -2.00  NQ=   6.50
1050623 1150   ES=  -2.00  NQ=   6.50
1050623 1155   ES=  -2.75  NQ=   6.00
1050623 1200   ES=  -3.25  NQ=   4.50
1050623 1205   ES=  -3.25  NQ=   5.00
1050623 1210   ES=  -4.25  NQ=   2.50
1050623 1215   ES=  -4.25  NQ=   1.50
1050623 1220   ES=  -4.50  NQ=   1.50
1050623 1225   ES=  -4.50  NQ=   0.50
1050623 1230   ES=  -4.50  NQ=   0.00
1050623 1235   ES=  -5.00  NQ=  -2.00
1050623 1240   ES=  -8.50  NQ=  -9.00
```

```
1050623 1245  ES=   -8.25  NQ=   -9.00
1050623 1250  ES= -10.50  NQ= -13.50
1050623 1255  ES= -10.50  NQ= -14.50
1050623 1300  ES= -10.50  NQ= -15.00
1050623 1305  ES= -11.00  NQ= -15.00
1050623 1310  ES= -10.25  NQ= -13.50
1050623 1315  ES= -11.75  NQ= -17.00
1050623 1320  ES=   -9.25  NQ= -13.00
1050623 1325  ES= -10.00  NQ= -13.50
1050623 1330  ES= -10.75  NQ= -14.00
1050623 1335  ES= -10.50  NQ= -13.50
1050623 1340  ES=   -9.50  NQ= -11.50
1050623 1345  ES= -10.75  NQ= -14.00
1050623 1350  ES= -10.25  NQ= -13.50
1050623 1355  ES= -11.75  NQ= -15.00
1050623 1400  ES= -11.00  NQ= -14.50
1050623 1405  ES= -12.00  NQ= -14.50
1050623 1410  ES= -14.00  NQ= -18.00
1050623 1415  ES= -12.75  NQ= -14.00
1050623 1420  ES= -13.25  NQ= -15.50
1050623 1425  ES= -13.50  NQ= -16.50
1050623 1430  ES= -14.75  NQ= -19.50
1050623 1435  ES= -15.75  NQ= -21.50
1050623 1440  ES= -14.25  NQ= -19.00
1050623 1445  ES= -14.50  NQ= -20.50
1050623 1450  ES= -14.75  NQ= -20.00
1050623 1455  ES= -16.00  NQ= -22.00
```

<u>1050623 1500 ES= -16.50 NQ=-22.00</u> • ← **STOP**

```
1050623 1505  ES= -17.00  NQ= -21.00
1050623 1510  ES= -17.25  NQ= -22.00
1050623 1515  ES= -17.75  NQ= -22.50
```

3) @ 0910 ES +ve S, NQ -ve S and absvalue(NQ) >= absvalue(ES) then wait → anytime NQ >= 13 then Long ("Long 2a"). We call this Opposite Day 3.

(At 09:10, when ES is up single digit, NQ is down single digit, and the absolute value of NQ is greater than or equal to absolute value of ES, then we wait till when NQ is up 13 points, and Long ES)

$$
\begin{array}{cc}
\text{ES} & \text{NQ} \\
\text{+ve S} & \text{-ve S} \\
|\text{ES}| \;\; <= & |\text{NQ}| \\
\downarrow \text{wait until} & \\
\end{array}
$$

NQ >= 13, Long with stop.

Explanation to rule 3: Opposite Day 3:

Contrary to items (a) and (b) at 09:10, ES +ve NQ -ve, NQ -ve, after 40 minutes of market opening, cannot lead ES down, there is high probability that ES leads NQ up, so we Long with stop.

Example:

i)　2002 / 8 / 8

1020808	835	ES=	-0.50	NQ=	-8.00
1020808	840	ES=	1.25	NQ=	-11.00
1020808	845	ES=	7.50	NQ=	-5.50
1020808	850	ES=	8.50	NQ=	-2.00
1020808	855	ES=	8.00	NQ=	-4.00
1020808	900	ES=	6.75	NQ=	-7.00
1020808	905	ES=	6.25	NQ=	-9.00
1020808	**910**	**ES=**	**6.75**	**NQ=**	**-9.00**

(OPPOSITE DAY 3)

1020808	915	ES=	6.00	NQ=	-9.00
1020808	920	ES=	1.25	NQ=	-13.00
1020808	925	ES=	-1.50	NQ=	-17.50
1020808	930	ES=	1.75	NQ=	-14.00
1020808	935	ES=	3.25	NQ=	-12.00
1020808	940	ES=	2.00	NQ=	-12.50
1020808	945	ES=	1.00	NQ=	-15.50

```
1020808  950  ES=  -0.25  NQ= -16.00
1020808  955  ES=   1.50  NQ= -13.50
1020808 1000  ES=   1.75  NQ= -12.50
1020808 1005  ES=   5.75  NQ=  -7.00
1020808 1010  ES=   6.50  NQ=  -3.50
1020808 1015  ES=   4.50  NQ=  -7.50
1020808 1020  ES=   7.00  NQ=  -4.00
1020808 1025  ES=   7.00  NQ=  -4.00
1020808 1030  ES=   9.25  NQ=   1.50
1020808 1035  ES=  10.75  NQ=   3.50
1020808 1040  ES=  11.25  NQ=   7.00
1020808 1045  ES=   9.50  NQ=   2.00
1020808 1050  ES=   8.75  NQ=   1.00
1020808 1055  ES=   7.25  NQ=  -2.50
1020808 1100  ES=   9.75  NQ=   0.50
1020808 1105  ES=   9.50  NQ=  -1.00
1020808 1110  ES=   9.75  NQ=   0.00
1020808 1115  ES=  10.75  NQ=   0.50
1020808 1120  ES=   9.75  NQ=   0.50
1020808 1125  ES=  10.00  NQ=   0.00
1020808 1130  ES=  10.75  NQ=   1.50
1020808 1135  ES=  10.75  NQ=   0.50
1020808 1140  ES=  11.00  NQ=   1.00
1020808 1145  ES=  10.25  NQ=   0.50
1020808 1150  ES=   9.25  NQ=  -3.50
1020808 1155  ES=   9.75  NQ=  -2.50
1020808 1200  ES=   9.50  NQ=  -3.50
1020808 1205  ES=   9.75  NQ=  -3.00
1020808 1210  ES=  10.75  NQ=  -1.00
1020808 1215  ES=  14.25  NQ=   5.00
1020808 1220  ES=  13.50  NQ=   3.00
1020808 1225  ES=  14.50  NQ=   5.50
1020808 1230  ES=  17.75  NQ=  11.00
```

1020808 1235 ES= 19.00 NQ= 15.50 ← **LONG**

```
1020808 1240  ES=  18.25  NQ=  13.50
```

```
1020808 1245  ES=  17.50  NQ=  11.50
1020808 1250  ES=  19.50  NQ=  16.00
1020808 1255  ES=  16.75  NQ=  13.50
1020808 1300  ES=  17.00  NQ=  12.50
1020808 1305  ES=  17.50  NQ=  14.50
1020808 1310  ES=  16.25  NQ=  13.00
1020808 1315  ES=  17.75  NQ=  15.00
1020808 1320  ES=  17.75  NQ=  15.00
1020808 1325  ES=  19.00  NQ=  16.00
1020808 1330  ES=  22.00  NQ=  20.00
1020808 1335  ES=  22.00  NQ=  21.00
1020808 1340  ES=  21.25  NQ=  17.50
1020808 1345  ES=  21.50  NQ=  18.50
1020808 1350  ES=  25.25  NQ=  23.50
1020808 1355  ES=  25.00  NQ=  25.00
1020808 1400  ES=  27.00  NQ=  25.50
1020808 1405  ES=  27.75  NQ=  28.00
1020808 1410  ES=  27.50  NQ=  27.00
1020808 1415  ES=  26.50  NQ=  25.50
1020808 1420  ES=  24.00  NQ=  23.00
1020808 1425  ES=  25.25  NQ=  23.50
1020808 1430  ES=  26.75  NQ=  27.00
1020808 1435  ES=  29.50  NQ=  30.00
1020808 1440  ES=  29.25  NQ=  29.50
1020808 1445  ES=  28.25  NQ=  26.00
1020808 1450  ES=  29.75  NQ=  29.00
1020808 1455  ES=  28.00  NQ=  27.50
```

1020808 1500 ES= 29.50 NQ= 29.00 • ← **STOP**

```
1020808 1505  ES=  29.00  NQ=  29.50
1020808 1510  ES=  30.00  NQ=  29.50
1020808 1515  ES=  29.25  NQ=  29.50
```

ii) 2004 / 1 / 26

```
1040126  835  ES=   0.25  NQ=  -2.00
1040126  840  ES=   1.25  NQ=  -1.00
```

1040126	845	ES=	1.75	NQ=	0.00
1040126	850	ES=	2.50	NQ=	2.50
1040126	855	ES=	2.25	NQ=	0.50
1040126	900	ES=	2.25	NQ=	0.50
1040126	905	ES=	0.00	NQ=	-6.50
1040126	**910**	**ES=**	**1.25**	**NQ=**	**-4.50**

(OPPOSTIE DAY 3)

1040126	915	ES=	1.25	NQ=	-3.50
1040126	920	ES=	1.25	NQ=	-5.00
1040126	925	ES=	2.75	NQ=	-2.00
1040126	930	ES=	0.00	NQ=	-6.50
1040126	935	ES=	0.50	NQ=	-5.50
1040126	940	ES=	1.25	NQ=	-4.00
1040126	945	ES=	0.50	NQ=	-7.00
1040126	950	ES=	2.00	NQ=	-3.50
1040126	955	ES=	2.75	NQ=	-2.00
1040126	1000	ES=	2.75	NQ=	-2.50
1040126	1005	ES=	2.75	NQ=	-0.50
1040126	1010	ES=	1.50	NQ=	-4.00
1040126	1015	ES=	1.25	NQ=	-4.50
1040126	1020	ES=	1.50	NQ=	-3.00
1040126	1025	ES=	0.25	NQ=	-4.50
1040126	1030	ES=	0.75	NQ=	-4.00
1040126	1035	ES=	0.50	NQ=	-4.50
1040126	1040	ES=	0.75	NQ=	-4.50
1040126	1045	ES=	1.25	NQ=	-4.00
1040126	1050	ES=	1.00	NQ=	-4.00
1040126	1055	ES=	1.25	NQ=	-3.50
1040126	1100	ES=	1.50	NQ=	-3.00
1040126	1105	ES=	1.25	NQ=	-3.50
1040126	1110	ES=	2.75	NQ=	-1.50
1040126	1115	ES=	2.50	NQ=	-1.50
1040126	1120	ES=	2.25	NQ=	-2.50
1040126	1125	ES=	2.25	NQ=	-2.00
1040126	1130	ES=	2.50	NQ=	-2.00

```
1040126 1135  ES=    1.50  NQ=  -3.50
1040126 1140  ES=    0.75  NQ=  -5.00
1040126 1145  ES=    0.75  NQ=  -5.00
1040126 1150  ES=    1.25  NQ=  -3.50
1040126 1155  ES=    2.25  NQ=  -1.50
1040126 1200  ES=    2.25  NQ=  -2.00
1040126 1205  ES=    1.75  NQ=  -3.00
1040126 1210  ES=    1.75  NQ=  -3.00
1040126 1215  ES=    2.25  NQ=  -2.50
1040126 1220  ES=    2.25  NQ=  -2.00
1040126 1225  ES=    3.00  NQ=  -1.00
1040126 1230  ES=    2.75  NQ=  -0.50
1040126 1235  ES=    2.75  NQ=   0.50
1040126 1240  ES=    3.25  NQ=   1.50
1040126 1245  ES=    3.00  NQ=   0.00
1040126 1250  ES=    3.25  NQ=   1.00
1040126 1255  ES=    3.00  NQ=   1.00
1040126 1300  ES=    2.25  NQ=   0.00
1040126 1305  ES=    3.25  NQ=   1.00
1040126 1310  ES=    3.50  NQ=   1.50
1040126 1315  ES=    4.00  NQ=   2.00
1040126 1320  ES=    4.00  NQ=   2.50
1040126 1325  ES=    6.00  NQ=   6.50
1040126 1330  ES=    6.25  NQ=   7.00
1040126 1335  ES=    7.50  NQ=   9.00
1040126 1340  ES=    7.50  NQ=  11.00
1040126 1345  ES=    8.00  NQ=  11.50
1040126 1350  ES=    8.50  NQ=  12.50
1040126 1355  ES=    7.75  NQ=  10.50
```

1040126 1400 ES=   8.75 NQ= 13.00 • ← **LONG**

```
1040126 1405  ES=    9.00  NQ=  13.50
1040126 1410  ES=    9.00  NQ=  13.00
1040126 1415  ES=   10.25  NQ=  14.50
1040126 1420  ES=   11.75  NQ=  19.00
1040126 1425  ES=   11.50  NQ=  19.50
```

```
1040126 1430  ES=  11.75  NQ=  19.50
1040126 1435  ES=  12.00  NQ=  19.50
1040126 1440  ES=  11.75  NQ=  19.00
1040126 1445  ES=  12.00  NQ=  18.50
1040126 1450  ES=  13.75  NQ=  22.50
1040126 1455  ES=  14.25  NQ=  22.00
```
1040126 1500 ES= 13.75 NQ= 21.50 ← **STOP**
```
1040126 1505  ES=  14.50  NQ=  22.50
1040126 1510  ES=  14.25  NQ=  23.00
1040126 1515  ES=  14.25  NQ=  21.50
```

**4) @ 0910 ES +ve S, NQ -ve S and absvalue(ES) >
absvalue(NQ) then wait → anytime NQ >= 13 then Long
("Long 2b").**

**(At 09:10, when you see ES is up and NQ is down from
yesterday's closing, and both are in single digit, and absolute
value of ES is greater than the absolute value of NQ, wait till
NQ is up 13 points from yesterday's closing, then Long ES.)**

$$ES \qquad NQ$$
$$+ve\ S \qquad -ve\ S$$
$$|ES| \quad > \quad |NQ|$$
$$\downarrow \text{wait until}$$
$$NQ >= 13, \text{Long with stop.}$$

Explanation to rule 4: Opposite Day 4:

Ditto item (c), trading rules are same for RC 5, but for RC 7, 8
traders need to separate (c), (d) condition and trade differently.
You will see the difference in RC 5++ system or trading rules
using RC 8 indicator to trade the same condition with better results.
RC 5++ system's hypothetical result will be shown by end of this
chapter.

Example:
i) 2002 / 10 / 1
```
1021001  835  ES=  8.50  NQ=  11.50
1021001  840  ES=  6.50  NQ=   9.50
```

1021001	845	ES=	6.00	NQ=	5.50
1021001	850	ES=	3.25	NQ=	2.00
1021001	855	ES=	3.00	NQ=	-0.50
1021001	900	ES=	4.00	NQ=	1.00
1021001	905	ES=	8.00	NQ=	4.00
1021001	**910**	**ES=**	**3.75**	**NQ=**	**-1.00**

(OPPOSITE DAY 4)

1021001	915	ES=	-1.00	NQ=	-7.50
1021001	920	ES=	0.25	NQ=	-5.50
1021001	925	ES=	-2.00	NQ=	-8.50
1021001	930	ES=	-0.50	NQ=	-8.00
1021001	935	ES=	3.50	NQ=	-3.50
1021001	940	ES=	2.75	NQ=	-6.00
1021001	945	ES=	3.25	NQ=	-3.50
1021001	950	ES=	5.75	NQ=	1.00
1021001	955	ES=	4.25	NQ=	-1.50
1021001	1000	ES=	3.00	NQ=	-3.50
1021001	1005	ES=	4.00	NQ=	-3.00
1021001	1010	ES=	0.75	NQ=	-7.50
1021001	1015	ES=	1.00	NQ=	-7.50
1021001	1020	ES=	0.75	NQ=	-7.50
1021001	1025	ES=	2.00	NQ=	-5.50
1021001	1030	ES=	0.75	NQ=	-5.50
1021001	1035	ES=	1.75	NQ=	-5.50
1021001	1040	ES=	2.75	NQ=	-4.50
1021001	1045	ES=	1.00	NQ=	-5.50
1021001	1050	ES=	2.25	NQ=	-3.50
1021001	1055	ES=	2.50	NQ=	-1.00
1021001	1100	ES=	1.50	NQ=	-3.00
1021001	1105	ES=	4.75	NQ=	2.50
1021001	1110	ES=	3.25	NQ=	0.00
1021001	1115	ES=	1.75	NQ=	-2.00
1021001	1120	ES=	4.00	NQ=	-1.00
1021001	1125	ES=	4.75	NQ=	0.50
1021001	1130	ES=	5.00	NQ=	-0.50

```
1021001 1135  ES=   6.00  NQ=   2.50
1021001 1140  ES=   5.75  NQ=   1.50
1021001 1145  ES=   6.50  NQ=   3.00
1021001 1150  ES=   8.00  NQ=   4.50
1021001 1155  ES=  11.25  NQ=   8.50
1021001 1200  ES=  11.00  NQ=   7.00
1021001 1205  ES=  10.50  NQ=   7.00
1021001 1210  ES=  10.50  NQ=   7.00
1021001 1215  ES=  14.00  NQ=  10.50
1021001 1220  ES=  15.50  NQ=  10.50
```
1021001 1225 ES= 18.00 NQ= 13.00 ← **LONG**
```
1021001 1230  ES=  18.25  NQ=  14.00
1021001 1235  ES=  16.75  NQ=  13.00
1021001 1240  ES=  16.25  NQ=  10.50
1021001 1245  ES=  15.75  NQ=  11.00
1021001 1250  ES=  18.00  NQ=  15.00
1021001 1255  ES=  15.00  NQ=  10.50
1021001 1300  ES=  15.75  NQ=  11.00
1021001 1305  ES=  14.50  NQ=   9.50
1021001 1310  ES=  15.75  NQ=  12.00
1021001 1315  ES=  16.00  NQ=  11.50
1021001 1320  ES=  18.25  NQ=  15.00
1021001 1325  ES=  22.00  NQ=  19.00
1021001 1330  ES=  21.00  NQ=  17.50
1021001 1335  ES=  21.75  NQ=  18.50
1021001 1340  ES=  24.00  NQ=  23.00
1021001 1345  ES=  23.00  NQ=  21.50
1021001 1350  ES=  22.00  NQ=  20.00
1021001 1355  ES=  22.50  NQ=  21.50
1021001 1400  ES=  20.25  NQ=  19.00
1021001 1405  ES=  21.00  NQ=  20.00
1021001 1410  ES=  24.25  NQ=  25.50
1021001 1415  ES=  25.50  NQ=  27.00
1021001 1420  ES=  25.75  NQ=  27.00
1021001 1425  ES=  26.75  NQ=  28.50
```

```
1021001 1430  ES=  31.00  NQ=  34.00
1021001 1435  ES=  30.50  NQ=  34.00
1021001 1440  ES=  32.00  NQ=  34.50
1021001 1445  ES=  31.75  NQ=  35.00
1021001 1450  ES=  30.75  NQ=  32.00
1021001 1455  ES=  30.50  NQ=  31.00
```
1021001 1500 ES= 33.50 NQ= 36.00 • ← **STOP**
```
1021001 1505  ES=  33.00  NQ=  37.00
1021001 1510  ES=  37.25  NQ=  47.00
1021001 1515  ES=  39.50  NQ=  49.00
```

ii) 2003 / 7 / 25
```
1030725  835  ES=   2.00  NQ=   5.00
1030725  840  ES=   0.00  NQ=   0.00
1030725  845  ES=   1.50  NQ=   0.00
1030725  850  ES=   3.75  NQ=   2.50
1030725  855  ES=   4.75  NQ=   5.00
1030725  900  ES=   5.25  NQ=   4.50
1030725  905  ES=   4.75  NQ=   1.50
```
1030725   910 ES=   4.25 NQ= -1.00

                                     (OPPOSITE DAY 4)
```
1030725  915  ES=   2.25  NQ=  -5.50
1030725  920  ES=   3.50  NQ=  -3.50
1030725  925  ES=   3.25  NQ=  -3.00
1030725  930  ES=   1.00  NQ=  -6.50
1030725  935  ES=  -1.25  NQ= -11.50
1030725  940  ES=  -1.50  NQ= -10.50
1030725  945  ES=  -1.25  NQ= -11.00
1030725  950  ES=  -3.50  NQ= -14.00
1030725  955  ES=  -3.50  NQ= -13.00
1030725 1000  ES=  -2.50  NQ= -11.50
1030725 1005  ES=  -2.50  NQ= -11.00
1030725 1010  ES=   0.25  NQ=  -8.00
1030725 1015  ES=   0.50  NQ=  -4.50
1030725 1020  ES=   1.00  NQ=  -6.00
1030725 1025  ES=   1.00  NQ=  -6.00
```

```
1030725 1030  ES=   0.75  NQ=  -7.50
1030725 1035  ES=   0.25  NQ=  -9.50
1030725 1040  ES=   0.50  NQ=  -7.50
1030725 1045  ES=   2.50  NQ=  -3.50
1030725 1050  ES=   2.75  NQ=  -4.00
1030725 1055  ES=   3.75  NQ=  -0.50
1030725 1100  ES=   4.00  NQ=  -0.50
1030725 1105  ES=   4.75  NQ=   0.50
1030725 1110  ES=   4.25  NQ=  -1.50
1030725 1115  ES=   4.25  NQ=  -2.00
1030725 1120  ES=   5.00  NQ=  -1.50
1030725 1125  ES=   4.25  NQ=  -3.00
1030725 1130  ES=   3.50  NQ=  -4.00
1030725 1135  ES=   3.50  NQ=  -3.50
1030725 1140  ES=   4.00  NQ=  -2.50
1030725 1145  ES=   3.75  NQ=  -4.00
1030725 1150  ES=   4.75  NQ=  -1.00
1030725 1155  ES=   4.50  NQ=  -1.00
1030725 1200  ES=   4.50  NQ=  -1.00
1030725 1205  ES=   5.75  NQ=   2.00
1030725 1210  ES=   5.50  NQ=   0.50
1030725 1215  ES=   8.00  NQ=   2.50
1030725 1220  ES=   8.25  NQ=   1.50
1030725 1225  ES=   8.25  NQ=   3.00
1030725 1230  ES=   8.25  NQ=   3.50
1030725 1235  ES=   9.25  NQ=   9.00
```

1030725 1240 ES=   9.75 NQ= 13.00 • ← **LONG**

```
1030725 1245  ES=   9.25  NQ=  12.00
1030725 1250  ES=   9.25  NQ=  12.00
1030725 1255  ES=   8.25  NQ=   9.50
1030725 1300  ES=   7.75  NQ=   8.50
1030725 1305  ES=   8.50  NQ=  10.00
1030725 1310  ES=   8.25  NQ=  10.00
1030725 1315  ES=   8.00  NQ=   9.50
1030725 1320  ES=   8.50  NQ=  10.00
1030725 1325  ES=   7.25  NQ=   8.50
```

```
1030725 1330  ES=   8.50  NQ=   9.50
1030725 1335  ES=  11.75  NQ=  16.00
1030725 1340  ES=  12.25  NQ=  16.00
1030725 1345  ES=  12.00  NQ=  15.00
1030725 1350  ES=  12.50  NQ=  15.50
1030725 1355  ES=  14.50  NQ=  19.50
1030725 1400  ES=  14.00  NQ=  19.00
1030725 1405  ES=  14.75  NQ=  20.50
1030725 1410  ES=  15.50  NQ=  21.50
1030725 1415  ES=  15.00  NQ=  20.00
1030725 1420  ES=  14.25  NQ=  16.50
1030725 1425  ES=  14.00  NQ=  18.00
1030725 1430  ES=  15.50  NQ=  22.00
1030725 1435  ES=  15.75  NQ=  21.50
1030725 1440  ES=  14.50  NQ=  19.00
1030725 1445  ES=  16.00  NQ=  21.00
1030725 1450  ES=  16.50  NQ=  22.50
1030725 1455  ES=  16.75  NQ=  23.00
```
1030725 1500 ES= 17.00 NQ= 24.50 • ← STOP
```
1030725 1505  ES=  16.50  NQ=  26.00
1030725 1510  ES=  16.50  NQ=  26.00
1030725 1515  ES=  16.75  NQ=  26.50
```

5) @ 0910 ES -ve S, NQ -ve S and NQ is more -ve than ES, wait → anytime NQ <= -20 then Short ("Short 3a"), Normal Negative Single Day.

(At 09:10, when ES is down and NQ is also down, both single digits, and NQ is down more than ES, i.e. if ES is down 10 points, NQ down 15 points, then NQ is down more than ES, or NQ is more -ve than ES -ve. Wait till NQ is down more than 20 points from yesterday's closing, then Short ES.)

$$
\begin{array}{ccc}
\text{ES} & & \text{NQ} \\
\text{–ve S} & & \text{–ve S} \\
\text{ES} & > & \text{NQ} \\
& \downarrow \text{ wait until} & \\
& \text{NQ} <= -20 &
\end{array}
$$

Explanation to rule 5: Normal Negative Single Day:
(Negative Single refers to the NQ is negative single digit at
09:10, Normal means NQ is more -ve than ES -ve, i.e. NQ is
leading ES to -ve, so we call it normal.)
Both ES and NQ are -ve and in single digits. The trader just waits
until NQ is down to -20 or below, and then Shorts. It's a trend –
following strategy using NQ as indicator NQ < -20, it's difficult
for NQ to go back to +ve and lead ES up. Because the real down
trend has set. So we short when NQ is < -20. I say it's difficult for
NQ to move up but it may be possible. RC 5 trader still has to
monitor NQ movement to stop the short when NQ is moving up,
or reverse position to long if traders see NQ is moving further up.
We watch the NQ movement to trade ES at ease rather than just
looking at the ES prices moving up and down which has no trading
edge.

Example:
i)　2004 / 10 / 22

1041022	835	ES=	-1.25	NQ=	-1.50
1041022	840	ES=	-2.25	NQ=	-6.50
1041022	845	ES=	-0.75	NQ=	-3.50
1041022	850	ES=	-0.75	NQ=	-3.00
1041022	855	ES=	-2.25	NQ=	-7.50
1041022	900	ES=	-1.00	NQ=	-5.00
1041022	905	ES=	-2.00	NQ=	-8.00
1041022	**910**	**ES=**	**-2.50**	**NQ=**	**-9.00 (NORMAL NEGATIVE SINGLE DAY)**
1041022	915	ES=	-2.00	NQ=	-6.00
1041022	920	ES=	-2.75	NQ=	-9.00
1041022	925	ES=	-3.25	NQ=	-10.00
1041022	930	ES=	-3.00	NQ=	-11.00
1041022	935	ES=	-2.50	NQ=	-10.00
1041022	940	ES=	-4.75	NQ=	-13.00
1041022	945	ES=	-4.00	NQ=	-11.50
1041022	950	ES=	-3.75	NQ=	-12.00

```
1041022   955  ES=  -3.50  NQ=  -11.00
1041022  1000  ES=  -4.00  NQ=  -12.00
1041022  1005  ES=  -3.00  NQ=  -10.00
1041022  1010  ES=  -3.25  NQ=  -11.00
1041022  1015  ES=  -3.25  NQ=  -11.00
1041022  1020  ES=  -3.50  NQ=  -13.00
1041022  1025  ES=  -5.25  NQ=  -17.00
1041022  1030  ES=  -5.50  NQ=  -16.00
1041022  1035  ES=  -5.00  NQ=  -15.00
1041022  1040  ES=  -4.25  NQ=  -14.00
1041022  1045  ES=  -3.75  NQ=  -13.50
1041022  1050  ES=  -4.75  NQ=  -15.00
1041022  1055  ES=  -4.50  NQ=  -15.50
1041022  1100  ES=  -4.75  NQ=  -15.50
1041022  1105  ES=  -4.00  NQ=  -15.00
1041022  1110  ES=  -3.50  NQ=  -14.50
1041022  1115  ES=  -3.25  NQ=  -13.50
1041022  1120  ES=  -3.50  NQ=  -14.50
1041022  1125  ES=  -3.00  NQ=  -13.50
1041022  1130  ES=  -2.75  NQ=  -12.50
1041022  1135  ES=  -2.75  NQ=  -11.50
1041022  1140  ES=  -3.75  NQ=  -14.00
1041022  1145  ES=  -3.00  NQ=  -13.00
1041022  1150  ES=  -3.50  NQ=  -13.00
1041022  1155  ES=  -4.00  NQ=  -15.00
1041022  1200  ES=  -4.25  NQ=  -15.50
1041022  1205  ES=  -4.25  NQ=  -15.50
1041022  1210  ES=  -4.25  NQ=  -15.00
1041022  1215  ES=  -4.75  NQ=  -18.00
```

1041022 1220 ES= -5.75 NQ=-20.00 • ← **SHORT**

```
1041022  1225  ES=  -7.25  NQ=  -21.00
1041022  1230  ES=  -7.00  NQ=  -20.50
1041022  1235  ES=  -8.25  NQ=  -23.00
1041022  1240  ES=  -8.00  NQ=  -22.00
1041022  1245  ES=  -9.00  NQ=  -23.00
```

```
1041022 1250  ES=   -9.50  NQ= -24.00
1041022 1255  ES=   -9.50  NQ= -24.00
1041022 1300  ES=   -9.00  NQ= -23.00
1041022 1305  ES=   -8.75  NQ= -24.00
1041022 1310  ES=   -9.25  NQ= -26.50
1041022 1315  ES=   -9.25  NQ= -27.50
1041022 1320  ES=   -7.75  NQ= -25.50
1041022 1325  ES=   -8.00  NQ= -26.50
1041022 1330  ES=   -7.00  NQ= -25.00
1041022 1335  ES=   -7.00  NQ= -24.50
1041022 1340  ES=   -9.00  NQ= -28.00
1041022 1345  ES=   -9.50  NQ= -30.00
1041022 1350  ES=   -9.00  NQ= -29.00
1041022 1355  ES= -11.75  NQ= -32.50
1041022 1400  ES= -12.25  NQ= -33.50
1041022 1405  ES= -12.75  NQ= -33.00
1041022 1410  ES= -11.25  NQ= -31.00
1041022 1415  ES= -12.00  NQ= -33.50
1041022 1420  ES= -12.00  NQ= -32.50
1041022 1425  ES= -12.50  NQ= -33.00
1041022 1430  ES= -11.75  NQ= -32.50
1041022 1435  ES= -11.25  NQ= -31.00
1041022 1440  ES= -11.25  NQ= -31.50
1041022 1445  ES= -10.25  NQ= -29.50
1041022 1450  ES= -11.75  NQ= -32.50
1041022 1455  ES= -12.75  NQ= -35.00
```

1041022 1500 ES= -12.75 NQ=-33.50 • ← **STOP**

```
1041022 1505  ES= -12.50  NQ= -33.50
1041022 1510  ES= -12.25  NQ= -34.00
1041022 1515  ES= -13.00  NQ= -33.00
```

ii) 2005 / 8 /16
```
1050816  835  ES=   -3.50  NQ=   -7.00
1050816  840  ES=   -5.50  NQ= -10.50
1050816  845  ES=   -5.25  NQ=   -8.00
```

```
1050816  850  ES=  -5.25  NQ=  -8.50
1050816  855  ES=  -5.50  NQ=  -8.50
1050816  900  ES=  -5.50  NQ=  -8.50
1050816  905  ES=  -6.25  NQ=  -9.50
```

1050816 910 ES= -4.25 NQ= -8.00 (NORMAL
NEGATIVE SINGLE DAY)

```
1050816  915  ES=  -5.50  NQ= -11.00
1050816  920  ES=  -5.25  NQ= -10.00
1050816  925  ES=  -5.00  NQ= -10.00
1050816  930  ES=  -5.25  NQ=  -9.00
1050816  935  ES=  -6.25  NQ= -14.00
1050816  940  ES=  -6.50  NQ= -13.50
1050816  945  ES=  -7.50  NQ= -15.00
1050816  950  ES=  -9.25  NQ= -18.00
1050816  955  ES=  -9.50  NQ= -17.00
1050816 1000  ES=  -9.75  NQ= -18.00
1050816 1005  ES= -10.00  NQ= -18.00
1050816 1010  ES=  -9.50  NQ= -17.50
1050816 1015  ES=  -9.50  NQ= -17.50
1050816 1020  ES=  -9.50  NQ= -16.50
1050816 1025  ES=  -9.00  NQ= -14.50
1050816 1030  ES=  -9.00  NQ= -15.00
1050816 1035  ES=  -9.00  NQ= -16.00
1050816 1040  ES=  -8.50  NQ= -15.50
1050816 1045  ES=  -9.00  NQ= -15.00
1050816 1050  ES=  -9.50  NQ= -16.00
1050816 1055  ES= -10.25  NQ= -17.00
1050816 1100  ES= -10.50  NQ= -18.00
1050816 1105  ES= -11.75  NQ= -19.00
1050816 1110  ES= -10.75  NQ= -16.00
1050816 1115  ES= -10.50  NQ= -15.50
1050816 1120  ES= -10.50  NQ= -15.50
1050816 1125  ES= -10.75  NQ= -17.00
1050816 1130  ES= -10.00  NQ= -15.00
1050816 1135  ES=  -9.75  NQ= -14.00
```

```
1050816 1140  ES= -10.00  NQ= -15.50
1050816 1145  ES= -10.50  NQ= -16.00
1050816 1150  ES= -10.50  NQ= -17.00
1050816 1155  ES= -10.25  NQ= -17.00
1050816 1200  ES= -10.25  NQ= -16.00
1050816 1205  ES= -10.25  NQ= -16.00
1050816 1210  ES= -10.50  NQ= -17.50
1050816 1215  ES= -10.00  NQ= -16.50
1050816 1220  ES=  -9.50  NQ= -16.00
1050816 1225  ES=  -9.25  NQ= -15.00
1050816 1230  ES= -10.25  NQ= -17.00
1050816 1235  ES= -10.25  NQ= -16.50
1050816 1240  ES= -10.75  NQ= -18.00
1050816 1245  ES= -11.00  NQ= -17.50
1050816 1250  ES= -10.75  NQ= -18.00
1050816 1255  ES= -10.75  NQ= -19.00
```

1050816 1300 ES= -11.75 NQ=-22.00 • ← **SHORT**

```
1050816 1305  ES= -11.00  NQ= -21.50
1050816 1310  ES= -12.25  NQ= -22.00
1050816 1315  ES= -12.75  NQ= -24.50
1050816 1320  ES= -12.50  NQ= -23.50
1050816 1325  ES= -12.25  NQ= -23.00
1050816 1330  ES= -12.50  NQ= -23.00
1050816 1335  ES= -12.00  NQ= -22.50
1050816 1340  ES= -11.25  NQ= -22.00
1050816 1345  ES= -11.25  NQ= -22.00
1050816 1350  ES= -11.75  NQ= -23.00
1050816 1355  ES= -11.75  NQ= -22.00
1050816 1400  ES= -11.25  NQ= -21.50
1050816 1405  ES= -11.00  NQ= -21.50
1050816 1410  ES= -10.75  NQ= -22.00
1050816 1415  ES= -11.50  NQ= -23.50
1050816 1420  ES= -12.50  NQ= -24.50
1050816 1425  ES= -15.25  NQ= -27.50
1050816 1430  ES= -15.25  NQ= -28.00
```

```
1050816 1435  ES= -16.00  NQ= -29.00
1050816 1440  ES= -16.50  NQ= -29.50
1050816 1445  ES= -14.25  NQ= -26.50
1050816 1450  ES= -15.00  NQ= -26.50
1050816 1455  ES= -16.00  NQ= -28.00
```
1050816 1500 ES= -17.00 NQ=-27.00 • ← STOP
```
1050816 1505  ES= -17.00  NQ= -24.50
1050816 1510  ES= -16.50  NQ= -24.50
1050816 1515  ES= -16.50  NQ= -24.00
```

6) @ 0910 ES -ve S, NQ -ve S and ES < NQ (means ES is more -ve than NQ -ve) then wait → anytime NQ <= -8 then Short ("Short 3b".)

(At 09:10, when ES and NQ are both down single digit, and ES is down more than NQ, wait till NQ is down to negative 8 points or more, then Short ES.)

$$\begin{array}{cc} ES & NQ \\ -ve\ S & -ve\ S \\ ES\ \ \ < & NQ \\ \downarrow \text{wait until} \\ NQ <= -8 \end{array}$$

Explanation to rule 6: Abnormal Negative Single Day:
(At 09:10, NQ is -ve single, so it is a Single Negative Day, but this time ES is more -ve than NQ -ve which makes it an Abnormal Day.) We wait, when NQ is -ve 8 or more -ve, then we Short with a Stop.

Example:
i) 2002 / 8 / 5
```
    1020805  835  ES= -2.75  NQ= -5.00
    1020805  840  ES= -4.00  NQ= -2.50
    1020805  845  ES= -4.00  NQ= -0.50
    1020805  850  ES= -3.75  NQ= -0.50
    1020805  855  ES= -7.75  NQ= -4.00
    1020805  900  ES= -6.75  NQ= -3.50
```

```
1020805   905  ES=  -7.75   NQ=  -5.00
1020805   910  ES=  -8.00   NQ=  -4.50 (ABNORMAL
                                       NEGATIVE SINGLE DAY )
1020805   915  ES=  -5.50   NQ=  -1.50
1020805   920  ES=  -5.25   NQ=  -1.00
1020805   925  ES=  -6.75   NQ=  -2.00
1020805   930  ES=  -7.25   NQ=  -5.50
1020805   935  ES=  -6.75   NQ=  -5.50
1020805   940  ES=  -9.00   NQ=  -9.50  •  ← SHORT
1020805   945  ES=  -8.50   NQ= -10.00
1020805   950  ES=  -6.50   NQ=  -9.50
1020805   955  ES=  -9.00   NQ= -14.50
1020805  1000  ES= -12.50   NQ=  18.50
1020805  1005  ES= -13.00   NQ= -22.50
1020805  1010  ES= -14.50   NQ= -23.00
1020805  1015  ES= -14.75   NQ= -24.50
1020805  1020  ES= -15.00   NQ= -24.00
1020805  1025  ES= -14.00   NQ= -23.00
1020805  1030  ES= -13.00   NQ= -21.50
1020805  1035  ES= -14.25   NQ= -22.00
1020805  1040  ES= -17.50   NQ= -24.50
1020805  1045  ES= -16.50   NQ= -24.50
1020805  1050  ES= -16.00   NQ= -23.00
1020805  1055  ES= -14.75   NQ= -21.00
1020805  1100  ES= -15.75   NQ= -22.00
1020805  1105  ES= -14.50   NQ= -20.50
1020805  1110  ES= -16.00   NQ= -23.00
1020805  1115  ES= -16.50   NQ= -23.50
1020805  1120  ES= -19.75   NQ= -26.50
1020805  1125  ES= -18.25   NQ= -25.50
1020805  1130  ES= -18.50   NQ= -24.50
1020805  1135  ES= -19.25   NQ= -26.00
1020805  1140  ES= -21.50   NQ= -27.50
1020805  1145  ES= -21.75   NQ= -27.50
1020805  1150  ES= -20.25   NQ= -25.50
```

```
1020805 1155  ES= -21.50  NQ= -27.00
1020805 1200  ES= -21.75  NQ= -28.00
1020805 1205  ES= -19.50  NQ= -26.50
1020805 1210  ES= -18.00  NQ= -25.50
1020805 1215  ES= -16.50  NQ= -24.50
1020805 1220  ES= -16.75  NQ= -24.50
1020805 1225  ES= -16.25  NQ= -22.00
1020805 1230  ES= -16.75  NQ= -22.50
1020805 1235  ES= -17.50  NQ= -24.00
1020805 1240  ES= -17.50  NQ= -24.00
1020805 1245  ES= -16.50  NQ= -23.00
1020805 1250  ES= -19.25  NQ= -24.50
1020805 1255  ES= -19.00  NQ= -23.50
1020805 1300  ES= -19.75  NQ= -26.00
1020805 1305  ES= -21.00  NQ= -28.50
1020805 1310  ES= -21.25  NQ= -28.00
1020805 1315  ES= -20.75  NQ= -28.50
1020805 1320  ES= -23.25  NQ= -33.00
1020805 1325  ES= -21.50  NQ= -31.00
1020805 1330  ES= -25.00  NQ= -35.00
1020805 1335  ES= -24.25  NQ= -33.50
1020805 1340  ES= -24.75  NQ= -34.50
1020805 1345  ES= -23.00  NQ= -32.00
1020805 1350  ES= -23.00  NQ= -31.50
1020805 1355  ES= -23.00  NQ= -32.50
1020805 1400  ES= -24.25  NQ= -32.50
1020805 1405  ES= -27.00  NQ= -35.50
1020805 1410  ES= -26.25  NQ= -36.00
1020805 1415  ES= -26.00  NQ= -35.00
1020805 1420  ES= -27.50  NQ= -34.50
1020805 1425  ES= -23.00  NQ= -31.00
1020805 1430  ES= -26.25  NQ= -35.50
1020805 1435  ES= -27.75  NQ= -35.00
1020805 1440  ES= -28.50  NQ= -35.50
1020805 1445  ES= -28.75  NQ= -35.00
```

1020805 1450 ES= -31.50 NQ= -37.00
1020805 1455 ES= -31.00 NQ= -36.00
1020805 1500 ES= -31.50 NQ=-36.50 • ← **STOP**
1020805 1505 ES= -32.25 NQ= -35.50
1020805 1510 ES= -31.00 NQ= -35.00
1020805 1515 ES= -30.25 NQ= -32.50

ii) 2005 / 4 / 28
1050428   835 ES= -2.75 NQ= -1.50
1050428   840 ES= -4.00 NQ= -2.50
1050428   845 ES= -5.50 NQ= -3.50
1050428   850 ES= -7.75 NQ= -5.50
1050428   855 ES= -8.00 NQ= -7.00
1050428   900 ES= -7.50 NQ= -5.00
1050428   905 ES= -5.75 NQ= -3.50
1050428   910 ES= -6.25 NQ= -3.50 (ABNORMAL
NEGATIVE SINGLE DAY)
1050428   915 ES= -4.50 NQ= -2.00
1050428   920 ES= -5.00 NQ= -3.00
1050428   925 ES= -2.75 NQ= -2.00
1050428   930 ES= -2.50 NQ= -1.50
1050428   935 ES= -1.00 NQ=   2.00
1050428   940 ES= -2.75 NQ= -1.50
1050428   945 ES= -3.25 NQ= -4.00
1050428   950 ES= -3.25 NQ= -3.00
1050428   955 ES= -5.25 NQ= -5.50
1050428 1000 ES= -4.25 NQ= -3.50
1050428 1005 ES= -4.00 NQ= -3.50
1050428 1010 ES= -3.75 NQ= -3.00
1050428 1015 ES= -4.50 NQ= -3.00
1050428 1020 ES= -2.75 NQ= -0.50
1050428 1025 ES= -3.00 NQ= -2.00
1050428 1030 ES= -4.75 NQ= -3.50
1050428 1035 ES= -6.50 NQ= -7.50
1050428 1040 ES= -6.00 NQ= -7.00
1050428 1045 ES= -6.50 NQ= -7.00

1050428 1050 ES=   -5.75 NQ=   -6.00
1050428 1055 ES=   -5.75 NQ=   -6.50
1050428 1100 ES=   -6.25 NQ=   -7.50
1050428 1105 ES=   -6.00 NQ=   -6.50
1050428   1110   ES=   -7.00   NQ=   -8.00 ← **SHORT**
1050428 1115 ES=   -7.50 NQ=   -9.00
1050428 1120 ES=   -7.00 NQ=   -8.50
1050428 1125 ES=   -7.25 NQ=   -8.50
1050428 1130 ES=   -6.50 NQ=   -7.50
1050428 1135 ES=   -6.00 NQ=   -7.00
1050428 1140 ES=   -6.00 NQ=   -7.00
1050428 1145 ES=   -5.75 NQ=   -5.50
1050428 1150 ES=   -5.75 NQ=   -5.00
1050428 1155 ES=   -5.75 NQ=   -5.00
1050428 1200 ES=   -6.00 NQ=   -6.00
1050428 1205 ES=   -6.75 NQ=   -6.50
1050428 1210 ES=   -6.50 NQ=   -5.50
1050428 1215 ES=   -6.50 NQ=   -6.50
1050428 1220 ES=   -7.00 NQ=   -8.50
1050428 1225 ES=   -6.50 NQ=   -7.00
1050428 1230 ES=   -7.00 NQ=   -7.00
1050428 1235 ES=   -7.50 NQ=   -8.00
1050428 1240 ES=   -7.25 NQ=   -7.00
1050428 1245 ES=   -6.50 NQ=   -6.50
1050428 1250 ES=   -6.25 NQ=   -6.50
1050428 1255 ES=   -5.25 NQ=   -4.00
1050428 1300 ES=   -3.75 NQ=   -1.50
1050428 1305 ES=   -4.00 NQ=   -1.50
1050428 1310 ES=   -6.50 NQ=   -3.50
1050428 1315 ES=   -7.00 NQ=   -4.00
1050428 1320 ES=   -7.75 NQ=   -7.00
1050428 1325 ES= -10.25 NQ=   -9.00
1050428 1330 ES= -10.75 NQ= -10.50
1050428 1335 ES= -10.50 NQ= -11.00
1050428 1340 ES=   -9.75 NQ=   -9.50
1050428 1345 ES=   -9.50 NQ= -10.00

```
1050428 1350   ES= -11.00   NQ= -12.50
1050428 1355   ES=  -9.75   NQ= -10.50
1050428 1400   ES=  -9.00   NQ=  -9.50
1050428 1405   ES=  -9.75   NQ= -10.50
1050428 1410   ES= -10.00   NQ= -10.50
1050428 1415   ES= -10.75   NQ= -11.00
1050428 1420   ES= -10.25   NQ= -10.00
1050428 1425   ES=  -9.00   NQ=  -9.00
1050428 1430   ES= -10.00   NQ= -10.00
1050428 1435   ES= -11.00   NQ= -12.00
1050428 1440   ES= -11.25   NQ= -11.50
1050428 1445   ES= -10.50   NQ= -11.00
1050428 1450   ES= -11.75   NQ= -12.50
1050428 1455   ES= -12.00   NQ= -12.50
```
1050428 1500   ES= -13.50   NQ= -13.00 ← **STOP**
```
1050428 1505   ES= -13.25   NQ= -12.50
1050428 1510   ES= -14.25   NQ= -12.50
1050428 1515   ES= -15.00   NQ= -14.50
```

7) @ 0910 ES +ve S, NQ +ve S and NQ more +ve than ES
+ve, then wait → anytime
      1) NQ>=10 points (compare to NQ at 0910), then
          Long ("Long 4a") OR
      2) NQ <= -13 then Short ("Short 4a")

(At 09:10, when ES and NQ are up, both up single digits
compared to yesterday's closing. NQ is up more than ES, wait
for one of the conditions, if you see NQ up 15 points or more,
then Long ES. If you see NQ down 13 points or more, then
Short ES.)

$$\begin{array}{ccc} ES & & NQ \\ +ve\ S & & +ve\ S \\ ES & <= & NQ \end{array}$$

       ↓ wait until

       NQ >= 10 point Long OR

       NQ <= -13 Short, whichever comes first.

Explanation to rule 7: Normal Positive Single Day:
(Positive Single refer to 09:10, NQ is positive and single digit,
it is also normal because NQ +ve is more +ve than ES +ve.)
At 09:10 both ES and NQ are +ve, so if NQ >= 10 point compare
to NQ at 09:10, the up-trend is confirmed, then Long. If NQ <=
-13, the down-trend is established, then Short. Again, RC traders
who know how to read the NQ movement through practice are
able to cut loss quickly or ride with profit.

Example ("Long 4a"):
i)   2005 / 3 / 30

1050330	835	ES=	2.75	NQ=	2.50
1050330	840	ES=	3.75	NQ=	5.50
1050330	845	ES=	4.50	NQ=	5.50
1050330	850	ES=	3.25	NQ=	3.00
1050330	855	ES=	3.00	NQ=	1.50
1050330	900	ES=	3.00	NQ=	2.00
1050330	905	ES=	4.00	NQ=	6.50
1050330	910	ES=	5.50	NQ=	8.50
1050330	**915**	**ES=**	**4.25**	**NQ=**	**7.00 (NORMAL POSITIVE SINGLE DAY)**
1050330	920	ES=	4.75	NQ=	7.50
1050330	925	ES=	4.75	NQ=	7.50
1050330	930	ES=	5.00	NQ=	9.50
1050330	935	ES=	6.00	NQ=	10.50
1050330	940	ES=	6.50	NQ=	12.00
1050330	945	ES=	6.50	NQ=	12.00
1050330	950	ES=	7.00	NQ=	15.00
1050330	955	ES=	6.75	NQ=	15.00
1050330	1000	ES=	6.50	NQ=	14.50
1050330	1005	ES=	6.50	NQ=	13.50
1050330	1010	ES=	6.25	NQ=	14.00
1050330	1015	ES=	6.00	NQ=	13.00
1050330	1020	ES=	7.00	NQ=	16.00
1050330	1025	ES=	5.75	NQ=	13.00

```
1050330 1030  ES=   6.75  NQ=  14.00
1050330 1035  ES=   7.00  NQ=  14.50
1050330 1040  ES=   6.75  NQ=  14.00
1050330 1045  ES=   8.00  NQ=  17.00
```
1050330 1050 ES=   9.25 NQ= 19.00 • ← **LONG**
```
1050330 1055  ES=   9.00  NQ=  19.50
1050330 1100  ES=  10.25  NQ=  21.50
1050330 1105  ES=  10.75  NQ=  22.00
1050330 1110  ES=  10.50  NQ=  21.50
1050330 1115  ES=  10.75  NQ=  21.00
1050330 1120  ES=  10.75  NQ=  20.50
1050330 1125  ES=  10.75  NQ=  20.50
1050330 1130  ES=  11.25  NQ=  21.00
1050330 1135  ES=  11.25  NQ=  21.50
1050330 1140  ES=  11.00  NQ=  21.50
1050330 1145  ES=  11.00  NQ=  21.00
1050330 1150  ES=  11.50  NQ=  21.50
1050330 1155  ES=  11.75  NQ=  22.00
1050330 1200  ES=  11.00  NQ=  20.50
1050330 1205  ES=  10.50  NQ=  20.00
1050330 1210  ES=  10.75  NQ=  20.50
1050330 1215  ES=  11.50  NQ=  21.00
1050330 1220  ES=  11.00  NQ=  19.50
1050330 1225  ES=  11.25  NQ=  20.50
1050330 1230  ES=  11.75  NQ=  20.00
1050330 1235  ES=  12.00  NQ=  20.50
1050330 1240  ES=  11.50  NQ=  20.00
1050330 1245  ES=  10.75  NQ=  19.00
1050330 1250  ES=  10.25  NQ=  19.50
1050330 1255  ES=   9.75  NQ=  18.50
1050330 1300  ES=  11.25  NQ=  19.50
1050330 1305  ES=  12.25  NQ=  21.50
1050330 1310  ES=  12.00  NQ=  21.50
1050330 1315  ES=  12.50  NQ=  21.50
1050330 1320  ES=  10.75  NQ=  19.00
```

```
1050330 1325  ES=   9.25  NQ=  16.50
1050330 1330  ES=   9.50  NQ=  17.50
1050330 1335  ES=  11.00  NQ=  18.00
1050330 1340  ES=  10.25  NQ=  17.50
1050330 1345  ES=   9.50  NQ=  15.00
1050330 1350  ES=  10.00  NQ=  16.00
1050330 1355  ES=   9.75  NQ=  15.50
1050330 1400  ES=  10.50  NQ=  17.50
1050330 1405  ES=  12.00  NQ=  19.00
1050330 1410  ES=  11.75  NQ=  18.00
1050330 1415  ES=  11.25  NQ=  17.00
1050330 1420  ES=  11.75  NQ=  18.50
1050330 1425  ES=  12.00  NQ=  18.50
1050330 1430  ES=  12.00  NQ=  19.00
1050330 1435  ES=  11.50  NQ=  18.00
1050330 1440  ES=  12.75  NQ=  19.50
1050330 1445  ES=  12.75  NQ=  19.50
1050330 1450  ES=  14.50  NQ=  22.00
1050330 1455  ES=  14.25  NQ=  21.00
```
1050330 1500 ES= 15.00 NQ= 22.00 • ← STOP
```
1050330 1505  ES=  14.75  NQ=  22.00
1050330 1510  ES=  15.50  NQ=  23.00
1050330 1515  ES=  15.50  NQ=  22.50
```

ii) 2006 / 1 / 3
```
1060103   835  ES=   6.75  NQ=  10.50
1060103   840  ES=   6.25  NQ=   7.50
1060103   845  ES=   7.00  NQ=  10.00
1060103   850  ES=   5.75  NQ=  10.00
1060103   855  ES=   4.75  NQ=   8.00
1060103   900  ES=   6.00  NQ=   9.00
1060103   905  ES=   4.50  NQ=   7.50
```
1060103   910 ES=   2.75 NQ=   4.00
```
1060103   915  ES=   2.50  NQ=  -0.50
1060103   920  ES=   3.00  NQ=   1.00
```

```
1060103  925 ES=  1.25 NQ= -3.00
1060103  930 ES=  1.00 NQ= -4.00
1060103  935 ES=  0.25 NQ= -4.00
1060103  940 ES= -1.00 NQ= -7.50
1060103  945 ES=  0.50 NQ= -3.50
1060103  950 ES=  1.00 NQ= -2.00
1060103  955 ES=  1.00 NQ= -1.50
1060103 1000 ES=  1.25 NQ= -1.00
1060103 1005 ES=  1.00 NQ= -1.00
1060103 1010 ES=  1.50 NQ=  0.00
1060103 1015 ES=  1.50 NQ= -0.50
1060103 1020 ES=  2.25 NQ=  1.00
1060103 1025 ES=  2.25 NQ=  0.50
1060103 1030 ES=  2.25 NQ=  1.00
1060103 1035 ES=  2.75 NQ=  1.50
1060103 1040 ES=  3.25 NQ=  4.50
1060103 1045 ES=  3.50 NQ=  4.50
1060103 1050 ES=  3.00 NQ=  4.00
1060103 1055 ES=  3.00 NQ=  4.00
1060103 1100 ES=  4.50 NQ=  7.50
1060103 1105 ES=  3.50 NQ=  6.50
1060103 1110 ES=  5.00 NQ= 10.00
1060103 1115 ES=  4.75 NQ=  9.00
1060103 1120 ES=  3.75 NQ=  7.50
1060103 1125 ES=  3.75 NQ=  8.50
1060103 1130 ES=  3.50 NQ=  7.50
1060103 1135 ES=  3.25 NQ=  8.00
1060103 1140 ES=  3.50 NQ=  7.50
1060103 1145 ES=  3.25 NQ=  6.50
1060103 1150 ES=  5.00 NQ=  8.50
1060103 1155 ES=  4.50 NQ=  8.50
1060103 1200 ES=  4.25 NQ=  7.50
1060103 1205 ES=  4.50 NQ=  8.00
1060103 1210 ES=  4.50 NQ=  8.00
1060103 1215 ES=  3.75 NQ=  6.00
```

```
1060103 1220  ES=   4.00  NQ=   6.50
1060103 1225  ES=   3.25  NQ=   5.50
1060103 1230  ES=   3.75  NQ=   6.00
1060103 1235  ES=   3.50  NQ=   5.50
1060103 1240  ES=   4.00  NQ=   6.50
1060103 1245  ES=   4.50  NQ=   7.50
1060103 1250  ES=   4.75  NQ=   8.50
1060103 1255  ES=   4.75  NQ=   7.50
1060103 1300  ES=   4.25  NQ=   7.50
```

1060103 1305 ES=   8.25 NQ= 14.00 ← **LONG**

```
1060103 1310  ES=   9.75  NQ=  18.00
1060103 1315  ES=  10.25  NQ=  20.50
1060103 1320  ES=  11.75  NQ=  22.50
1060103 1325  ES=  10.75  NQ=  21.50
1060103 1330  ES=  12.00  NQ=  24.00
1060103 1335  ES=  14.50  NQ=  28.50
1060103 1340  ES=  14.75  NQ=  30.00
1060103 1345  ES=  15.75  NQ=  31.50
1060103 1350  ES=  16.00  NQ=  30.00
1060103 1355  ES=  15.75  NQ=  31.00
1060103 1400  ES=  16.25  NQ=  31.00
1060103 1405  ES=  20.00  NQ=  39.50
1060103 1410  ES=  21.00  NQ=  41.00
1060103 1415  ES=  21.25  NQ=  42.00
1060103 1420  ES=  20.75  NQ=  41.00
1060103 1425  ES=  20.75  NQ=  41.50
1060103 1430  ES=  21.25  NQ=  42.50
1060103 1435  ES=  23.25  NQ=  44.50
1060103 1440  ES=  23.00  NQ=  42.50
1060103 1445  ES=  22.75  NQ=  42.50
1060103 1450  ES=  22.00  NQ=  40.00
1060103 1455  ES=  21.25  NQ=  38.50
```

1060103 1500 ES= 22.50 NQ= 38.50 • ← **STOP**

```
1060103 1505  ES=  23.00  NQ=  37.50
1060103 1510  ES=  23.25  NQ=  39.50
1060103 1515  ES=  21.75  NQ=  40.50
```

Example ("Short 4a"):
i)   2004 / 4 / 20

1040420	835	ES=	2.25	NQ=	3.00
1040420	840	ES=	2.75	NQ=	4.00
1040420	845	ES=	2.50	NQ=	4.00
1040420	850	ES=	2.75	NQ=	4.50
1040420	855	ES=	3.75	NQ=	7.50
1040420	900	ES=	4.75	NQ=	9.00
1040420	905	ES=	4.25	NQ=	9.00
1040420	**910**	**ES=**	**4.00**	**NQ=**	**8.50**
1040420	915	ES=	3.50	NQ=	8.00
1040420	920	ES=	3.50	NQ=	6.50
1040420	925	ES=	3.25	NQ=	6.50
1040420	930	ES=	3.75	NQ=	6.50
1040420	935	ES=	3.50	NQ=	6.00
1040420	940	ES=	3.50	NQ=	6.00
1040420	945	ES=	4.25	NQ=	8.00
1040420	950	ES=	4.25	NQ=	9.00
1040420	955	ES=	2.75	NQ=	7.00
1040420	1000	ES=	1.50	NQ=	4.50
1040420	1005	ES=	1.00	NQ=	3.00
1040420	1010	ES=	0.50	NQ=	3.50
1040420	1015	ES=	1.25	NQ=	3.00
1040420	1020	ES=	0.50	NQ=	2.00
1040420	1025	ES=	1.50	NQ=	3.50
1040420	1030	ES=	1.00	NQ=	1.00
1040420	1035	ES=	0.75	NQ=	2.00
1040420	1040	ES=	1.00	NQ=	3.00
1040420	1045	ES=	1.00	NQ=	2.50
1040420	1050	ES=	0.25	NQ=	0.50
1040420	1055	ES=	-0.50	NQ=	-0.50
1040420	1100	ES=	-1.25	NQ=	-2.50
1040420	1105	ES=	-0.50	NQ=	-2.00
1040420	1110	ES=	-0.50	NQ=	-2.00
1040420	1115	ES=	-0.75	NQ=	-2.50

```
1040420 1120  ES=   0.00  NQ=  -1.50
1040420 1125  ES=  -0.75  NQ=  -3.50
1040420 1130  ES=   0.00  NQ=  -3.50
1040420 1135  ES=   0.50  NQ=  -2.00
1040420 1140  ES=   0.50  NQ=  -2.00
1040420 1145  ES=   0.50  NQ=  -1.00
1040420 1150  ES=   0.75  NQ=  -1.00
1040420 1155  ES=   0.75  NQ=  -1.00
1040420 1200  ES=   0.00  NQ=  -3.50
1040420 1205  ES=  -0.50  NQ=  -5.00
1040420 1210  ES=   0.00  NQ=  -4.00
1040420 1215  ES=   0.00  NQ=  -4.00
1040420 1220  ES=   0.50  NQ=  -2.50
1040420 1225  ES=   0.25  NQ=  -2.50
1040420 1230  ES=  -0.25  NQ=  -3.50
1040420 1235  ES=   1.00  NQ=  -1.00
1040420 1240  ES=   1.50  NQ=   0.00
1040420 1245  ES=   1.75  NQ=   1.50
1040420 1250  ES=   1.00  NQ=   0.00
1040420 1255  ES=   1.00  NQ=   0.00
1040420 1300  ES=   1.50  NQ=   1.50
1040420 1305  ES=   0.75  NQ=  -1.00
1040420 1310  ES=   0.75  NQ=  -1.00
1040420 1315  ES=   0.25  NQ=  -2.00
1040420 1320  ES=   0.50  NQ=  -2.00
1040420 1325  ES=   1.25  NQ=  -1.00
1040420 1330  ES=   1.50  NQ=  -0.50
1040420 1335  ES=  -0.50  NQ=  -4.00
1040420 1340  ES=  -1.50  NQ=  -8.50
1040420 1345  ES=  -2.25  NQ=  -8.00
1040420 1350  ES=  -3.75  NQ= -11.50
1040420 1355  ES=  -4.00  NQ= -10.50
```

1040420 1400 ES= -5.25 NQ= -13.00 • ← **SHORT**

```
1040420 1405  ES=  -6.50  NQ= -15.50
1040420 1410  ES=  -5.25  NQ= -14.00
```

```
1040420 1415  ES=   -5.50  NQ= -14.50
1040420 1420  ES=   -3.75  NQ= -11.00
1040420 1425  ES=   -5.25  NQ= -13.50
1040420 1430  ES=   -6.50  NQ= -16.00
1040420 1435  ES= -10.00  NQ= -21.00
1040420 1440  ES=   -9.75  NQ= -21.00
1040420 1445  ES= -12.25  NQ= -26.50
1040420 1450  ES= -12.50  NQ= -26.00
1040420 1455  ES= -14.00  NQ= -29.00
```
1040420 1500 ES= -16.50 NQ= -31.50 • ← **STOP**
```
1040420 1505  ES= -19.50  NQ= -35.00
1040420 1510  ES= -18.25  NQ= -33.50
1040420 1515  ES= -18.75  NQ= -33.50
```

ii)   2005 / 1 / 4
```
1050104  835  ES=   1.00  NQ=   2.50
1050104  840  ES=   0.50  NQ=   1.50
1050104  845  ES=  -0.50  NQ=   0.50
1050104  850  ES=   0.00  NQ=   2.50
1050104  855  ES=  -0.25  NQ=   1.50
1050104  900  ES=  -1.25  NQ=  -1.00
1050104  905  ES=   0.00  NQ=   1.50
```
1050104 910 ES=   1.50 NQ=   5.50 (NORMAL
                        POSITIVE SINGLE DAY)
```
1050104  915  ES=   0.75  NQ=   3.00
1050104  920  ES=   0.25  NQ=   2.50
1050104  925  ES=  -2.50  NQ=  -3.50
1050104  930  ES=  -2.75  NQ=  -1.50
1050104  935  ES=  -3.25  NQ=  -5.50
1050104  940  ES=  -3.00  NQ=  -5.50
1050104  945  ES=  -3.50  NQ=  -6.50
1050104  950  ES=  -3.75  NQ= -10.50
1050104  955  ES=  -3.75  NQ= -10.50
1050104 1000  ES=  -4.00  NQ= -12.00
1050104 1005  ES=  -4.50  NQ= -12.50
```

```
1050104 1010  ES=  -4.75  NQ= -12.50
1050104 1015  ES=  -4.50  NQ= -11.00
1050104 1020  ES=  -3.50  NQ=  -9.50
1050104 1025  ES=  -4.00  NQ= -11.00
1050104 1030  ES=  -4.00  NQ= -10.50
1050104 1035  ES=  -3.50  NQ= -10.50
1050104 1040  ES=  -3.00  NQ=  -8.50
1050104 1045  ES=  -3.50  NQ= -10.50
1050104 1050  ES=  -4.25  NQ= -10.50
1050104 1055  ES=  -4.50  NQ= -12.00
1050104 1100  ES=  -4.50  NQ= -12.50
```
1050104 1105 ES= -5.75 NQ= -16.00 • ← **SHORT**
```
1050104 1110  ES=  -6.00  NQ= -15.50
1050104 1115  ES=  -8.25  NQ= -21.00
1050104 1120  ES=  -7.75  NQ= -22.50
1050104 1125  ES=  -7.50  NQ= -22.50
1050104 1130  ES=  -7.25  NQ= -23.00
1050104 1135  ES=  -6.50  NQ= -21.00
1050104 1140  ES=  -6.75  NQ= -21.50
1050104 1145  ES=  -7.50  NQ= -23.00
1050104 1150  ES=  -6.50  NQ= -21.00
1050104 1155  ES=  -6.50  NQ= -21.50
1050104 1200  ES=  -8.25  NQ= -23.00
1050104 1205  ES=  -7.25  NQ= -22.50
1050104 1210  ES=  -6.75  NQ= -21.50
1050104 1215  ES=  -6.25  NQ= -21.00
1050104 1220  ES=  -7.00  NQ= -22.00
1050104 1225  ES=  -7.00  NQ= -22.50
1050104 1230  ES=  -7.00  NQ= -22.50
1050104 1235  ES=  -7.25  NQ= -22.50
1050104 1240  ES=  -7.75  NQ= -23.50
1050104 1245  ES=  -7.50  NQ= -23.50
1050104 1250  ES=  -7.25  NQ= -22.00
1050104 1255  ES=  -7.75  NQ= -24.00
1050104 1300  ES=  -8.25  NQ= -25.50
```

```
1050104 1305  ES=  -9.75  NQ= -28.00
1050104 1310  ES= -12.25  NQ= -33.50
1050104 1315  ES= -11.50  NQ= -31.50
1050104 1320  ES= -12.50  NQ= -32.00
1050104 1325  ES= -13.50  NQ= -35.50
1050104 1330  ES= -15.00  NQ= -35.50
1050104 1335  ES= -14.75  NQ= -35.00
1050104 1340  ES= -16.00  NQ= -38.00
1050104 1345  ES= -16.75  NQ= -40.50
1050104 1350  ES= -18.50  NQ= -40.00
1050104 1355  ES= -17.75  NQ= -39.50
1050104 1400  ES= -15.50  NQ= -37.00
1050104 1405  ES= -16.00  NQ= -37.00
1050104 1410  ES= -15.50  NQ= -36.50
1050104 1415  ES= -15.75  NQ= -36.00
1050104 1420  ES= -16.25  NQ= -35.00
1050104 1425  ES= -16.50  NQ= -37.00
1050104 1430  ES= -16.50  NQ= -34.50
1050104 1435  ES= -15.00  NQ= -31.50
1050104 1440  ES= -14.75  NQ= -30.50
1050104 1445  ES= -14.75  NQ= -31.00
1050104 1450  ES= -16.25  NQ= -33.00
1050104 1455  ES= -16.50  NQ= -32.50
```
1050104 1500 ES= -16.50 NQ=-33.50 • ← **STOP**
```
1050104 1505  ES= -15.50  NQ= -32.00
1050104 1510  ES= -15.75  NQ= -33.00
1050104 1515  ES= -15.50  NQ= -32.50
```

8) @ 0910 ES +ve S, NQ +ve S and ES +ve is more +ve than
   NQ +ve), then Short immediately ("Short 4b").
(At 09:10, when ES is up and NQ is up, both up single digit.
ES is up more than NQ compared to yesterday's closing.
We Short with stop.)

ES	NQ
+ve S	+ve S
ES	>	NQ

Explanation to Rule 8: Abnormal Positive Single Day:
(At 09:10, NQ is +ve single, it is Abnormal because ES +ve is
more +ve than NQ +ve.) If NQ +ve is more +ve than ES +ve,
then it is Normal.

At 09:10, both ES and NQ are +ve, but ES is more +ve than NQ
+ve, which indicates NQ is not leading ES up. Good chance that
NQ will lead ES down, so we Short.

Example:
i)   2004 / 7 / 21

1040721	835	ES=	1.25	NQ=	3.00
1040721	840	ES=	1.25	NQ=	3.00
1040721	845	ES=	2.00	NQ=	5.00
1040721	850	ES=	1.75	NQ=	3.50
1040721	855	ES=	0.75	NQ=	0.00
1040721	900	ES=	0.75	NQ=	-1.50
1040721	905	ES=	1.00	NQ=	-1.50
1040721	**910**	**ES=**	**1.25**	**NQ=**	**0.00 (ABNORMAL POSITIVE SINGLE DAY, SHORT)**
1040721	915	ES=	2.00	NQ=	1.50
1040721	920	ES=	3.75	NQ=	4.00
1040721	925	ES=	2.50	NQ=	1.00
1040721	930	ES=	2.50	NQ=	1.00
1040721	935	ES=	2.25	NQ=	0.50
1040721	940	ES=	1.75	NQ=	-1.50
1040721	945	ES=	2.50	NQ=	-1.00
1040721	950	ES=	1.50	NQ=	-1.50

```
1040721   955  ES=    2.00  NQ=   -1.50
1040721  1000  ES=    1.50  NQ=   -2.00
1040721  1005  ES=   -0.25  NQ=   -6.50
1040721  1010  ES=   -0.50  NQ=   -6.00
1040721  1015  ES=   -0.25  NQ=   -6.00
1040721  1020  ES=   -1.00  NQ=   -7.50
1040721  1025  ES=   -0.25  NQ=   -5.50
1040721  1030  ES=   -0.25  NQ=   -5.00
1040721  1035  ES=   -0.25  NQ=   -5.50
1040721  1040  ES=    0.00  NQ=   -5.00
1040721  1045  ES=   -1.00  NQ=   -6.00
1040721  1050  ES=   -0.50  NQ=   -5.50
1040721  1055  ES=   -1.25  NQ=   -6.00
1040721  1100  ES=   -2.25  NQ=   -9.50
1040721  1105  ES=   -2.75  NQ=  -10.00
1040721  1110  ES=   -3.00  NQ=  -13.50
1040721  1115  ES=   -3.25  NQ=  -14.00
1040721  1120  ES=   -4.00  NQ=  -15.50
1040721  1125  ES=   -3.75  NQ=  -15.50
1040721  1130  ES=   -3.50  NQ=  -14.00
1040721  1135  ES=   -4.00  NQ=  -15.50
1040721  1140  ES=   -3.00  NQ=  -14.00
1040721  1145  ES=   -2.75  NQ=  -14.00
1040721  1150  ES=   -2.00  NQ=  -12.50
1040721  1155  ES=   -2.75  NQ=  -13.00
1040721  1200  ES=   -3.00  NQ=  -14.00
1040721  1205  ES=   -3.25  NQ=  -15.50
1040721  1210  ES=   -2.25  NQ=  -14.00
1040721  1215  ES=   -2.75  NQ=  -14.50
1040721  1220  ES=   -4.25  NQ=  -19.00
1040721  1225  ES=   -5.00  NQ=  -21.00
1040721  1230  ES=   -5.25  NQ=  -20.50
1040721  1235  ES=   -5.25  NQ=  -20.50
1040721  1240  ES=   -5.00  NQ=  -20.50
1040721  1245  ES=   -5.75  NQ=  -23.00
```

```
1040721 1250  ES=  -6.75  NQ= -24.50
1040721 1255  ES=  -6.75  NQ= -23.00
1040721 1300  ES=  -6.75  NQ= -23.50
1040721 1305  ES=  -8.75  NQ= -25.50
1040721 1310  ES=  -8.00  NQ= -24.50
1040721 1315  ES=  -8.50  NQ= -24.50
1040721 1320  ES=  -7.50  NQ= -23.00
1040721 1325  ES=  -8.00  NQ= -23.00
1040721 1330  ES=  -8.25  NQ= -24.50
1040721 1335  ES=  -8.75  NQ= -25.00
1040721 1340  ES=  -8.25  NQ= -24.50
1040721 1345  ES=  -7.50  NQ= -22.50
1040721 1350  ES=  -7.50  NQ= -22.00
1040721 1355  ES=  -8.50  NQ= -24.00
1040721 1400  ES=  -9.75  NQ= -26.50
1040721 1405  ES= -12.00  NQ= -30.00
1040721 1410  ES= -12.00  NQ= -30.00
1040721 1415  ES= -12.50  NQ= -31.50
1040721 1420  ES= -11.75  NQ= -31.50
1040721 1425  ES= -12.75  NQ= -32.50
1040721 1430  ES= -12.50  NQ= -33.50
1040721 1435  ES= -12.25  NQ= -31.50
1040721 1440  ES= -13.75  NQ= -33.00
1040721 1445  ES= -15.25  NQ= -34.00
1040721 1450  ES= -17.00  NQ= -36.50
1040721 1455  ES= -16.75  NQ= -34.00
```

<u>1040721 1500 ES= -18.75 NQ=-36.50</u> • ← **STOP**

```
1040721 1505  ES= -20.75  NQ= -40.50
1040721 1510  ES= -20.25  NQ= -39.00
1040721 1515  ES= -21.00  NQ= -41.50
```

ii) 2005 / 6 / 7
```
1050607  835  ES=   2.50  NQ=   1.00
1050607  840  ES=   3.75  NQ=   2.00
1050607  845  ES=   4.25  NQ=   2.50
```

1050607	850	ES=	5.75	NQ=	5.00
1050607	855	ES=	6.00	NQ=	5.00
1050607	900	ES=	6.75	NQ=	6.00
1050607	905	ES=	6.75	NQ=	6.50
1050607	**910**	**ES=**	**8.75**	**NQ=**	**8.50 (ABNORMAL**

POSITIVE SINGLE DAY, SHORT)

1050607	915	ES=	9.00	NQ=	11.00
1050607	920	ES=	9.50	NQ=	13.00
1050607	925	ES=	9.75	NQ=	13.50
1050607	930	ES=	10.50	NQ=	14.50
1050607	935	ES=	10.25	NQ=	13.50
1050607	940	ES=	10.25	NQ=	12.50
1050607	945	ES=	10.50	NQ=	14.00
1050607	950	ES=	9.75	NQ=	12.50
1050607	955	ES=	9.50	NQ=	11.00
1050607	1000	ES=	10.25	NQ=	12.00
1050607	1005	ES=	9.75	NQ=	12.00
1050607	1010	ES=	10.00	NQ=	12.00
1050607	1015	ES=	9.75	NQ=	10.50
1050607	1020	ES=	9.50	NQ=	10.00
1050607	1025	ES=	9.50	NQ=	9.50
1050607	1030	ES=	9.75	NQ=	11.00
1050607	1035	ES=	10.50	NQ=	11.00
1050607	1040	ES=	10.25	NQ=	10.00
1050607	1045	ES=	10.00	NQ=	9.50
1050607	1050	ES=	10.50	NQ=	11.50
1050607	1055	ES=	11.50	NQ=	13.00
1050607	1100	ES=	11.25	NQ=	12.50
1050607	1105	ES=	10.50	NQ=	11.00
1050607	1110	ES=	10.50	NQ=	10.50
1050607	1115	ES=	10.25	NQ=	10.50
1050607	1120	ES=	9.75	NQ=	9.50
1050607	1125	ES=	9.75	NQ=	9.50
1050607	1130	ES=	10.00	NQ=	9.50
1050607	1135	ES=	10.00	NQ=	10.50

1050607 1140 ES= 10.00 NQ=   9.50
1050607 1145 ES= 10.00 NQ= 10.00
1050607 1150 ES= 10.25 NQ= 10.50
1050607 1155 ES= 10.25 NQ= 10.50
1050607 1200 ES= 10.75 NQ= 11.50
1050607 1205 ES= 10.50 NQ= 10.50
1050607 1210 ES= 10.75 NQ= 10.50
1050607 1215 ES= 10.75 NQ= 11.00
1050607 1220 ES= 10.25 NQ= 10.50
1050607 1225 ES=   9.75 NQ=   9.50
1050607 1230 ES=   9.75 NQ=   8.50
1050607 1235 ES=   8.75 NQ=   6.00
1050607 1240 ES=   9.50 NQ=   6.50
1050607 1245 ES=   9.25 NQ=   6.00
1050607 1250 ES=   9.25 NQ=   5.00
1050607 1255 ES=   8.25 NQ=   2.50
1050607 1300 ES=   8.25 NQ=   2.50
1050607 1305 ES=   7.50 NQ= -2.00
1050607 1310 ES=   7.00 NQ= -2.50
1050607 1315 ES=   3.50 NQ= -7.00
1050607 1320 ES=   5.00 NQ= -7.50
1050607 1325 ES=   4.25 NQ= -8.00
1050607 1330 ES=   4.00 NQ= -8.00
1050607 1335 ES=   4.25 NQ= -8.00
1050607 1340 ES=   6.00 NQ= -3.50
1050607 1345 ES=   5.50 NQ= -5.00
1050607 1350 ES=   5.00 NQ= -5.00
1050607 1355 ES=   5.75 NQ= -3.50
1050607 1400 ES=   5.00 NQ= -5.00
1050607 1405 ES=   3.75 NQ= -9.00
1050607 1410 ES=   3.75 NQ= -8.50
1050607 1415 ES=   3.25 NQ= -9.50
1050607 1420 ES=   3.50 NQ= -8.00
1050607 1425 ES=   3.50 NQ= -7.50
1050607 1430 ES=   2.25 NQ= -10.00

```
1050607 1435  ES=   1.25  NQ= -11.50
1050607 1440  ES=   1.50  NQ= -11.50
1050607 1445  ES=   0.75  NQ= -13.00
1050607 1450  ES=   1.25  NQ= -12.00
1050607 1455  ES=   0.50  NQ= -12.50
```
1050607 1500 ES= -0.25 NQ= -12.00 • ← STOP
```
1050607 1505  ES=  -0.25  NQ= -12.00
1050607 1510  ES=   0.50  NQ= -11.50
1050607 1515  ES=   0.75  NQ= -12.00
```

9) @ 0910 ES -ve S and NQ between -10 to -25 then wait →
anytime NQ down 10 points (compare to 0910) then Short
("Short 5a").
(At 09:10, ES is down single digit, NQ is down double digit.
Wait for NQ to be down by 10 or more points compared to
the value at 09:10, then Short ES.)

           ES   NQ
        -ve S   -ve D (between -25 to -10)
               ↓ wait until
               NQ down 10pt (compare 0910 NQ)

Explanation to rule 9: Normal Negative Double Day:
(09:10, NQ is -ve double digit, so we call it negative double,
and it is more -ve than ES -ve, so it is a Normal Day.)
At 09:10, ES is -ve single digit and NQ is -ve double digit. NQ is
very -ve, chances of leading ES -ve to more -ve are high. So we
wait for NQ to be down 10 points, turn to more -ve, then we
Short (trend – following strategy using NQ as an indicator to trade
ES.)

Example:
i)   2003 / 9 / 24
```
     1030924  835  ES=   1.25  NQ=   0.00
     1030924  840  ES=  -0.50  NQ=  -7.50
     1030924  845  ES=   0.75  NQ=  -5.50
     1030924  850  ES=   1.25  NQ=  -4.00
```

1030924 855 ES=   0.00 NQ= -7.00
1030924 900 ES= -1.00 NQ= -8.50
1030924 905 ES= -1.25 NQ= -9.00
1030924 910 ES=-2.00 NQ= -10.50 (NORMAL
NEGATIVE DOUBLE DAY)
1030924 915 ES= -2.50 NQ= -10.00
1030924 920 ES= -2.75 NQ= -11.50
1030924 925 ES= -2.50 NQ= -10.50
1030924 930 ES= -2.75 NQ= -11.00
1030924 935 ES= -2.00 NQ= -10.50
1030924 940 ES= -1.75 NQ= -9.00
1030924 945 ES= -1.75 NQ= -6.50
1030924 950 ES= -1.75 NQ= -7.50
1030924 955 ES= -1.50 NQ= -5.50
1030924 1000 ES= -3.00 NQ= -10.50
1030924 1005 ES= -3.00 NQ= -9.00
1030924 1010 ES= -2.75 NQ= -8.50
1030924 1015 ES= -1.75 NQ= -7.00
1030924 1020 ES= -2.25 NQ= -8.00
1030924 1025 ES= -3.25 NQ= -9.50
1030924 1030 ES= -4.25 NQ= -12.00
1030924 1035 ES= -4.50 NQ= -11.50
1030924 1040 ES= -5.50 NQ= -13.50
1030924 1045 ES= -6.00 NQ= -16.00
1030924 1050 ES= -6.50 NQ= -17.50
1030924 1055 ES= -7.50 NQ= -19.50
1030924 1100 ES=   -8.50 NQ=-20.50 • ← SHORT
1030924 1105 ES= -9.00 NQ= -25.00
1030924 1110 ES= -11.25 NQ= -30.50
1030924 1115 ES= -11.75 NQ= -31.00
1030924 1120 ES= -11.50 NQ= -27.50
1030924 1125 ES= -11.00 NQ= -26.00
1030924 1130 ES= -11.75 NQ= -29.00
1030924 1135 ES= -11.25 NQ= -27.50
1030924 1140 ES= -11.00 NQ= -27.50

1030924 1145 ES= -13.75 NQ= -34.00
1030924 1150 ES= -14.50 NQ= -35.00
1030924 1155 ES= -15.00 NQ= -35.00
1030924 1200 ES= -13.25 NQ= -30.50
1030924 1205 ES= -14.00 NQ= -32.00
1030924 1210 ES= -13.75 NQ= -32.00
1030924 1215 ES= -13.75 NQ= -32.50
1030924 1220 ES= -12.75 NQ= -31.50
1030924 1225 ES= -14.75 NQ= -36.00
1030924 1230 ES= -15.00 NQ= -36.50
1030924 1235 ES= -13.75 NQ= -33.50
1030924 1240 ES= -14.25 NQ= -33.00
1030924 1245 ES= -15.25 NQ= -36.00
1030924 1250 ES= -16.50 NQ= -37.50
1030924 1255 ES= -16.00 NQ= -36.50
1030924 1300 ES= -15.25 NQ= -36.00
1030924 1305 ES= -15.25 NQ= -35.00
1030924 1310 ES= -14.75 NQ= -35.00
1030924 1315 ES= -13.75 NQ= -31.50
1030924 1320 ES= -15.25 NQ= -35.00
1030924 1325 ES= -15.25 NQ= -35.50
1030924 1330 ES= -14.75 NQ= -36.00
1030924 1335 ES= -15.00 NQ= -35.00
1030924 1340 ES= -14.50 NQ= -35.50
1030924 1345 ES= -14.25 NQ= -34.00
1030924 1350 ES= -14.75 NQ= -35.50
1030924 1355 ES= -15.25 NQ= -36.00
1030924 1400 ES= -16.25 NQ= -38.50
1030924 1405 ES= -15.75 NQ= -37.50
1030924 1410 ES= -16.00 NQ= -39.00
1030924 1415 ES= -15.50 NQ= -37.50
1030924 1420 ES= -15.75 NQ= -39.50
1030924 1425 ES= -15.25 NQ= -38.50
1030924 1430 ES= -16.75 NQ= -42.00
1030924 1435 ES= -15.50 NQ= -39.00

```
1030924 1440  ES= -16.50  NQ= -42.50
1030924 1445  ES= -17.00  NQ= -45.50
1030924 1450  ES= -17.25  NQ= -45.00
1030924 1455  ES= -18.00  NQ= -46.50
```
1030924 1500 ES= -17.75 NQ=-45.50 • ← STOP
```
1030924 1505  ES= -18.50  NQ= -46.00
1030924 1510  ES= -18.00  NQ= -49.00
1030924 1515  ES= -18.50  NQ= -51.50
```

ii) 2005 / 10 / 27
```
1051027  835  ES=  -1.75  NQ=  -6.50
1051027  840  ES=  -2.75  NQ=  -6.00
1051027  845  ES=  -3.00  NQ=  -6.50
1051027  850  ES=  -3.50  NQ=  -7.50
1051027  855  ES=  -4.00  NQ=  -8.00
1051027  900  ES=  -2.75  NQ=  -8.50
1051027  905  ES=  -3.50  NQ=  -8.00
```
1051027 910 ES= -4.25 NQ= -10.50 (NORMAL
                              NEGATIVE DOUBLE DAY)
```
1051027  915  ES=  -3.75  NQ= -11.00
1051027  920  ES=  -3.00  NQ=  -9.50
1051027  925  ES=  -4.25  NQ= -12.50
1051027  930  ES=  -4.50  NQ= -12.50
1051027  935  ES=  -6.00  NQ= -14.50
1051027  940  ES=  -6.50  NQ= -17.00
1051027  945  ES=  -6.50  NQ= -17.50
1051027  950  ES=  -7.25  NQ= -18.50
1051027  955  ES=  -6.75  NQ= -16.00
1051027 1000  ES=  -6.50  NQ= -17.50
1051027 1005  ES=  -5.50  NQ= -16.50
1051027 1010  ES=  -5.00  NQ= -16.00
1051027 1015  ES=  -6.00  NQ= -17.50
1051027 1020  ES=  -5.00  NQ= -15.50
1051027 1025  ES=  -4.00  NQ= -15.00
1051027 1030  ES=  -4.75  NQ= -15.00
```

```
1051027 1035  ES=  -6.00  NQ= -16.50
1051027 1040  ES=  -6.25  NQ= -16.50
1051027 1045  ES=  -6.50  NQ= -16.50
1051027 1050  ES=  -6.50  NQ= -17.00
1051027 1055  ES=  -6.50  NQ= -18.00
1051027 1100  ES=  -6.25  NQ= -17.00
1051027 1105  ES=  -5.25  NQ= -15.00
1051027 1110  ES=  -4.50  NQ= -15.50
1051027 1115  ES=  -5.25  NQ= -15.50
1051027 1120  ES=  -5.50  NQ= -16.00
1051027 1125  ES=  -4.75  NQ= -15.00
1051027 1130  ES=  -4.75  NQ= -14.50
1051027 1135  ES=  -4.25  NQ= -15.00
1051027 1140  ES=  -4.25  NQ= -15.00
1051027 1145  ES=  -5.00  NQ= -15.50
1051027 1150  ES=  -5.75  NQ= -16.50
1051027 1155  ES=  -5.25  NQ= -16.50
1051027 1200  ES=  -4.50  NQ= -15.00
1051027 1205  ES=  -4.50  NQ= -15.00
1051027 1210  ES=  -5.00  NQ= -16.50
1051027 1215  ES=  -7.00  NQ= -18.50
```

1051027 1220 ES= -8.25 NQ=-22.50 • ← **SHORT**

```
1051027 1225  ES=  -8.25  NQ= -22.50
1051027 1230  ES=  -9.50  NQ= -25.00
1051027 1235  ES=  -8.75  NQ= -23.50
1051027 1240  ES=  -7.75  NQ= -22.00
1051027 1245  ES=  -8.00  NQ= -22.00
1051027 1250  ES=  -7.75  NQ= -21.50
1051027 1255  ES=  -7.75  NQ= -20.50
1051027 1300  ES=  -6.75  NQ= -19.50
1051027 1305  ES=  -7.00  NQ= -20.50
1051027 1310  ES=  -7.50  NQ= -21.50
1051027 1315  ES=  -7.25  NQ= -21.00
1051027 1320  ES=  -7.25  NQ= -21.00
1051027 1325  ES=  -7.75  NQ= -22.00
```

```
1051027 1330  ES=   -8.25  NQ= -23.50
1051027 1335  ES=   -8.00  NQ= -22.50
1051027 1340  ES=   -9.25  NQ= -24.50
1051027 1345  ES=   -8.50  NQ= -24.00
1051027 1350  ES=   -8.25  NQ= -23.00
1051027 1355  ES=   -8.75  NQ= -24.50
1051027 1400  ES= -10.50  NQ= -28.00
1051027 1405  ES= -10.75  NQ= -27.50
1051027 1410  ES= -12.00  NQ= -28.00
1051027 1415  ES= -12.75  NQ= -33.00
1051027 1420  ES= -12.25  NQ= -31.50
1051027 1425  ES= -11.50  NQ= -30.00
1051027 1430  ES= -13.00  NQ= -32.50
1051027 1435  ES= -12.00  NQ= -30.50
1051027 1440  ES= -12.00  NQ= -29.50
1051027 1445  ES= -11.50  NQ= -28.00
1051027 1450  ES= -11.75  NQ= -28.50
1051027 1455  ES= -13.25  NQ= -31.50
```
1051027 1500 ES= -14.50 NQ=-35.00 • ← **STOP**
```
1051027 1505  ES= -14.25  NQ= -33.00
1051027 1510  ES= -14.50  NQ= -33.00
1051027 1515  ES= -13.50  NQ= -30.00
```

10)   @ 0910 ES +ve S and NQ between 10 and 25 then wait
      → anytime 1) NQ up 12 points (compare to 0910) then
      Long ("Long 6a") or 2) NQ down 10 points (compare to
      0910) then Short ("Short 6a").

(At 09:10, ES is up single digit, NQ is up 10 points to 25 points.
Wait when NQ up 12 points or more, then Long ES. Or if NQ
down 10 points or more, then Short ES, whichever comes first.)

ES   NQ
+ve S   +ve D (between 10 and 25)
          ↓ wait until
NQ up 12pt (compare 0910 NQ), Long with stop
                    OR

NQ down 10 points (compare 0910 NQ) Short with stop. Whichever comes first.

Explanation to rule 10: Normal Positive Double Day:
(09:10, NQ is +ve double digit, and NQ +ve double is more +ve than ES +ve single, so it is Normal Positive Double Day.)
At 09:10, when NQ $> = 12$ point or more, we Long ES. When NQ $< = 10$ points or more, we Short ES (We use NQ trend and not ES trend.)

Example ("Long 6a"):
i) 2003 / 5 / 27

1030527	835	ES=	-5.25	NQ=	-7.00
1030527	840	ES=	-5.25	NQ=	-5.00
1030527	845	ES=	-4.75	NQ=	-1.50
1030527	850	ES=	-3.75	NQ=	0.00
1030527	855	ES=	-2.75	NQ=	4.00
1030527	900	ES=	-1.75	NQ=	4.00
1030527	905	ES=	1.00	NQ=	9.00
1030527	**910**	**ES=**	**1.75**	**NQ=**	**11.50** (NORMAL POSITIVE DOUBLE DAY)
1030527	915	ES=	1.50	NQ=	12.50
1030527	920	ES=	4.25	NQ=	16.50
1030527	925	ES=	4.75	NQ=	17.50
1030527	**930**	**ES=**	**7.50**	**NQ=**	**23.50** • ← LONG
1030527	935	ES=	8.75	NQ=	23.50
1030527	940	ES=	8.75	NQ=	22.50
1030527	945	ES=	8.75	NQ=	24.50
1030527	950	ES=	10.25	NQ=	26.00
1030527	955	ES=	10.50	NQ=	27.00
1030527	1000	ES=	11.50	NQ=	29.00
1030527	1005	ES=	11.00	NQ=	30.50
1030527	1010	ES=	12.25	NQ=	32.50
1030527	1015	ES=	10.25	NQ=	30.50
1030527	1020	ES=	11.00	NQ=	29.50
1030527	1025	ES=	10.50	NQ=	29.00

1030527 1030 ES= 11.50 NQ= 31.00
1030527 1035 ES= 11.50 NQ= 31.00
1030527 1040 ES= 10.75 NQ= 30.00
1030527 1045 ES= 11.75 NQ= 32.00
1030527 1050 ES= 12.25 NQ= 33.00
1030527 1055 ES= 11.50 NQ= 32.00
1030527 1100 ES= 11.25 NQ= 32.00
1030527 1105 ES= 12.75 NQ= 33.50
1030527 1110 ES= 12.75 NQ= 34.00
1030527 1115 ES= 12.50 NQ= 33.00
1030527 1120 ES= 13.25 NQ= 34.50
1030527 1125 ES= 14.25 NQ= 36.00
1030527 1130 ES= 14.00 NQ= 35.50
1030527 1135 ES= 13.75 NQ= 36.00
1030527 1140 ES= 13.25 NQ= 34.00
1030527 1145 ES= 13.25 NQ= 33.50
1030527 1150 ES= 12.75 NQ= 33.50
1030527 1155 ES= 13.00 NQ= 34.00
1030527 1200 ES= 12.75 NQ= 33.50
1030527 1205 ES= 12.50 NQ= 33.00
1030527 1210 ES= 13.50 NQ= 34.50
1030527 1215 ES= 13.50 NQ= 35.00
1030527 1220 ES= 13.50 NQ= 35.00
1030527 1225 ES= 14.25 NQ= 36.00
1030527 1230 ES= 15.00 NQ= 38.50
1030527 1235 ES= 16.25 NQ= 39.00
1030527 1240 ES= 15.75 NQ= 38.00
1030527 1245 ES= 16.00 NQ= 37.50
1030527 1250 ES= 16.00 NQ= 37.00
1030527 1255 ES= 16.25 NQ= 37.00
1030527 1300 ES= 15.00 NQ= 36.50
1030527 1305 ES= 15.25 NQ= 36.50
1030527 1310 ES= 14.25 NQ= 34.50
1030527 1315 ES= 14.50 NQ= 35.00
1030527 1320 ES= 14.25 NQ= 35.00
1030527 1325 ES= 14.75 NQ= 36.50

```
1030527 1330  ES=  14.00  NQ=  36.00
1030527 1335  ES=  14.75  NQ=  36.50
1030527 1340  ES=  15.00  NQ=  37.00
1030527 1345  ES=  16.00  NQ=  38.50
1030527 1350  ES=  15.25  NQ=  37.00
1030527 1355  ES=  15.75  NQ=  38.00
1030527 1400  ES=  16.75  NQ=  40.00
1030527 1405  ES=  17.25  NQ=  40.00
1030527 1410  ES=  17.25  NQ=  40.00
1030527 1415  ES=  17.00  NQ=  40.00
1030527 1420  ES=  16.75  NQ=  38.50
1030527 1425  ES=  16.75  NQ=  39.00
1030527 1430  ES=  18.50  NQ=  42.00
1030527 1435  ES=  19.00  NQ=  42.50
1030527 1440  ES=  18.75  NQ=  42.50
1030527 1445  ES=  19.50  NQ=  43.00
1030527 1450  ES=  20.50  NQ=  44.00
1030527 1455  ES=  19.50  NQ=  42.00
```

1030527 1500 ES= 19.00 NQ= 41.00 • ← **STOP**

```
1030527 1505  ES=  18.25  NQ=  42.50
1030527 1510  ES=  18.00  NQ=  42.00
1030527 1515  ES=  17.00  NQ=  41.00
```

ii) 2005 / 4 / 21

```
1050421  835  ES=  10.25  NQ=  15.50
1050421  840  ES=  11.00  NQ=  16.50
1050421  845  ES=  10.25  NQ=  15.00
1050421  850  ES=   8.25  NQ=  13.00
1050421  855  ES=   9.50  NQ=  14.50
1050421  900  ES=  11.75  NQ=  20.00
1050421  905  ES=   9.00  NQ=  15.50
```

1050421 910 ES= 8.75 NQ= 15.50 (NORMAL POSITIVE DOUBLE DAY)

```
1050421  915  ES=   9.25  NQ=  17.00
1050421  920  ES=   7.00  NQ=  10.50
1050421  925  ES=   7.75  NQ=  12.00
```

```
1050421   930  ES=   7.50  NQ=  12.50
1050421   935  ES=   8.50  NQ=  16.50
1050421   940  ES=   8.25  NQ=  14.50
1050421   945  ES=   7.00  NQ=  12.50
1050421   950  ES=   7.25  NQ=  13.00
1050421   955  ES=   8.50  NQ=  16.00
1050421  1000  ES=   8.00  NQ=  16.00
1050421  1005  ES=   7.00  NQ=  14.00
1050421  1010  ES=   7.00  NQ=  13.50
1050421  1015  ES=   6.50  NQ=  12.00
1050421  1020  ES=   5.75  NQ=   9.50
1050421  1025  ES=   6.00  NQ=  10.50
1050421  1030  ES=   6.50  NQ=  12.50
1050421  1035  ES=   7.25  NQ=  13.50
1050421  1040  ES=   8.25  NQ=  14.50
1050421  1045  ES=   9.50  NQ=  16.50
1050421  1050  ES=   9.75  NQ=  16.50
1050421  1055  ES=   9.25  NQ=  18.50
1050421  1100  ES=   9.25  NQ=  18.50
1050421  1105  ES=  11.75  NQ=  21.50
1050421  1110  ES=  12.00  NQ=  22.00
1050421  1115  ES=  13.50  NQ=  24.50
1050421  1120  ES=  13.00  NQ=  24.50
1050421  1125  ES=  13.75  NQ=  25.50
1050421  1130  ES=  13.25  NQ=  24.50
1050421  1135  ES=  13.00  NQ=  24.00
1050421  1140  ES=  13.00  NQ=  23.50
1050421  1145  ES=  12.50  NQ=  22.50
1050421  1150  ES=  14.00  NQ=  25.00
1050421  1155  ES=  11.75  NQ=  21.50
1050421  1200  ES=  12.25  NQ=  22.00
1050421  1205  ES=  12.25  NQ=  22.00
1050421  1210  ES=  13.00  NQ=  22.50
1050421  1215  ES=  13.50  NQ=  23.00
1050421  1220  ES=  14.25  NQ=  24.50
```

```
1050421 1225  ES=  14.00  NQ=  23.50
1050421 1230  ES=  13.50  NQ=  22.50
1050421 1235  ES=  14.00  NQ=  23.50
1050421 1240  ES=  15.00  NQ=  25.50
1050421 1245  ES=  16.00  NQ=  26.50
1050421 1250  ES=  16.50  NQ=  27.00
1050421 1255  ES=  15.75  NQ=  25.50
```
1050421 1300 ES= 16.50 NQ= 27.50 • ← **LONG**
```
1050421 1305  ES=  16.25  NQ=  28.00
1050421 1310  ES=  17.00  NQ=  29.50
1050421 1315  ES=  17.75  NQ=  31.00
1050421 1320  ES=  19.50  NQ=  31.50
1050421 1325  ES=  20.25  NQ=  33.00
1050421 1330  ES=  19.75  NQ=  33.00
1050421 1335  ES=  18.50  NQ=  31.50
1050421 1340  ES=  18.75  NQ=  31.00
1050421 1345  ES=  18.50  NQ=  31.50
1050421 1350  ES=  18.75  NQ=  31.00
1050421 1355  ES=  19.25  NQ=  32.00
1050421 1400  ES=  18.75  NQ=  30.50
1050421 1405  ES=  19.00  NQ=  32.00
1050421 1410  ES=  19.75  NQ=  32.50
1050421 1415  ES=  19.25  NQ=  32.00
1050421 1420  ES=  19.50  NQ=  32.50
1050421 1425  ES=  18.75  NQ=  33.50
1050421 1430  ES=  20.25  NQ=  35.50
1050421 1435  ES=  21.25  NQ=  38.00
1050421 1440  ES=  21.25  NQ=  37.00
1050421 1445  ES=  21.00  NQ=  35.50
1050421 1450  ES=  20.25  NQ=  34.00
1050421 1455  ES=  20.00  NQ=  33.00
```
1050421 1500 ES= 21.75 NQ= 37.50 • ← **STOP**
```
1050421 1505  ES=  23.25  NQ=  38.00
1050421 1510  ES=  23.25  NQ=  37.50
1050421 1515  ES=  21.75  NQ=  34.50
```

Example ("Short 6a"):

i) 2003 / 12 / 15

    1031215 835 ES= 8.75 NQ= 20.00

    1031215 840 ES= 7.75 NQ= 18.50

    1031215 845 ES= 6.75 NQ= 15.00

    1031215 850 ES= 7.25 NQ= 15.50

    1031215 855 ES= 5.00 NQ= 12.00

    1031215 900 ES= 5.25 NQ= 12.50

    1031215 905 ES= 6.25 NQ= 14.50

1031215 910 ES= 5.75 NQ= 14.50 (NORMAL POSITIVE DOUBLE DAY)

    1031215 915 ES= 4.50 NQ= 10.50

    1031215 920 ES= 5.25 NQ= 12.50

    1031215 925 ES= 5.75 NQ= 13.50

    1031215 930 ES= 5.00 NQ= 12.00

    1031215 935 ES= 5.25 NQ= 11.50

    1031215 940 ES= 5.50 NQ= 13.50

    1031215 945 ES= 5.75 NQ= 15.50

    1031215 950 ES= 5.75 NQ= 14.00

    1031215 955 ES= 5.50 NQ= 13.00

    1031215 1000 ES= 4.50 NQ= 9.00

    1031215 1005 ES= 4.25 NQ= 9.00

    1031215 1010 ES= 3.50 NQ= 6.50

    1031215 1015 ES= 3.50 NQ= 6.00

1031215 1020 ES= 3.00 NQ= 3.00 ← SHORT

    1031215 1025 ES= 3.25 NQ= 4.50

    1031215 1030 ES= 4.25 NQ= 7.00

    1031215 1035 ES= 4.50 NQ= 7.50

    1031215 1040 ES= 4.25 NQ= 6.50

    1031215 1045 ES= 5.50 NQ= 10.00

    1031215 1050 ES= 5.75 NQ= 10.00

    1031215 1055 ES= 5.25 NQ= 9.00

    1031215 1100 ES= 5.50 NQ= 9.00

    1031215 1105 ES= 5.00 NQ= 7.50

    1031215 1110 ES= 4.75 NQ= 7.50

```
1031215 1115  ES=   4.25  NQ=   6.50
1031215 1120  ES=   4.50  NQ=   7.00
1031215 1125  ES=   5.25  NQ=   9.00
1031215 1130  ES=   4.25  NQ=   6.00
1031215 1135  ES=   3.75  NQ=   5.00
1031215 1140  ES=   3.50  NQ=   3.00
1031215 1145  ES=   3.25  NQ=   1.50
1031215 1150  ES=   3.50  NQ=   1.50
1031215 1155  ES=   3.50  NQ=   0.00
1031215 1200  ES=   3.75  NQ=   0.50
1031215 1205  ES=   3.75  NQ=   1.00
1031215 1210  ES=   3.75  NQ=   0.50
1031215 1215  ES=   3.75  NQ=   1.00
1031215 1220  ES=   3.00  NQ=  -1.50
1031215 1225  ES=   2.25  NQ=  -5.00
1031215 1230  ES=   1.25  NQ=  -6.00
1031215 1235  ES=   1.00  NQ=  -7.50
1031215 1240  ES=   2.25  NQ=  -4.50
1031215 1245  ES=   2.00  NQ=  -3.00
1031215 1250  ES=   3.00  NQ=  -1.50
1031215 1255  ES=   2.25  NQ=  -3.00
1031215 1300  ES=   0.75  NQ=  -6.00
1031215 1305  ES=   1.50  NQ=  -3.00
1031215 1310  ES=   1.00  NQ=  -5.00
1031215 1315  ES=   2.75  NQ=  -2.50
1031215 1320  ES=   1.75  NQ=  -4.00
1031215 1325  ES=   2.75  NQ=  -1.50
1031215 1330  ES=   2.50  NQ=   0.00
1031215 1335  ES=   2.00  NQ=   0.00
1031215 1340  ES=   2.75  NQ=   1.50
1031215 1345  ES=   1.25  NQ=  -0.50
1031215 1350  ES=   0.50  NQ=  -3.00
1031215 1355  ES=  -0.25  NQ=  -4.50
1031215 1400  ES=  -2.00  NQ=  -7.00
1031215 1405  ES=  -1.75  NQ=  -4.50
1031215 1410  ES=  -1.50  NQ=  -4.00
```

```
1031215 1415  ES=   -1.75  NQ=   -6.50
1031215 1420  ES=   -2.75  NQ=   -9.50
1031215 1425  ES=   -2.00  NQ=   -8.50
1031215 1430  ES=   -2.75  NQ=  -10.50
1031215 1435  ES=   -2.75  NQ=  -11.00
1031215 1440  ES=   -4.25  NQ=  -14.50
1031215 1445  ES=   -6.00  NQ=  -20.50
1031215 1450  ES=   -5.75  NQ=  -19.50
1031215 1455  ES=   -5.50  NQ=  -20.50
```

1031215 1500 ES=   -6.00 NQ= -21.50 • ← **STOP**

```
1031215 1505  ES=   -5.50  NQ=  -22.50
1031215 1510  ES=   -5.50  NQ=  -21.50
1031215 1515  ES=   -5.50  NQ=  -19.50
```

ii) 2004 / 10 / 19

```
1041019  835  ES=    3.00  NQ=    9.50
1041019  840  ES=    3.25  NQ=    9.50
1041019  845  ES=    3.25  NQ=   11.50
1041019  850  ES=    4.25  NQ=   13.50
1041019  855  ES=    3.75  NQ=   11.50
1041019  900  ES=    2.50  NQ=   10.00
1041019  905  ES=    5.00  NQ=   16.50
```

1041019   910 ES=   4.75 NQ= 14.50 (NORMAL
POSITIVE DOUBLE DAY)

```
1041019  915  ES=    5.00  NQ=   17.00
1041019  920  ES=    3.75  NQ=   15.00
1041019  925  ES=    3.50  NQ=   15.50
1041019  930  ES=    2.50  NQ=   13.00
1041019  935  ES=    1.75  NQ=   13.00
1041019  940  ES=    1.75  NQ=   13.00
1041019  945  ES=    1.75  NQ=   15.50
1041019  950  ES=    1.50  NQ=   15.50
1041019  955  ES=    1.75  NQ=   15.50
1041019 1000  ES=    0.75  NQ=   12.50
1041019 1005  ES=    0.00  NQ=    9.50
1041019 1010  ES=   -1.25  NQ=    7.50
```

```
1041019 1015  ES=   -1.25  NQ=    8.50
1041019 1020  ES=   -2.50  NQ=    6.50
1041019 1025  ES=   -2.50  NQ=    7.50
1041019 1030  ES=   -2.75  NQ=    7.00
1041019 1035  ES=   -1.50  NQ=    9.50
1041019 1040  ES=   -1.75  NQ=    9.50
1041019 1045  ES=   -1.75  NQ=    9.50
1041019 1050  ES=   -3.00  NQ=    6.50
1041019 1055  ES=   -2.50  NQ=    7.50
1041019 1100  ES=   -2.00  NQ=    8.00
1041019 1105  ES=   -1.00  NQ=   11.00
1041019 1110  ES=   -1.25  NQ=    9.00
1041019 1115  ES=   -1.00  NQ=    9.50
1041019 1120  ES=   -0.75  NQ=    9.00
1041019 1125  ES=    0.00  NQ=   10.50
1041019 1130  ES=   -0.25  NQ=   10.00
1041019 1135  ES=   -1.00  NQ=    9.00
1041019 1140  ES=   -0.50  NQ=    9.50
1041019 1145  ES=   -0.50  NQ=    9.00
1041019 1150  ES=   -1.25  NQ=    8.50
1041019 1155  ES=   -1.75  NQ=    7.50
1041019 1200  ES=   -1.25  NQ=    8.00
1041019 1205  ES=   -2.25  NQ=    6.00
```

1041019   1210   ES=   -2.75   NQ=   4.50 • **← SHORT**

```
1041019 1215  ES=   -2.25  NQ=    5.50
1041019 1220  ES=   -1.75  NQ=    6.50
1041019 1225  ES=   -2.25  NQ=    6.50
1041019 1230  ES=   -1.25  NQ=    8.00
1041019 1235  ES=   -1.00  NQ=    9.00
1041019 1240  ES=   -1.25  NQ=   10.00
1041019 1245  ES=   -2.50  NQ=    8.00
1041019 1250  ES=   -3.75  NQ=    5.50
1041019 1255  ES=   -4.25  NQ=    4.50
1041019 1300  ES=   -4.75  NQ=    2.00
1041019 1305  ES=   -5.25  NQ=    2.00
1041019 1310  ES=   -6.25  NQ=    0.00
```

```
1041019 1315  ES=   -6.25  NQ=   -2.00
1041019 1320  ES=   -6.75  NQ=   -2.00
1041019 1325  ES=   -5.75  NQ=   -0.50
1041019 1330  ES=   -6.25  NQ=   -1.50
1041019 1335  ES=   -6.50  NQ=   -2.50
1041019 1340  ES=   -6.50  NQ=   -2.00
1041019 1345  ES=   -6.00  NQ=   -1.50
1041019 1350  ES=   -6.75  NQ=   -3.00
1041019 1355  ES=   -7.50  NQ=   -5.50
1041019 1400  ES=   -7.75  NQ=   -4.50
1041019 1405  ES=   -7.25  NQ=   -4.00
1041019 1410  ES=   -7.75  NQ=   -4.00
1041019 1415  ES=   -7.50  NQ=   -3.00
1041019 1420  ES=   -8.25  NQ=   -5.50
1041019 1425  ES=   -7.50  NQ=   -3.50
1041019 1430  ES=   -8.25  NQ=   -5.50
1041019 1435  ES=   -7.75  NQ=   -2.50
1041019 1440  ES=   -6.75  NQ=   -1.50
1041019 1445  ES=   -7.75  NQ=   -2.50
1041019 1450  ES=   -9.00  NQ=   -6.00
1041019 1455  ES=   -9.00  NQ=   -7.50
```
1041019 1500 ES= -9.25 NQ= -8.00 • ← **STOP**
```
1041019 1505  ES=   -9.50  NQ=   -8.00
1041019 1510  ES=  -10.75  NQ=  -12.00
1041019 1515  ES=   -9.25  NQ=  -10.50
```

**11) @ 0910 ES +ve D (>=10) and NQ +ve (>=10) then wait
→ anytime NQ down 10 points (compared to 0910) then
Short ("Short 7a").**

**(At 09:10, ES is up double digits, NQ is also up double digits.
Wait when NQ is down 10 points, then Short ES.)**

ES	NQ
+ve D	+ve D (>= 10)

↓ wait until

NQ down 10pt (compare 0910 NQ) Short

Explanation to rule 11 : Positive Double Double Day:
(Both ES and NQ are +ve double digit at 09:10.)
At 09:10, both ES and NQ are +ve double digit; this happened
often in 2001 and 2002, it may happen again in the future. Since
both are up so much at 09:10, we watch NQ down 10 points and
we Short. (Countertrend strategy.)

Example:
i) 2003 / 4 / 7

```
     1030407   835  ES=  21.25  NQ=  43.00
     1030407   840  ES=  20.00  NQ=  38.50
     1030407   845  ES=  21.00  NQ=  40.50
     1030407   850  ES=  23.50  NQ=  44.00
     1030407   855  ES=  23.75  NQ=  43.00
     1030407   900  ES=  22.75  NQ=  42.50
     1030407   905  ES=  21.50  NQ=  41.50
```
1030407   910 ES= 24.25 NQ= 43.50 (DOUBLE
                                  DOUBLE POSITIVE DAY)
```
     1030407   915  ES=  24.75  NQ=  43.00
     1030407   920  ES=  25.50  NQ=  41.50
     1030407   925  ES=  25.00  NQ=  42.00
     1030407   930  ES=  24.50  NQ=  41.00
     1030407   935  ES=  23.00  NQ=  37.50
     1030407   940  ES=  21.25  NQ=  35.50
     1030407   945  ES=  20.50  NQ=  35.50
     1030407   950  ES=  20.75  NQ=  35.50
     1030407   955  ES=  18.25  NQ=  35.00
```
1030407 1000 ES= 16.75 NQ= 32.50 • ← SHORT
```
     1030407  1005  ES=  17.50  NQ=  34.50
     1030407  1010  ES=  16.75  NQ=  33.50
     1030407  1015  ES=  17.00  NQ=  34.00
     1030407  1020  ES=  18.75  NQ=  35.00
     1030407  1025  ES=  18.50  NQ=  34.50
     1030407  1030  ES=  20.25  NQ=  36.50
     1030407  1035  ES=  17.75  NQ=  35.50
```

```
1030407 1040  ES=  18.25  NQ=  35.50
1030407 1045  ES=  18.00  NQ=  35.00
1030407 1050  ES=  19.25  NQ=  37.00
1030407 1055  ES=  16.75  NQ=  35.50
1030407 1100  ES=  17.25  NQ=  35.50
1030407 1105  ES=  16.00  NQ=  34.00
1030407 1110  ES=  17.50  NQ=  34.00
1030407 1115  ES=  15.25  NQ=  31.00
1030407 1120  ES=  16.75  NQ=  32.00
1030407 1125  ES=  16.75  NQ=  31.50
1030407 1130  ES=  17.75  NQ=  33.00
1030407 1135  ES=  18.25  NQ=  33.50
1030407 1140  ES=  18.00  NQ=  33.50
1030407 1145  ES=  18.75  NQ=  33.50
1030407 1150  ES=  17.25  NQ=  32.50
1030407 1155  ES=  17.25  NQ=  31.50
1030407 1200  ES=  17.00  NQ=  30.00
1030407 1205  ES=  16.75  NQ=  31.00
1030407 1210  ES=  17.00  NQ=  31.00
1030407 1215  ES=  17.75  NQ=  31.50
1030407 1220  ES=  18.25  NQ=  32.50
1030407 1225  ES=  18.00  NQ=  32.50
1030407 1230  ES=  18.00  NQ=  33.50
1030407 1235  ES=  18.25  NQ=  33.50
1030407 1240  ES=  16.50  NQ=  31.50
1030407 1245  ES=  16.00  NQ=  31.00
1030407 1250  ES=  16.00  NQ=  31.00
1030407 1255  ES=  16.00  NQ=  31.50
1030407 1300  ES=  17.00  NQ=  32.50
1030407 1305  ES=  17.50  NQ=  33.00
1030407 1310  ES=  16.75  NQ=  33.00
1030407 1315  ES=  15.75  NQ=  31.50
1030407 1320  ES=  15.50  NQ=  31.00
1030407 1325  ES=  16.00  NQ=  31.50
1030407 1330  ES=  13.25  NQ=  28.50
```

1030407 1335 ES= 12.75 NQ= 27.50
1030407 1340 ES= 13.25 NQ= 27.50
1030407 1345 ES= 13.75 NQ= 28.50
1030407 1350 ES= 14.00 NQ= 28.00
1030407 1355 ES= 12.00 NQ= 25.50
1030407 1400 ES= 10.25 NQ= 21.50
1030407 1405 ES=   8.75 NQ= 19.00
1030407 1410 ES= 10.00 NQ= 19.00
1030407 1415 ES=   9.75 NQ= 20.50
1030407 1420 ES=   7.00 NQ= 15.00
1030407 1425 ES=   8.50 NQ= 17.00
1030407 1430 ES=   6.75 NQ= 15.00
1030407 1435 ES=   3.50 NQ=   9.00
1030407 1440 ES=   4.25 NQ= 10.50
1030407 1445 ES=   4.00 NQ= 12.50
1030407 1450 ES=   0.50 NQ=   7.00
1030407 1455 ES=   2.50 NQ= 10.00
1030407 1500 ES=   0.50 NQ=   7.00 • ← **STOP**
1030407 1505 ES= -0.50 NQ=   4.50
1030407 1510 ES= -0.50 NQ=   3.50
1030407 1515 ES= -1.50 NQ=   1.50

ii) 2004 / 5 / 19

1040519 835 ES=   8.50 NQ= 17.00
1040519 840 ES=   9.00 NQ= 15.50
1040519 845 ES=   8.25 NQ= 15.50
1040519 850 ES= 10.25 NQ= 18.00
1040519 855 ES= 10.25 NQ= 18.00
1040519 900 ES= 10.00 NQ= 17.50
1040519 905 ES= 11.50 NQ= 19.50
1040519 910 ES= 13.50 NQ= 23.50 (DOUBLE
DOUBLE POSITIVE DAY)
1040519 915 ES= 12.75 NQ= 23.00
1040519 920 ES= 14.25 NQ= 26.00
1040519 925 ES= 13.75 NQ= 25.00

```
1040519  930  ES=  13.75  NQ=  25.50
1040519  935  ES=  14.50  NQ=  26.00
1040519  940  ES=  14.50  NQ=  29.00
1040519  945  ES=  14.75  NQ=  29.50
1040519  950  ES=  13.75  NQ=  27.50
1040519  955  ES=  14.00  NQ=  27.50
1040519 1000  ES=  13.75  NQ=  28.00
1040519 1005  ES=  14.00  NQ=  27.50
1040519 1010  ES=  13.75  NQ=  27.00
1040519 1015  ES=  14.25  NQ=  28.50
1040519 1020  ES=  13.75  NQ=  28.00
1040519 1025  ES=  13.50  NQ=  27.50
1040519 1030  ES=  14.00  NQ=  27.00
1040519 1035  ES=  13.00  NQ=  24.50
1040519 1040  ES=  12.50  NQ=  24.00
1040519 1045  ES=  12.50  NQ=  24.00
1040519 1050  ES=  12.75  NQ=  24.50
1040519 1055  ES=  13.25  NQ=  26.00
1040519 1100  ES=  13.50  NQ=  26.50
1040519 1105  ES=  13.00  NQ=  26.00
1040519 1110  ES=  13.75  NQ=  27.00
1040519 1115  ES=  13.50  NQ=  27.00
1040519 1120  ES=  13.25  NQ=  26.00
1040519 1125  ES=  13.25  NQ=  26.50
1040519 1130  ES=  14.25  NQ=  28.50
1040519 1135  ES=  12.75  NQ=  27.00
1040519 1140  ES=  13.00  NQ=  26.50
1040519 1145  ES=  11.75  NQ=  24.50
1040519 1150  ES=  11.75  NQ=  24.50
1040519 1155  ES=  12.00  NQ=  25.00
1040519 1200  ES=  12.25  NQ=  25.50
1040519 1205  ES=  12.00  NQ=  25.00
1040519 1210  ES=  12.00  NQ=  24.50
1040519 1215  ES=  12.00  NQ=  24.50
1040519 1220  ES=  12.00  NQ=  24.50
```

```
1040519 1225  ES=  12.25  NQ=  25.50
1040519 1230  ES=  11.25  NQ=  23.50
1040519 1235  ES=  11.25  NQ=  24.00
1040519 1240  ES=  11.75  NQ=  24.00
1040519 1245  ES=  12.50  NQ=  26.50
1040519 1250  ES=  12.50  NQ=  25.50
1040519 1255  ES=  13.00  NQ=  26.50
1040519 1300  ES=  13.25  NQ=  27.00
1040519 1305  ES=  13.00  NQ=  26.50
1040519 1310  ES=  12.25  NQ=  26.00
1040519 1315  ES=  11.25  NQ=  25.00
1040519 1320  ES=  10.50  NQ=  24.00
1040519 1325  ES=  10.50  NQ=  24.00
1040519 1330  ES=   7.25  NQ=  20.00
1040519 1335  ES=   7.75  NQ=  18.50
1040519 1340  ES=   7.75  NQ=  20.00
1040519 1345  ES=   7.75  NQ=  20.00
1040519 1350  ES=   6.50  NQ=  18.00
1040519 1355  ES=   6.75  NQ=  18.00
1040519 1400  ES=   5.50  NQ=  16.00
```
1040519 1405 ES=   4.50 NQ= 13.00 • ← **SHORT**
```
1040519 1410  ES=   5.25  NQ=  15.00
1040519 1415  ES=   4.25  NQ=  13.00
1040519 1420  ES=   4.75  NQ=  13.50
1040519 1425  ES=   2.25  NQ=   9.50
1040519 1430  ES=   2.00  NQ=   8.00
1040519 1435  ES=   0.25  NQ=   4.00
1040519 1440  ES=   1.00  NQ=   6.50
1040519 1445  ES=   1.25  NQ=   6.50
1040519 1450  ES=  -1.75  NQ=   0.00
1040519 1455  ES=  -0.75  NQ=   2.50
```
1040519 1500 ES= -2.25 NQ=   0.00 • ← **STOP**
```
1040519 1505  ES=  -2.50  NQ=  -2.50
1040519 1510  ES=  -3.25  NQ=  -3.00
1040519 1515  ES=  -3.75  NQ=  -3.00
```

12) @ 0910 ES -ve D (<= -10) and NQ -ve D (<= -10) then wait → anytime NQ up 10 points (compare to 0910) then Long ("Long 7b").

(At 09:10, when ES is down double digits, NQ is also down double digits. Wait for NQ to be up by 10 points, then Long ES.)

ES   NQ

-ve D   -ve D (<= -10)

↓ wait until

NQ up 10 point (compare 0910 NQ), Long with stop

Explanation of rule 12 : Double Double Negative Day:

(At 09:10, both ES and NQ are -ve double digits). Market is down a lot at too early a stage at 09:10. So we wait when NQ is up, then we Long with stop. We do not Short on this day.

Example:

i) 2002 / 9 / 9

    1020909   835   ES= -7.50   NQ= -10.00
    1020909   840   ES= -8.00   NQ= -10.00
    1020909   845   ES= -7.50   NQ= -9.50
    1020909   850   ES= -7.75   NQ= -10.50
    1020909   855   ES= -8.25   NQ= -11.50
    1020909   900   ES= -8.50   NQ= -13.00
    1020909   905   ES= -10.00   NQ= -16.00
    1020909   910   ES= -10.00   NQ= -18.50 (DOUBLE
                                    DOUBLE NEGATIVE DAY)
    1020909   915   ES= -9.75   NQ= -16.00
    1020909   920   ES= -8.75   NQ= -15.50
    1020909   925   ES= -9.00   NQ= -16.50
    1020909   930   ES= -10.00   NQ= -16.50
    1020909   935   ES= -11.25   NQ= -17.50
    1020909   940   ES= -10.75   NQ= -17.50
    1020909   945   ES= -9.75   NQ= -17.00
    1020909   950   ES= -9.75   NQ= -16.00
    1020909   955   ES= -8.50   NQ= -13.50

```
1020909 1000 ES= -7.50 NQ= -12.00
1020909 1005 ES= -6.25 NQ= -11.50
1020909 1010 ES= -5.00 NQ= -10.50
1020909 1015 ES= -6.00 NQ= -12.50
1020909 1020 ES= -6.00 NQ= -14.00
1020909 1025 ES= -8.00 NQ= -15.00
1020909 1030 ES= -9.25 NQ= -15.50
1020909 1035 ES= -9.25 NQ= -14.50
1020909 1040 ES= -9.50 NQ= -14.00
1020909 1045 ES= -8.75 NQ= -14.50
1020909 1050 ES= -9.00 NQ= -13.50
1020909 1055 ES= -8.25 NQ= -13.50
1020909 1100 ES= -9.25 NQ= -14.50
1020909 1105 ES= -8.00 NQ= -13.50
1020909 1110 ES= -7.50 NQ= -13.00
1020909 1115 ES= -7.25 NQ= -12.00
1020909 1120 ES= -6.25 NQ= -12.00
1020909 1125 ES= -6.25 NQ= -11.50
1020909 1130 ES= -6.25 NQ= -11.50
1020909 1135 ES= -6.00 NQ= -11.00
1020909 1140 ES= -6.25 NQ= -11.50
1020909 1145 ES= -5.50 NQ= -10.50
```

1020909 1150 ES= -4.00 NQ= -7.50 • ← **LONG**

```
1020909 1155 ES= -2.75 NQ= -6.50
1020909 1200 ES= -1.25 NQ= -2.50
1020909 1205 ES=  0.00 NQ=  0.00
1020909 1210 ES= -1.25 NQ= -2.00
1020909 1215 ES= -1.50 NQ= -2.00
1020909 1220 ES= -0.75 NQ= -1.00
1020909 1225 ES=  0.00 NQ=  0.00
1020909 1230 ES=  2.25 NQ=  4.50
1020909 1235 ES=  1.75 NQ=  4.50
1020909 1240 ES=  1.00 NQ=  3.50
1020909 1245 ES=  1.75 NQ=  5.00
1020909 1250 ES=  2.50 NQ=  8.00
```

```
1020909 1255  ES=   0.25  NQ=   4.50
1020909 1300  ES=   0.50  NQ=   6.00
1020909 1305  ES=   2.00  NQ=   7.50
1020909 1310  ES=   5.00  NQ=  12.00
1020909 1315  ES=   6.25  NQ=  13.00
1020909 1320  ES=   4.50  NQ=  10.00
1020909 1325  ES=   9.75  NQ=  16.50
1020909 1330  ES=   9.50  NQ=  16.50
1020909 1335  ES=  10.25  NQ=  16.50
1020909 1340  ES=   9.75  NQ=  15.50
1020909 1345  ES=   8.75  NQ=  13.50
1020909 1350  ES=   9.00  NQ=  14.00
1020909 1355  ES=  10.75  NQ=  17.50
1020909 1400  ES=  11.50  NQ=  17.00
1020909 1405  ES=  10.00  NQ=  15.00
1020909 1410  ES=   9.50  NQ=  14.50
1020909 1415  ES=   9.00  NQ=  13.00
1020909 1420  ES=  12.50  NQ=  19.00
1020909 1425  ES=  11.00  NQ=  17.00
1020909 1430  ES=   9.50  NQ=  15.00
1020909 1435  ES=   9.50  NQ=  15.00
1020909 1440  ES=   9.50  NQ=  14.50
1020909 1445  ES=  10.25  NQ=  14.00
1020909 1450  ES=  11.25  NQ=  17.00
1020909 1455  ES=  11.50  NQ=  17.50
```

1020909 1500 ES=   7.50 NQ= 11.50 • ← **STOP**

```
1020909 1505  ES=   7.50  NQ=  11.50
1020909 1510  ES=   6.25  NQ=  10.00
1020909 1515  ES=   6.00  NQ=   7.50
```

ii) 2003 / 7 / 1

```
1030701  835  ES=  -4.75  NQ=  -8.50
1030701  840  ES=  -4.50  NQ=  -8.00
1030701  845  ES=  -4.50  NQ= -10.00
1030701  850  ES=  -3.75  NQ=  -8.50
```

1030701   855 ES=   -4.25 NQ= -10.00
1030701   900 ES=   -5.00 NQ=   -9.50
1030701   905 ES= -10.50 NQ= -18.50
1030701   910 ES= -11.50 NQ= -21.50 (DOUBLE
                                    DOUBLE NEGATIVE DAY)
1030701   915 ES= -10.25 NQ= -19.50
1030701   920 ES= -10.25 NQ= -19.00
1030701   925 ES=   -8.25 NQ= -16.50
1030701   930 ES=   -7.75 NQ= -15.50
1030701   935 ES=   -9.25 NQ= -16.00
1030701   940 ES=   -9.75 NQ= -17.00
1030701   945 ES= -11.00 NQ= -20.50
1030701   950 ES= -10.50 NQ= -20.00
1030701   955 ES= -11.25 NQ= -21.00
1030701 1000 ES= -10.25 NQ= -20.50
1030701 1005 ES=   -9.75 NQ= -20.00
1030701 1010 ES=   -8.75 NQ= -18.00
1030701 1015 ES=   -9.25 NQ= -17.50
1030701 1020 ES=   -8.50 NQ= -17.50
1030701 1025 ES=   -8.25 NQ= -18.00
1030701 1030 ES=   -7.00 NQ= -16.50
1030701 1035 ES=   -7.25 NQ= -16.50
1030701 1040 ES=   -6.50 NQ= -15.50
1030701 1045 ES=   -7.75 NQ= -17.50
1030701 1050 ES=   -8.50 NQ= -17.00
1030701 1055 ES=   -8.00 NQ= -15.50
1030701 1100 ES=   -7.25 NQ= -14.00
1030701 1105 ES=   -8.75 NQ= -15.50
1030701 1110 ES=   -9.00 NQ= -16.50
1030701 1115 ES=   -9.25 NQ= -16.50
1030701 1120 ES= -10.00 NQ= -18.00
1030701 1125 ES=   -9.50 NQ= -16.50
1030701 1130 ES=   -9.50 NQ= -16.50
1030701 1135 ES=   -9.50 NQ= -17.50
1030701 1140 ES=   -9.25 NQ= -18.50

```
1030701 1145    ES=   -9.75   NQ= -18.50
1030701 1150    ES=   -9.00   NQ= -18.00
1030701 1155    ES=   -9.00   NQ= -17.00
1030701 1200    ES=   -7.25   NQ= -14.50
```
1030701 1205   ES=   -4.25   NQ= -11.50 • ← **LONG**
```
1030701 1210    ES=   -4.75   NQ= -12.00
1030701 1215    ES=   -3.50   NQ=  -9.50
1030701 1220    ES=   -3.50   NQ=  -9.50
1030701 1225    ES=   -3.75   NQ=  -9.50
1030701 1230    ES=   -2.00   NQ=  -7.50
1030701 1235    ES=   -2.50   NQ=  -8.50
1030701 1240    ES=   -3.50   NQ=  -9.50
1030701 1245    ES=   -3.50   NQ=  -9.50
1030701 1250    ES=   -4.00   NQ= -11.00
1030701 1255    ES=   -3.75   NQ= -10.50
1030701 1300    ES=   -3.25   NQ= -10.50
1030701 1305    ES=   -3.50   NQ= -11.00
1030701 1310    ES=   -3.25   NQ= -11.00
1030701 1315    ES=   -3.00   NQ=  -8.50
1030701 1320    ES=   -1.75   NQ=  -6.00
1030701 1325    ES=    0.75   NQ=   1.50
1030701 1330    ES=    2.00   NQ=   5.50
1030701 1335    ES=    2.75   NQ=   7.50
1030701 1340    ES=    3.25   NQ=   5.50
1030701 1345    ES=    5.25   NQ=  12.00
1030701 1350    ES=    4.50   NQ=  10.00
1030701 1355    ES=    5.50   NQ=  11.00
1030701 1400    ES=    4.75   NQ=  10.50
1030701 1405    ES=    5.25   NQ=   9.00
1030701 1410    ES=    5.25   NQ=   8.50
1030701 1415    ES=    6.75   NQ=  12.50
1030701 1420    ES=    7.50   NQ=  13.50
1030701 1425    ES=    7.00   NQ=  12.50
1030701 1430    ES=    8.25   NQ=  13.50
1030701 1435    ES=    7.25   NQ=  11.50
1030701 1440    ES=    6.50   NQ=   8.50
1030701 1445    ES=    6.75   NQ=  10.00
1030701 1450    ES=    7.75   NQ=  13.00
```

```
1030701 1455  ES=  8.50  NQ=  16.00
1030701 1500  ES=  7.75  NQ=  15.00  •  ← STOP
1030701 1505  ES=  8.50  NQ=  16.50
1030701 1510  ES=  8.25  NQ=  16.00
1030701 1515  ES=  8.25  NQ=  17.00
```

Traders can use ES and NQ data from any quote machine, write down the data of ES and NQ every five minutes, and trade accordingly. Using the TradeStation platform will get five minutes data automatically and one need not use a pen and a note book to write it down like I did years ago. There are advantages in writing down as explained elsewhere in this book. I have traded without TradeStation for many years, and I discovered these strategies without TradeStation. TradeStation is just a tool which is more convenient for data generation. That's all.

Given below is the hypothetical performance of RC 5 System after back test by TradeStation. We must verify the above trading method with TradeStation back test since 2001. Do not use any strategies or trading methods without verifying their efficacy.

Hypothetical Performance Report of RC 5 Seminar
(No commission and slippage included)
Net profit: $44,275.00
Profit factor: 1.97
Percent profitable: 69.19%
Average trade net profit: $69.94

TradeStation Performance Summary			Collapse ⌃
	All Trades	**Long Trades**	**Short Trades**
Total Net Profit	$44,275.00	$10,525.00	$33,750.00
Gross Profit	$89,687.50	$25,800.00	$63,887.50
Gross Loss	($45,412.50)	($15,275.00)	($30,137.50)
Profit Factor	1.97	1.69	2.12
Open Position P/L	$0.00	$0.00	$0.00
Select Total Net Profit	$31,750.00	$6,987.50	$24,762.50
Select Gross Profit	$77,162.50	$22,262.50	$54,900.00
Select Gross Loss	($45,412.50)	($15,275.00)	($30,137.50)
Select Profit Factor	1.70	1.46	1.82
Adjusted Total Net Profit	$36,650.77	$6,307.40	$27,402.21
Adjusted Gross Profit	$85,402.07	$23,554.40	$60,235.29
Adjusted Gross Loss	($48,751.29)	($17,246.99)	($32,833.08)
Adjusted Profit Factor	1.75	1.37	1.83
Total Number of Trades	633	197	436
Percent Profitable	69.19%	67.01%	70.18%
Winning Trades	438	132	306
Losing Trades	185	60	125
Even Trades	10	5	5
Avg. Trade Net Profit	$69.94	$53.43	$77.41
Avg. Winning Trade	$204.77	$195.45	$208.78
Avg. Losing Trade	($245.47)	($254.58)	($241.10)
Ratio Avg. Win:Avg. Loss	0.83	0.77	0.87
Largest Winning Trade	$1,700.00	$1,400.00	$1,700.00
Largest Losing Trade	($500.00)	($500.00)	($500.00)
Largest Winner as % of Gross Profit	1.90%	5.43%	2.66%
Largest Loser as % of Gross Loss	1.10%	3.27%	1.66%
Net Profit as % of Largest Loss	8855.00%	2105.00%	6750.00%
Select Net Profit as % of Largest Loss	6350.00%	1397.50%	4952.50%
Adjusted Net Profit as % of Largest Loss	7330.15%	1261.48%	5480.44%
Max. Consecutive Winning Trades	13	8	15
Max. Consecutive Losing Trades	4	4	4
Avg. Bars in Total Trades	40.29	34.32	42.99
Avg. Bars in Winning Trades	40.23	36.53	41.82
Avg. Bars in Losing Trades	41.09	31.15	45.86
Avg. Bars in Even Trades	28.30	14.20	42.40

Table 12.1 Hypothetical Performance Report of RC 5 Seminar

Source: Created by TradeStation

Continue from page 170

Max. Shares/Contracts Held	1	1	1
Total Shares/Contracts Held	633	197	436
Account Size Required	$2,112.50	$1,925.00	$2,112.50
Total Slippage	$0.00	$0.00	$0.00
Total Commission	$0.00	$0.00	$0.00
Return on Initial Capital	44.27%		
Annual Rate of Return	7.34%		
Buy & Hold Return	(6.70%)		
Return on Account	2095.86%		
Avg. Monthly Return	$516.88		
Std. Deviation of Monthly Return	$769.75		
Return Retracement Ratio	0.31		
RINA Index	3750.12		
Sharpe Ratio	0.62		
K-Ratio	n/a		
Trading Period	4 Yrs, 11 Mths, 28 Dys, 2 Hrs, 30 Mins		
Percent of Time in the Market	4.75%		
Time in the Market	2 Mths, 25 Dys, 15 Hrs		
Longest Flat Period	16 Dys, 20 Hrs, 20 Mins		
Max. Equity Run-up	$45,375.00		
Date of Max. Equity Run-up	05/19/06 10:15		
Max. Equity Run-up as % of Initial Capital	45.38%		

Max. Drawdown (Intra-day Peak to Valley)

Value	($2,462.50)	($2,325.00)	($3,800.00)
Date	12/17/04 14:00		
as % of Initial Capital	2.46%	2.33%	3.80%
Net Profit as % of Drawdown	1797.97%	452.69%	888.16%
Select Net Profit as % of Drawdown	1289.34%	300.54%	651.64%
Adjusted Net Profit as % of Drawdown	1488.36%	271.29%	721.11%

Max. Drawdown (Trade Close to Trade Close)

Value	($2,112.50)	($1,925.00)	($2,112.50)
Date	12/29/04 15:00		
as % of Initial Capital	2.11%	1.93%	2.11%
Net Profit as % of Drawdown	2095.86%	546.75%	1597.63%
Select Net Profit as % of Drawdown	1502.96%	362.99%	1172.19%
Adjusted Net Profit as % of Drawdown	1734.95%	327.66%	1297.15%
Max. Trade Drawdown	($587.50)	($587.50)	($500.00)

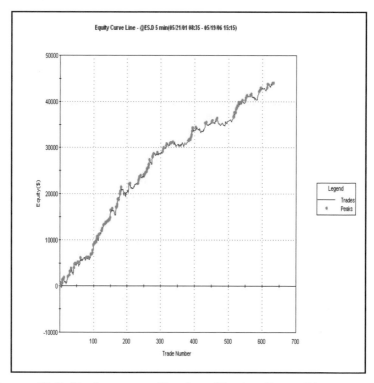

Figure 12.2 Performance Graphs - Equity Curve Line

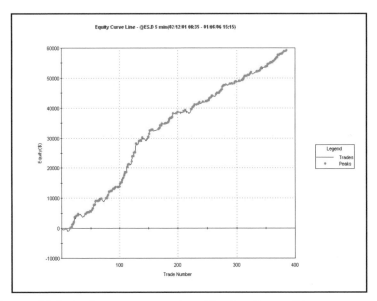

Figure 12.3 Performance graph – Equity Curve Line

Source: Created by TradeStation

If you use RC 8 indicator and strategy with the same market condition as shown above, the result will be different. How to convert RC 5 System to RC 5++ System will remain as a challenge to the readers. To save time and space, we just show the summary of the hypothetical report and the equity curve in Figure 12.3.

Hypothetical Performance Report of RC 5++ System
(No commission and slippage included)
Net profit: $57,385.00
Profit factor: 4.14
Percent profitable: 78.71%
Average trade net profit: $154.68

13

RC 5 Indicator and Easy Language Source Code

T his is the elucidation of the contents of Chapter 12 in a programming language. If you can follow it, you may use it to form a mechanical system that will help you observe and make improvements to suit your own trading needs.

Of course, the easiest way is to have a TradeStation platform set up. Then insert an indicator that shows ES and NQ five minutes value.

The Indicator Source Code

```
Inputs: PriceES(Close of Data1),
          PriceNDQ(Close of Data4);
Vars:   ESLevel(0), NDQLevel(0), ESYDC(0), NDQYDC(0),
        Started(FALSE);
        if Date<>Date[1] then
        begin
            ESYDC = Close[1];
            NDQYDC = PriceNDQ[1];
            Started=TRUE;
        end;
        if Started then
        begin
            ESLevel              =Close-ESYDC;
            NDQLevel     =PriceNDQ-NDQYDC;
        end;
        Plot1(ESLevel,"es");
        Plot2(NDQLevel,"ndq");
        Plot3(0,"zero");
```

```
if Date<>Date[1] then
begin
        Print(" ");
        Print(" ");
end;
Print(Date:10:0,Time:6:0," ES=",ESLevel," NQ=",
NDQLevel);
```

The Source Code used in TradeStation

An easier option is to write out an Easy Language file to get the signals of these strategies. **If traders use the TradeStation platform, this RC 5 can turn into a mechanical system, getting signals generated by TradeStation. This is more convenient. Traders could look at the signals and then monitor the NQ to improve trading.**

```
vars:        EarlyStartOffset(20),
             StartOffset(40),
             EndOffset(15),
             LastTradeOffset(30),
             Stop_Width(0),
             Stop_Price(0),
             HalfDay(false),
      StopLoss(10),
             RevStopLoss(5);
Inputs:      PriceDJI(Close of Data2),
                 PriceIVX(Close of Data3),
                 PriceNDQ(Close of Data4);
      HalfDay = RC_Halfday(date);
if HalfDay = false then
begin
Vars:  EarlyStartTimeMins(0), StartTimeMins(0),
       EndTimeMins(0), LastTradeMins(0);
Vars:  MP(0),EP(0),ED1(0),ED2(0),NTToday(0),MPP(0);
       if CurrentBar=1 then
       begin
```

```
EarlyStartTimeMins=TimeToMinutes(Sess1StartTime)+EarlyStartOffset;
StartTimeMins=TimeToMinutes(Sess1StartTime)+StartOffset;
EndTimeMins  =TimeToMinutes(Sess1EndTime)-EndOffset;
LastTradeMins  =TimeToMinutes(Sess1EndTime)-
LastTradeOffset;
        end;
        MP=MarketPosition;
        EP=EntryPrice;
        ED1=EntryDate(1);
        ED2=EntryDate(2);
        MPP=MaxContractProfit(0)/BigPointValue;
        NTToday=0;
        if ED1=Date then NTToday=1;
        if ED2=Date then NTToday=2;
        if MP<>0 then NTToday=NTToday+1;
Vars:  DateOK(False), TimeOK(False), Tmins(0);
Vars:  ESLevel(0), NDQLevel(0), ESYDC(0), NDQYDC(0),
        Started(FALSE);
Vars:  HaveTraded(0), ES(0);
        if Date<>Date[1] then
        begin
                ESYDC      = Close[1];
                NDQYDC     = PriceNDQ[1];
                Started = TRUE;
                DateOK  = False;
    TimeOK  = FALSE;
        end;
        if Started then
        begin
                ESLevel       =Close-ESYDC;
                NDQLevel      =PriceNDQ-NDQYDC;
        end;
        Tmins=TimeToMinutes(Time);
Vars:  Priority(False),NTrade(false);
```

```
Vars:   PS_NS(false),NS_PS(false),PS_PS(false),NS_NS(false);
Vars:   ES1(0),NDQ(0),NDQ1(0);
if Date<>Date[1] then
begin
                Priority    = false;
                DateOk      = false;

                PS_NS = false;
                NS_PS = false;
                PS_PS = false;
                NS_NS = false;
end;
if Tmins = StartTimeMins then
begin
if (ESLevel >= 0 and ESLevel < 10) and (NDQLevel < 0 and
NDQLevel > -10) then PS_NS= true;
if (ESLevel < 0 and ESLevel > -10) and (NDQLevel >= 0 and
NDQLevel < 10) then NS_PS = true;
if (ESLevel < 0 and ESLevel > -10) and (NDQLevel < 0 and
NDQLevel > -10) then NS_NS = true;
if (ESLevel >= 0 and ESLevel < 10) and (NDQLevel >= 0
and NDQLevel < 10) then PS_PS = true;
end;
if Tmins=EarlyStartTimeMins then
begin
        ES1 = ESLevel;
        NDQ1 = NDQLevel;
end;
Vars:   wait2a(false),wait2b(false);
Vars:   wait3a(false), wait3b(false),wait4a(false);
Vars:   wait5a(false),
wait5b(false),wait6a(false),wait7a(false),wait7b(false);
Vars:   wait8a(false), wait8b(false), NTrade3(false);
                if Date<>Date[1] then
                begin
```

```
                    wait2a = false;
                    wait2b = false;
                    wait3a = false;
                    wait3b = false;
                    wait4a = false;
                    wait5a = false;
                    wait5b = false;
                    wait6a = false;
                    wait7a = false;
                    wait7b = false;
                    wait8a = false;
                    wait8b = false;
                    NTrade3 = false;
               end;
if Tmins = StartTimeMins and Priority = false then
begin
     if NS_PS and absvalue(NDQLevel) >= absvalue(ESLevel)
     and
     Priority = false then
     begin
                    Sell Short("Short 1a")this bar on close;
                    Priority = true;
                    Stop_Width = StopLoss;
          end;
     if NS_PS and absvalue(ESLevel) > absvalue(NDQLevel) and
     Priority = false then
          begin
                    Sell Short("Short 1b")this bar on close;
                    Priority = true;
                    Stop_Width = StopLoss;
          end;
     if PS_NS and absvalue(NDQLevel) >= absvalue(ESLevel)
     and
     Priority = false then
          begin
```

```
        NDQ = NDQLevel;
        wait2a = true;
        Priority = true;
    end;
    if PS_NS and absvalue(ESLevel) > absvalue(NDQLevel)
    and
Priority = false then
    begin
        NDQ = NDQLevel;
        wait2b = true;
        Priority = true;
    end;
    if NS_NS and NDQLevel <= ESLevel and Priority =
    false then
    begin
        NDQ = NDQLevel;
        wait3a = true;
        Priority = true;
    end;
if NS_NS and ESLevel < NDQLevel and Priority = false then
    begin
        wait3b = true;
        Priority = true;
    end;
    if PS_PS and NDQLevel >= ESLevel and Priority = false then
    begin
        wait4a = true;
        Priority = true;
        NDQ = NDQLevel;
    end;
if PS_PS and ESLevel > NDQLevel and Priority = false then
    begin
        Sell Short("Short 4b")this bar on close;
        Priority = true;
        Stop_Width = StopLoss;
```

```
        end;
    if ESLevel < 0 and ESLevel > -10 and NDQLevel <= -10
    and NDQLevel >= -25 and Priority = false then
        begin
                NDQ = NDQLevel;
                wait5a = true;
                Priority = true;
        end;
    if ESLevel >= 0 and ESLevel < 10 and NDQLevel >= 10
    and NDQLevel <= 25 and Priority = false then
        begin
                NDQ = NDQLevel;
                wait6a = true;
                Priority = true;
        end;
    if ESLevel >= 10 and NDQLevel >= 10 and Priority =
false then
        begin
                NDQ = NDQLevel;
                wait7a = true;
                Priority = true;
        end;
    if ESLevel <= -10 and NDQLevel <= -10 and Priority =
false then
        begin
                NDQ = NDQLevel;
                wait7b = true;
                Priority = true;
        end;
end;
if Tmins > StartTimeMins and Tmins < LastTradeMins and wait2a
then
begin
        if NDQLevel >= 13 and wait2a then
        begin
```

```
                Buy("Long 2a")this bar on close;
                wait2a = false;
                Priority = true;
                Stop_Width = StopLoss;
        end;
end;
if Tmins > StartTimeMins and Tmins < LastTradeMins and wait2b
then
begin
        if NDQLevel >= 13 and wait2b then
        begin
                Buy("Long 2b")this bar on close;
                wait2b = false;
                Priority = true;
                Stop_Width = StopLoss;
        end;
end;
if Tmins > StartTimeMins and Tmins <= LastTradeMins and
wait3a then
begin
        if NDQLevel <= -20 and wait3a then
        begin
                Sell Short("Short 3a")this bar on close;
                wait3a = false;
                Priority = true;
                Stop_Width = StopLoss;
        end;
end;
if Tmins > StartTimeMins and Tmins <= LastTradeMins and
wait3b then
begin
        if NDQLevel <= -8 and wait3b then
        begin
                Sell Short("Short 3b")this bar on close;
                wait3b = false;
```

```
                Priority = true;
                Stop_Width = StopLoss;
        end;
end;
if Tmins > StartTimeMins and Tmins <= LastTradeMins and
wait4a then
begin
        if NDQLevel-NDQ>= 10 and wait4a then
        begin
                Buy("Long 4a") this bar on close;
                wait4a = false;
                Priority = true;
                Stop_Width = StopLoss;
        end;
        if NDQLevel <= -13 and wait4a then
        begin
                Sell Short("Short 4a")this bar on close;
                wait4a = false;
                Priority = true;
                Stop_Width = StopLoss;
        end;
end;
if Tmins > StartTimeMins and Tmins < LastTradeMins and wait5a
then
begin
        if NDQ-NDQLevel >= 10 and wait5a then
        begin
                Sell Short("Short 5a")this bar on close;
                wait5a = false;
                Priority = true;
                Stop_Width = StopLoss;
    end;
end;
if Tmins > StartTimeMins and Tmins < LastTradeMins and wait6a
then
```

```
begin
        if NDQLevel-NDQ >= 12 and wait6a then
        begin
                Buy("Long 6a") this bar on close;
                wait6a = false;
                Priority = true;
                Stop_Width = StopLoss;
        end;
        if NDQ-NDQLevel >= 10 and wait6a then
        begin
                Sell Short("Short 6a")this bar on close;
                wait6a = false;
                Priority = true;
                Stop_Width = StopLoss;
        end;
end;
if Tmins > StartTimeMins and Tmins < LastTradeMins and wait7a
then
begin
        if NDQ-NDQLevel >= 10 and wait7a then
        begin
                Sell Short("Short 7a")this bar on close;
                wait7a = false;
                Priority = true;
                Stop_Width = StopLoss;
        end;
end;
if Tmins > StartTimeMins and Tmins < LastTradeMins and wait7b
then
begin
        if NDQLevel-NDQ >= 10 and wait7b then
        begin
                Buy("Long 7b") this bar on close;
                wait7b = false;
                Priority = true;
```

```
                Stop_Width = StopLoss;
        end;
end;
if MarketPosition = 1 and MPP >= 4 then
begin
                Stop_Price = EP + 0.75;
                Sell ("LBE") next bar Stop_Price Stop;
end;
if MarketPosition = -1 and MPP >= 4 then
begin
                Stop_Price = EP - 0.75;
                buy to cover ("SBE") next bar Stop_Price Stop;
end;
if MarketPosition = 1 then
begin
                Stop_Price = EP - Stop_Width;
                Sell ("L-Exit") next bar Stop_Price Stop;
end;
if MarketPosition = -1 then
begin
                Stop_Price = EP + Stop_Width;
                buy to cover ("S-Exit") next bar Stop_Price Stop;
end;
if Tmins>=EndTimeMins then
begin
                Sell("LEoD") this bar on close;
                Buy to Cover("SEoD") this bar on close;
end;
end;
```

RC HalfDay Function (included all FOMC day, half day like Christmas eve, and days that data is incorrect)
input:
    theDate(NumericSimple);
var:

```
  kNumSlots(100);
array:
  shortday[100](0);
if shortday[ kNumSlots-1 ] = 0 then begin
  for value1 = 1 to kNumSlots begin
    shortday[ value1 ] = value1;
  end;
  shortday[ 52 ] =  971006;
  shortday[ 53 ] =  971027;
  shortday[ 54 ] =  971128;
  shortday[ 55 ] =  971208;
  shortday[ 56 ] =  971224;
  shortday[ 57 ] =  971226;
  shortday[ 58 ] =  980529;
  shortday[ 59 ] =  980609;
  shortday[ 60 ] =  981127;
  shortday[ 61 ] =  981224;
  shortday[ 62 ] =  990111;
  shortday[ 63 ] =  990402;
  shortday[ 64 ] =  991126;
  shortday[ 65 ] =  991231;
  shortday[ 66 ] = 1000331;
  shortday[ 67 ] = 1000630;
  shortday[ 68 ] = 1000703;
  shortday[ 69 ] = 1000929;
  shortday[ 70 ] = 1001124;
  shortday[ 71 ] = 1001229;
  shortday[ 72 ] = 1010131;
  shortday[ 73 ] = 1010228;
  shortday[ 74 ] = 1010430;
  shortday[ 75 ] = 1010531;
  shortday[ 76 ] = 1010703;
  shortday[ 77 ] = 1010731;
  shortday[ 78 ] = 1010831;
  shortday[ 79 ] = 1010928;
```

```
    shortday[ 80 ] = 1011031;
    shortday[ 81 ] = 1011123;
    shortday[ 82 ] = 1011224;
    shortday[ 83 ] = 1020208;
    shortday[ 84 ] = 1020705;
    shortday[ 85 ] = 1021129;
    shortday[ 86 ] = 1021224;
    shortday[ 87 ] = 1030501;
    shortday[ 88 ] = 1030703;
    shortday[ 89 ] = 1030930;
    shortday[ 90 ] = 1031127;
    shortday[ 91 ] = 1031128;
    shortday[ 92 ] = 1031224;
    shortday[ 93 ] = 1031226;
    shortday[ 94 ] = 1041126;
    shortday[ 95 ] = 1050310;
    shortday[ 96 ] = 1050426;
    shortday[ 97 ] = 1051125;
    shortday[ 98 ] = 1060131;
    shortday[ 99 ] = 1060421;
end;
var:step(0),i(0),found(false);
i = kNumSlots/2; step = i; found = false;
while found = false and step >= 1 and shortday[ i ] <> theDate
begin
    step = step/2;
    var: diff(0);
    diff = theDate - shortday[ i ];
    if diff <> 0 then
        i = i + iff(diff>0, step, -step);
end;
RC_halfday = (shortday[ i ] = theDate);
```

14

A Quick Practice on RC 5 Strategies

T his chapter is meant for practicing the trading rules that were mentioned in chapter 12 (RC 5 Seminar).

After teaching the trading rules, we give out the mechanical system to show that the strategies that are taught can be verified and back tested. We only trade with strategies that can be verified. To practice the rules is a vital step in becoming a better trader. This applies to RC 5 strategies and system, as well as to your own trading strategies or system.

In order to make progress, you must master what you know, then think and practice to trade better then your present strategies or systems.

A) Exercises for readers, using 10 minutes bar instead of 5 minutes.
Practice Date:

1) 2002 / 06 / 06
    1020606 840 ES= -2.75 NQ= -11.50
    1020606 850 ES= -4.50 NQ= -16.00
    1020606 900 ES= -7.00 NQ= -18.50
    1020606 910 ES= -8.50 NQ=-25.00 (Normal Negative
                                         Double Day , rule # 9)
    1020606 920 ES= -11.00 NQ= -26.50
    1020606 930 ES= -9.00 NQ= -22.50
    1020606 940 ES= -11.00 NQ= -27.00
    1020606 950 ES= -9.00 NQ= -23.50
    1020606 1000 ES= -10.50 NQ= -23.00
    1020606 1010 ES= -15.50 NQ= -31.50
    1020606 1020 ES= -15.00 NQ= -32.00
    1020606 1030 ES= -16.25 NQ=-35.00 • ← SHORT

```
1020606 1040  ES=-16.75   NQ= -33.50
1020606 1050  ES=-15.75   NQ= -30.50
1020606 1100  ES=-14.75   NQ= -28.50
1020606 1110  ES=-15.00   NQ= -31.00
1020606 1120  ES=-14.75   NQ= -28.50
1020606 1130  ES=-16.50   NQ= -31.50
1020606 1140  ES=-17.75   NQ= -32.50
1020606 1150  ES=-18.50   NQ= -31.00
1020606 1200  ES=-16.50   NQ= -26.00
1020606 1210  ES=-16.50   NQ= -26.00
1020606 1220  ES=-14.00   NQ= -24.50
1020606 1230  ES=-13.50   NQ= -23.50
1020606 1240  ES=-14.75   NQ= -27.00
1020606 1250  ES=-14.75   NQ= -26.50
1020606 1300  ES=-15.50   NQ= -28.50
1020606 1310  ES=-17.00   NQ= -29.50
1020606 1320  ES=-15.50   NQ= -27.00
1020606 1330  ES=-17.00   NQ= -30.00
1020606 1340  ES=-17.50   NQ= -31.50
1020606 1350  ES=-21.25   NQ= -38.50
1020606 1400  ES=-21.50   NQ= -35.50
1020606 1410  ES=-21.75   NQ= -34.00
1020606 1420  ES=-21.75   NQ= -32.50
1020606 1430  ES=-19.00   NQ= -27.50
1020606 1440  ES=-21.50   NQ= -32.50
1020606 1450  ES=-20.00   NQ= -27.50
```

1020606 1500 ES=-21.00 NQ= -35.00 • ← **STOP**

```
1020606 1510  ES=-22.75   NQ= -34.00
1020606 1515  ES=-21.00   NQ= -30.00
```

Answer: "Short 5a" (Short at 1030, Stop at 1500)

2)2004 / 08 / 18
```
1040818  840  ES=  -2.50  NQ= -6.00
1040818  850  ES=  -1.50  NQ= -4.50
1040818  900  ES=  -1.75  NQ= -3.50
```

1040818	**910**	**ES=**	**0.50**	**NQ=**	**1.00 (Normal Positive**
					Single Day , rule # 7)
1040818	920	ES=	2.50	NQ=	7.00
1040818	930	ES=	2.25	NQ=	7.00
1040818	940	ES=	1.75	NQ=	7.00
1040818	**950**	**ES=**	**5.25**	**NQ=**	**15.00** • ← **LONG**
1040818	1000	ES=	4.00	NQ=	13.00
1040818	1010	ES=	2.50	NQ=	10.00
1040818	1020	ES=	3.75	NQ=	12.00
1040818	1030	ES=	4.00	NQ=	10.50
1040818	1040	ES=	3.25	NQ=	9.00
1040818	1050	ES=	3.25	NQ=	9.00
1040818	1100	ES=	4.00	NQ=	11.50
1040818	1110	ES=	3.50	NQ=	10.50
1040818	1120	ES=	3.50	NQ=	11.50
1040818	1130	ES=	4.25	NQ=	12.50
1040818	1140	ES=	4.25	NQ=	13.50
1040818	1150	ES=	4.00	NQ=	12.00
1040818	1200	ES=	3.50	NQ=	11.00
1040818	1210	ES=	3.25	NQ=	9.50
1040818	1220	ES=	3.50	NQ=	9.00
1040818	1230	ES=	3.00	NQ=	9.00
1040818	1240	ES=	4.25	NQ=	12.50
1040818	1250	ES=	5.00	NQ=	13.00
1040818	1300	ES=	4.75	NQ=	13.50
1040818	1310	ES=	7.75	NQ=	16.50
1040818	1320	ES=	8.75	NQ=	19.00
1040818	1330	ES=	8.50	NQ=	19.00
1040818	1340	ES=	7.75	NQ=	18.00
1040818	1350	ES=	9.50	NQ=	20.50
1040818	1400	ES=	9.25	NQ=	20.00
1040818	1410	ES=	9.00	NQ=	19.50
1040818	1420	ES=	9.00	NQ=	19.50
1040818	1430	ES=	9.75	NQ=	21.00
1040818	1440	ES=	9.75	NQ=	21.00

1040818 1450   ES=   11.50   NQ= 25.50
1040818   1500   ES= 11.75   NQ= 25.50 • ← STOP
1040818 1510   ES=   11.75   NQ= 23.50
1040818 1515   ES=   11.25   NQ= 23.00
Answer: "Long 4a" (Long at 0950, Stop at 1500)

3)2003 / 07 / 24
   1030724   840   ES=   6.25   NQ=   11.50
   1030724   850   ES=   2.75   NQ=   7.00
   1030724   900   ES=   4.00   NQ=   11.50
   1030724   910   ES=   8.00   NQ=   15.50 (Normal Positive
   Double Day ,rule # 10)
   1030724   920   ES=   9.75   NQ=   15.50
   1030724   930   ES=   8.25   NQ=   11.00
   1030724   940   ES=   7.25   NQ=   10.00
   1030724   950   ES=   4.75   NQ=   7.50
   1030724 1000   ES=   5.75   NQ=   8.50
   1030724 1010   ES=   6.50   NQ=   9.50
   1030724 1020   ES=   8.50   NQ=   13.50
   1030724 1030   ES=   8.50   NQ=   13.00
   1030724 1040   ES=   8.00   NQ=   12.50
   1030724 1050   ES=   6.50   NQ=   10.00
   1030724 1100   ES=   6.75   NQ=   10.50
   1030724 1110   ES=   6.25   NQ=   9.50
   1030724 1120   ES=   6.00   NQ=   8.00
   1030724 1130   ES=   6.25   NQ=   7.50
   1030724 1140   ES=   6.25   NQ=   9.00
   1030724 1150   ES=   5.00   NQ=   7.00
   1030724 1200   ES=   5.75   NQ=   8.00
   1030724 1210   ES=   6.50   NQ=   9.50
   1030724 1220   ES=   6.75   NQ=   10.50
   1030724 1230   ES=   6.50   NQ=   9.00
   1030724 1240   ES=   6.00   NQ=   8.50
   1030724 1250   ES=   6.50   NQ=   9.00
   1030724 1300   ES=   7.00   NQ=   10.00

```
1030724 1310  ES=   6.75  NQ=   9.50
```
1030724 1320 ES=   5.50 NQ=   5.50 ← **SHORT**
```
1030724 1330  ES=   1.75  NQ=   1.00
1030724 1340  ES=  -0.50  NQ=  -3.00
1030724 1350  ES=  -2.75  NQ=  -8.50
1030724 1400  ES=  -3.00  NQ=  -8.50
1030724 1410  ES=  -4.00  NQ=  -9.50
1030724 1420  ES=  -2.75  NQ=  -7.00
1030724 1430  ES=  -2.25  NQ=  -7.00
1030724 1440  ES=  -3.00  NQ=  -9.00
1030724 1450  ES=  -5.50  NQ= -15.50
```
1030724 1500 ES= -7.50 NQ= -19.00 • ← **STOP**
```
1030724 1510  ES=  -7.00  NQ= -18.00
1030724 1515  ES=  -7.25  NQ= -17.50
```
Answer: "Short 6a" (Short at 1320, Stop at 1500)

4)2003 / 02 / 12
```
1030212  840  ES=   0.50  NQ=   1.50
1030212  850  ES=  -3.00  NQ=  -2.00
1030212  900  ES=  -0.50  NQ=   3.00
```
1030212   910 ES= -1.75   NQ=   2.00 • ← **SHORT**
                                        (Opposite Day 1)
```
1030212  920  ES=  -2.25  NQ=   1.00
1030212  930  ES=  -4.75  NQ=  -2.50
1030212  940  ES=  -4.50  NQ=  -3.00
1030212  950  ES=  -4.00  NQ=  -2.00
1030212 1000  ES=  -5.25  NQ=  -3.00
1030212 1010  ES=  -5.75  NQ=  -3.50
1030212 1020  ES=  -7.00  NQ=  -5.00
1030212 1030  ES=  -6.50  NQ=  -4.50
1030212 1040  ES=  -5.50  NQ=  -3.00
1030212 1050  ES=  -5.25  NQ=  -1.50
1030212 1100  ES=  -3.50  NQ=  -1.00
1030212 1110  ES=  -5.00  NQ=  -3.50
1030212 1120  ES=  -5.00  NQ=  -3.00
```

```
1030212 1130  ES=   -5.25  NQ=   -3.00
1030212 1140  ES=   -5.00  NQ=   -2.00
1030212 1150  ES=   -6.50  NQ=   -5.00
1030212 1200  ES=   -5.25  NQ=   -3.50
1030212 1210  ES=   -7.00  NQ=   -6.50
1030212 1220  ES=   -8.00  NQ=   -8.50
1030212 1230  ES=   -8.75  NQ= -10.00
1030212 1240  ES=   -7.75  NQ=   -8.50
1030212 1250  ES=   -7.50  NQ=   -8.00
1030212 1300  ES=   -6.75  NQ=   -7.00
1030212 1310  ES=   -7.00  NQ=   -7.00
1030212 1320  ES=   -6.50  NQ=   -8.50
1030212 1330  ES=   -7.50  NQ=   -8.00
1030212 1340  ES=   -7.75  NQ=   -8.50
1030212 1350  ES=   -8.75  NQ=   -9.50
1030212 1400  ES=   -9.50  NQ= -11.00
1030212 1410  ES= -10.50  NQ= -12.00
1030212 1420  ES= -10.50  NQ= -11.00
1030212 1430  ES=   -9.75  NQ= -11.00
1030212 1440  ES= -11.00  NQ= -12.00
1030212 1450  ES= -10.25  NQ= -11.00
```

1030212 1500 ES=-12.50 NQ= -15.00 • ← STOP

```
1030212 1510  ES= -12.75  NQ= -15.50
1030212 1515  ES= -13.00  NQ= -15.00
```

Answer: "Short 1a" (Short at 0910, Stop at 1500)

5)2003 / 10 / 28

```
1031028  840  ES=   3.50  NQ=   9.50
1031028  850  ES=   3.25  NQ=   9.00
1031028  900  ES=   5.50  NQ= 13.00
```

1031028   910 ES=   5.25 NQ= 13.00 (Normal Positive
                                    Double Day rule # 10)

```
1031028  920  ES=   6.50  NQ= 16.50
1031028  930  ES=   6.00  NQ= 15.50
1031028  940  ES=   4.75  NQ= 14.50
```

```
1031028   950  ES=    4.50  NQ=  13.00
1031028  1000  ES=    5.00  NQ=  14.50
1031028  1010  ES=    3.75  NQ=  12.00
1031028  1020  ES=    5.00  NQ=  15.50
1031028  1030  ES=    4.75  NQ=  15.50
1031028  1040  ES=    5.00  NQ=  15.50
1031028  1050  ES=    4.50  NQ=  15.50
1031028  1100  ES=    4.50  NQ=  16.00
1031028  1110  ES=    5.25  NQ=  19.00
1031028  1120  ES=    4.00  NQ=  17.50
1031028  1130  ES=    4.25  NQ=  17.00
1031028  1140  ES=    3.75  NQ=  17.50
1031028  1150  ES=    4.75  NQ=  19.00
1031028  1200  ES=    4.75  NQ=  18.50
1031028  1210  ES=    4.75  NQ=  19.50
1031028  1220  ES=    4.25  NQ=  19.00
1031028  1230  ES=    4.50  NQ=  19.50
1031028  1240  ES=    4.25  NQ=  19.00
1031028  1250  ES=    5.50  NQ=  22.50
1031028  1300  ES=    5.50  NQ=  22.00
1031028  1310  ES=    5.25  NQ=  20.00
1031028  1320  ES=    4.75  NQ=  20.00
1031028  1330  ES=    6.00  NQ=  22.50
1031028  1340  ES=    5.00  NQ=  20.50
```

1031028 1350 ES=   9.00 NQ= 27.50 • ← **LONG**
```
1031028  1400  ES=    9.25  NQ=  29.50
1031028  1410  ES=    9.25  NQ=  28.50
1031028  1420  ES=    9.75  NQ=  30.50
1031028  1430  ES=   10.75  NQ=  31.50
1031028  1440  ES=   12.75  NQ=  37.50
1031028  1450  ES=   13.25  NQ=  40.00
```
1031028 1500 ES=   14.75 NQ= 44.50 • ← **STOP**
```
1031028  1510  ES=   15.25  NQ=  46.50
1031028  1515  ES=   14.00  NQ=  46.50
```
Answer: "Long 6a" (Long at 1350, Stop at 1500)

B) Further practice for readers (using RC 5 strategies, all data start at 09:10 US central time). The readers have to find the historical data to practice.

1)	2005 / 01 / 13	ES = -1 and NQ = 1
2)	2004 / 10 / 22	ES = -2.75 and NQ = -9
3)	2003 / 11 / 12	ES = +2.5 and NQ = +9.5
4)	2005 / 04 / 01	ES = +4.75 and NQ = +3
5)	2004 / 01 / 26	ES = +1.25 and NQ = -4.5
6)	2004 / 04 / 20	ES = +3.75 and NQ = +8.5
7)	2005 / 10 / 27	ES = -4.25 and NQ = -10.5
8)	2003 / 07 / 01	ES = -11.5 and NQ = +21.5
9)	2004 / 12 / 01	ES = +5.75 and NQ = +10
10)	2005 / 01 / 04	ES = +1.5 and NQ = +5.5
11)	2006 / 02 / 28	ES = -5.25 and NQ = -2.5
12)	2003 / 04 / 07	ES = +24 and NQ = +43
13)	2005 / 06 / 23	ES = -4.25 and NQ = 0
14)	2002 / 10 / 01	ES = +3.75 and NQ = -1
15)	2006 / 02 / 09	ES = +6 and NQ = +12
16)	2006 / 04 / 07	ES = -0.5 and NQ = +1.25
17)	2006 / 01 / 20	ES = -2.75 and NQ = -7.5
18)	2006 / 03 / 29	ES = +0.75 and NQ = +3.5
19)	2006 / 05 / 01	ES = +3.25 and NQ = +3
20)	2006 / 05 / 11	ES = -6 and NQ = -12.25

Answer:
1) Short 1a
2) Short 3a
3) Long 4a
4) Short 4b
5) Long 2a
6) Short 4a
7) Short 5a
8) Long 7b
9) Long 6a
10) Short 4a

11) Short 3b
12) Short 7a
13) Short 1b
14) Long 2b
15) Short 6a
16) Short 1a
17) Short 3a
18) Long 4a
19) Short 4b
20) Short 5a

C) Advance thinking for RC 5 strategies

If you have studied RC 5 thoroughly and have practiced with the historical data of ES and NQ or used TradeStation print log to study, you will recognize that at 09:10, there are some situations that are not covered. They happened frequently in the past and I am sure they will happen in the future too.

It is when ES is single digit positive or negative (compared to yesterday's close) and NQ is double digit and positive.

Example: 09:10   ES +5   NQ + 16
              Or
              09:10   ES -3   NQ + 20
              Or
              09:10   ES -0.5   NQ +13

Trading Dates with this 09:10 market condition for reader to check and Practice.

(You may use RC 5 indicator insert in TS, and get the data from print log).

1)   2005 / 12 / 21
2)   2005 / 12 / 01
3)   2005 / 09 / 06
4)   2005 / 08 / 22
5)   2005 / 06 / 01
6)   2005 / 04 / 21

7) 2005 / 03 / 23
8) 2005 / 02 / 04
9) 2004 / 12 / 03
10) 2004 / 10 / 19
11) 2004 / 10 / 04
12) 2004 / 08 / 17
13) 2004 / 08 / 16
14) 2004 / 07 / 29
15) 2004 / 07 / 27

If you can find new trading strategies for this market condition, please back test. If the result is good, then try to observe your method in actual trading. Strategies must have logic (Like the explanation that I gave under each RC 5 trading rules. If you cannot find out good strategies for a market condition, what will you do when it happens? Just don't trade. Trade only with a statistical edge combined with a sound logic).

After RC 5, forget about all the strategies that I told you! Develop better strategies than RC 5 to trade the market. If you succeed, you are on your way to mastery over trading.

15

How to Trade Better than RC 5?

Mastering the logic and strategies of RC 5 is only the first step of successful trading. You need to aim to trade better than RC 5.

The key is the NQ indicator. Watch the movement of the NQ after your entry.

A) After you have a Long entry using RC 5, monitor the NQ. If NQ continues to move up after your Long, then the trade is good. If NQ moves down, then you have to watch carefully. If NQ moves down even further, then get out immediately and do not wait for the 10 point protective stop to get hit. Thus, you can cut loss quicker than RC 5.

B) And if you have a Short entry using RC 5, you monitor the NQ. If NQ continues to move down after your Short, then the trade is good. If you see the NQ move up further, then get out immediately without waiting for the 10 point stop to get hit. Here again, you cut loss quicker than RC 5.

C) After you have a Long or a Short entry using RC 5, monitor the NQ, if NQ continues the trend as your entry − that is, if it moves up after a Long and moves down after a Short − then your trade is good. Practice and learn to add more contracts that is, average up while you are winning. Thus, you are adding more profit to your trade.

Remember the order. First learn to cut loss quickly and then learn to ride with profit by averaging up while you are winning. Above all, practice relentlessly. Soon you will find yourself trading better than RC 5.

Below is an example for easier assimilation on cutting losses quicker than RC 5 and riding with more profit using RC 5 entry.

Examples: Cut Loss Quick

Example (1) Short 1a – 2006/3/15 (-$275.00)

```
1030701 1210  ES=  -4.75  NQ= -12.00
1060315  835  ES=   0.00  NQ=   4.00
1060315  840  ES=  -0.25  NQ=   4.00
1060315  845  ES=  -1.50  NQ=   1.50
1060315  850  ES=  -1.75  NQ=   0.50
1060315  855  ES=  -1.50  NQ=   1.00
1060315  900  ES=  -0.50  NQ=   3.50
1060315  905  ES=  -0.25  NQ=   3.50
```
1060315　910　ES=　-0.25　NQ=　3.00 ← **RC 5 Short 1a**
```
1060315  915  ES=  -1.00  NQ=   0.50
1060315  920  ES=  -1.00  NQ=   1.50
1060315  925  ES=  -2.25  NQ=  -3.00
1060315  930  ES=  -1.50  NQ=   1.00
1060315  935  ES=  -1.00  NQ=   1.50
1060315  940  ES=  -0.75  NQ=   1.50
1060315  945  ES=  -0.75  NQ=   4.00
1060315  950  ES=  -1.75  NQ=   0.00
1060315  955  ES=  -2.75  NQ=  -3.00
1060315 1000  ES=  -2.50  NQ=  -3.00
1060315 1005  ES=  -2.00  NQ=  -2.50
1060315 1010  ES=  -2.00  NQ=  -2.00
1060315 1015  ES=  -1.75  NQ=  -2.00
1060315 1020  ES=  -2.00  NQ=  -2.50
1060315 1025  ES=  -1.75  NQ=  -3.50
1060315 1030  ES=  -1.75  NQ=  -3.50
1060315 1035  ES=  -1.75  NQ=  -3.50
1060315 1040  ES=  -2.00  NQ=  -3.50
1060315 1045  ES=  -3.00  NQ=  -4.00
1060315 1050  ES=  -3.25  NQ=  -4.50
```
1060315　1055　ES=　-3.25　NQ=　-4.50
```
1060315 1100  ES=  -3.00  NQ=  -4.50
1060315 1105  ES=  -3.00  NQ=  -4.50
```

```
1060315 1110  ES=  -2.25  NQ=  -3.50
1060315 1115  ES=  -1.25  NQ=  -1.00
1060315 1120  ES=  -1.25  NQ=   0.50
1060315 1125  ES=  -1.75  NQ=  -1.00
1060315 1130  ES=  -2.00  NQ=  -3.00
1060315 1135  ES=  -1.75  NQ=  -3.00
1060315 1140  ES=  -1.75  NQ=  -3.00
1060315 1145  ES=  -1.25  NQ=  -2.50
1060315 1150  ES=  -1.50  NQ=  -2.50
1060315 1155  ES=  -1.25  NQ=  -1.50
1060315 1200  ES=  -1.25  NQ=  -1.00
1060315 1205  ES=  -1.25  NQ=  -1.50
1060315 1210  ES=  -1.00  NQ=  -1.00
1060315 1215  ES=  -1.50  NQ=  -2.50
1060315 1220  ES=  -1.25  NQ=  -1.00
1060315 1225  ES=  -1.50  NQ=  -2.00
1060315 1230  ES=  -1.25  NQ=  -1.50
1060315 1235  ES=  -1.50  NQ=  -2.00
1060315 1240  ES=  -1.25  NQ=  -2.00
1060315 1245  ES=  -1.25  NQ=  -1.50
1060315 1250  ES=  -0.50  NQ=   0.00
```

1060315 1255 ES=   0.25 NQ=   1.00

```
1060315 1300  ES=   0.00  NQ=   0.00
1060315 1305  ES=   0.00  NQ=   0.00
```

1060315 1310 ES=   1.75 NQ=   3.50

```
1060315 1315  ES=   2.75  NQ=   4.50
1060315 1320  ES=   4.00  NQ=   6.50
1060315 1325  ES=   4.50  NQ=   5.50
1060315 1330  ES=   4.50  NQ=   5.00
1060315 1335  ES=   4.25  NQ=   4.50
1060315 1340  ES=   4.50  NQ=   5.00
1060315 1345  ES=   4.50  NQ=   4.00
1060315 1350  ES=   3.50  NQ=   2.50
1060315 1355  ES=   3.25  NQ=   2.00
1060315 1400  ES=   3.50  NQ=   2.50
```

1060315	1405	ES=	3.75	NQ=	2.00
1060315	1410	ES=	3.50	NQ=	2.00
1060315	1415	ES=	4.25	NQ=	4.00
1060315	1420	ES=	4.75	NQ=	4.50
1060315	1425	ES=	6.00	NQ=	7.00
1060315	1430	ES=	5.50	NQ=	7.00
1060315	1435	ES=	5.50	NQ=	7.50
1060315	1440	ES=	6.50	NQ=	9.50
1060315	1445	ES=	5.00	NQ=	8.00
1060315	1450	ES=	4.75	NQ=	7.50
1060315	1455	ES=	5.00	NQ=	8.00
1060315	**1500**	**ES=**	**5.25**	**NQ=**	**10.00** ← **RC 5 Close**
1060315	1505	ES=	5.50	NQ=	10.00
1060315	1510	ES=	5.25	NQ=	10.00
1060315	1515	ES=	5.25	NQ=	10.00

Explanation:

At 09:10, RC 5 enters Short 1a. You start watching NQ closely:

09:10	ES -0.25	NQ +3
10:55	ES -3.25	NQ -4.5 (Trade looks fine)
12:55	ES +0.25	NQ +1.0

(Trade is not good, NQ from –ve to +ve, need to watch out)

13:10   ES +1.75   NQ +3.5 (Stop & CUT LOSS
                                                QUICKLY)

LOSS = -$100

We are able to cut loss quick and lose only $100 instead of $275.

Example (2) Short 1a – 2005/6/2 (-$250.00)

1050602	835	ES=	-2.75	NQ=	-1.50
1050602	840	ES=	-0.75	NQ=	3.50
1050602	845	ES=	-1.00	NQ=	4.50
1050602	850	ES=	-1.25	NQ=	3.50
1050602	855	ES=	-0.25	NQ=	5.50
1050602	900	ES=	-0.50	NQ=	4.00
1050602	905	ES=	0.00	NQ=	5.00

1050602	**910**	**ES=**	**-1.50**	**NQ=**	**2.50**	← **RC 5 Short 1a**
1050602	915	ES=	-0.75	NQ=	2.50	
1050602	920	ES=	-1.75	NQ=	1.00	
1050602	925	ES=	-1.50	NQ=	1.00	
1050602	930	ES=	-1.00	NQ=	2.50	
1050602	935	ES=	-1.75	NQ=	3.00	
1050602	940	ES=	-1.25	NQ=	3.00	
1050602	945	ES=	0.75	NQ=	7.00	
1050602	950	ES=	0.50	NQ=	5.00	
1050602	955	ES=	0.75	NQ=	4.50	
1050602	1000	ES=	0.25	NQ=	4.00	
1050602	1005	ES=	-0.25	NQ=	2.00	
1050602	**1010**	**ES=**	**0.00**	**NQ=**	**3.00**	
1050602	1015	ES=	0.25	NQ=	3.50	
1050602	1020	ES=	0.25	NQ=	4.50	
1050602	1025	ES=	-0.25	NQ=	4.50	
1050602	1030	ES=	0.50	NQ=	5.00	
1050602	1035	ES=	0.25	NQ=	5.00	
1050602	1040	ES=	1.00	NQ=	6.00	
1050602	1045	ES=	0.50	NQ=	5.00	
1050602	1050	ES=	0.50	NQ=	5.00	
1050602	1055	ES=	0.25	NQ=	5.00	
1050602	1100	ES=	0.50	NQ=	5.00	
1050602	1105	ES=	1.50	NQ=	6.00	
1050602	**1110**	**ES=**	**1.00**	**NQ=**	**6.00**	
1050602	1115	ES=	1.00	NQ=	6.50	
1050602	1120	ES=	1.00	NQ=	5.50	
1050602	1125	ES=	1.25	NQ=	6.50	
1050602	1130	ES=	1.50	NQ=	7.00	
1050602	1135	ES=	1.75	NQ=	8.00	
1050602	1140	ES=	1.50	NQ=	7.00	
1050602	1145	ES=	1.75	NQ=	7.50	
1050602	1150	ES=	1.25	NQ=	6.50	
1050602	1155	ES=	1.50	NQ=	8.00	
1050602	1200	ES=	1.25	NQ=	6.50	

```
1050602 1205  ES=   1.75  NQ=   7.00
1050602 1210  ES=   1.00  NQ=   5.50
1050602 1215  ES=   1.25  NQ=   6.50
1050602 1220  ES=   1.25  NQ=   6.50
1050602 1225  ES=   1.00  NQ=   6.00
1050602 1230  ES=   0.75  NQ=   5.50
1050602 1235  ES=   0.50  NQ=   5.50
1050602 1240  ES=   1.00  NQ=   6.00
1050602 1245  ES=  -0.25  NQ=   4.00
1050602 1250  ES=   0.25  NQ=   5.00
1050602 1255  ES=   1.00  NQ=   5.00
1050602 1300  ES=   0.75  NQ=   6.00
1050602 1305  ES=   1.50  NQ=   8.00
1050602 1310  ES=   1.25  NQ=   7.00
1050602 1315  ES=   1.00  NQ=   7.00
1050602 1320  ES=   1.50  NQ=   7.00
1050602 1325  ES=   2.00  NQ=   8.00
1050602 1330  ES=   2.75  NQ=   9.00
1050602 1335  ES=   2.75  NQ=   9.00
1050602 1340  ES=   2.50  NQ=   7.00
1050602 1345  ES=   2.50  NQ=   8.50
1050602 1350  ES=   2.25  NQ=   8.00
1050602 1355  ES=   3.75  NQ=  10.00
1050602 1400  ES=   3.00  NQ=  10.00
1050602 1405  ES=   3.00  NQ=   9.50
1050602 1410  ES=   2.25  NQ=   9.00
1050602 1415  ES=   2.50  NQ=  10.00
1050602 1420  ES=   2.75  NQ=   9.50
1050602 1425  ES=   2.50  NQ=   9.00
1050602 1430  ES=   3.00  NQ=  10.50
1050602 1435  ES=   2.50  NQ=   9.00
1050602 1440  ES=   3.75  NQ=  11.00
1050602 1445  ES=   4.25  NQ=  13.00
1050602 1450  ES=   3.50  NQ=  12.00
1050602 1455  ES=   3.25  NQ=  12.00
```

1050602 1500 ES= 3.50 NQ= 12.50 ← **RC 5 Close**
1050602 1505 ES= 3.25 NQ= 13.50
1050602 1510 ES= 3.50 NQ= 14.00
1050602 1515 ES= 3.75 NQ= 14.50

Explanation:

    09:10   ES -1.5   NQ +2.5

    10:10   ES 0   NQ +3

                (after an hour Short, NQ is up and not down, watch out)

    11:10   ES +1   NQ +6

(In an hour, ES is up and NQ is up further, we have shorted, so we close position and take a small loss)

    LOSS = -$125

We are able to cut loss quickly and lose only $125 instead of $250.

Example (3) Short 1a – 2004/4/22 (-$500.00)

    1040422 835 ES= -0.75 NQ= 4.50
    1040422 840 ES= -1.75 NQ= 2.50
    1040422 845 ES= -0.25 NQ= 6.50
    1040422 850 ES= 1.25 NQ= 10.00
    1040422 855 ES= 0.25 NQ= 7.50
    1040422 900 ES= 1.00 NQ= 9.00
    1040422 905 ES= 0.00 NQ= 8.50
    1040422 910 ES= -1.00 NQ= 5.00 ← **RC 5 Short 1a**
    1040422 915 ES= -1.75 NQ= 4.50
    1040422 920 ES= -0.25 NQ= 8.50
    1040422 925 ES= -1.50 NQ= 6.00
    1040422 930 ES= -1.75 NQ= 5.00
    1040422 935 ES= -1.25 NQ= 6.00
    1040422 940 ES= 0.75 NQ= 12.00
    1040422 945 ES= 2.00 NQ= 12.00
    1040422 950 ES= 1.50 NQ= 13.50
    1040422 955 ES= 2.50 NQ= 17.00
    1040422 1000 ES= 2.25 NQ= 17.00

```
1040422 1005  ES=    4.25  NQ=  19.50
```
1040422 1010 ES=   5.75 NQ= 21.00
```
1040422 1015  ES=    6.75  NQ=  22.50
```
1040422 1020 ES=   9.50 NQ= 30.00 ← **RC 5 Close**
```
1040422 1025  ES=   12.25  NQ=  32.50
1040422 1030  ES=   11.25  NQ=  29.50
1040422 1035  ES=   10.75  NQ=  29.00
1040422 1040  ES=   11.25  NQ=  29.00
1040422 1045  ES=   11.50  NQ=  30.00
1040422 1050  ES=   13.75  NQ=  36.00
1040422 1055  ES=   12.25  NQ=  31.50
1040422 1100  ES=   12.75  NQ=  31.50
1040422 1105  ES=   12.00  NQ=  30.50
1040422 1110  ES=   13.25  NQ=  32.50
1040422 1115  ES=   13.00  NQ=  32.50
1040422 1120  ES=   13.00  NQ=  32.50
1040422 1125  ES=   13.00  NQ=  31.50
1040422 1130  ES=   14.00  NQ=  33.00
1040422 1135  ES=   14.25  NQ=  34.00
1040422 1140  ES=   14.00  NQ=  33.50
1040422 1145  ES=   13.25  NQ=  33.50
1040422 1150  ES=   13.25  NQ=  33.00
1040422 1155  ES=   13.50  NQ=  34.00
1040422 1200  ES=   12.75  NQ=  32.50
1040422 1205  ES=   12.75  NQ=  33.00
1040422 1210  ES=   13.75  NQ=  35.00
1040422 1215  ES=   13.75  NQ=  35.00
1040422 1220  ES=   14.25  NQ=  38.00
1040422 1225  ES=   13.50  NQ=  35.00
1040422 1230  ES=   14.50  NQ=  37.50
1040422 1235  ES=   17.50  NQ=  39.50
1040422 1240  ES=   18.50  NQ=  40.00
1040422 1245  ES=   18.25  NQ=  39.50
1040422 1250  ES=   18.00  NQ=  39.50
1040422 1255  ES=   18.25  NQ=  40.50
```

```
1040422  1300  ES=  18.00   NQ=  39.50
1040422  1305  ES=  18.00   NQ=  39.00
1040422  1310  ES=  17.50   NQ=  39.00
1040422  1315  ES=  17.25   NQ=  38.00
1040422  1320  ES=  17.50   NQ=  39.50
1040422  1325  ES=  17.25   NQ=  39.00
1040422  1330  ES=  18.50   NQ=  41.00
1040422  1335  ES=  18.25   NQ=  40.00
1040422  1340  ES=  16.75   NQ=  39.00
1040422  1345  ES=  17.50   NQ=  39.50
1040422  1350  ES=  17.25   NQ=  39.50
1040422  1355  ES=  18.25   NQ=  40.00
1040422  1400  ES=  18.75   NQ=  41.50
1040422  1405  ES=  16.50   NQ=  38.00
1040422  1410  ES=  17.25   NQ=  39.00
1040422  1415  ES=  18.75   NQ=  40.00
1040422  1420  ES=  17.25   NQ=  38.50
1040422  1425  ES=  16.75   NQ=  36.50
1040422  1430  ES=  16.75   NQ=  36.50
1040422  1435  ES=  15.75   NQ=  35.00
1040422  1440  ES=  16.00   NQ=  36.00
1040422  1445  ES=  16.00   NQ=  36.50
1040422  1450  ES=  17.25   NQ=  39.00
1040422  1455  ES=  18.00   NQ=  40.00
1040422  1500  ES=  17.25   NQ=  38.50
1040422  1505  ES=  16.00   NQ=  39.00
1040422  1510  ES=  15.50   NQ=  38.00
1040422  1515  ES=  14.25   NQ=  37.00
```

Explanation:

| 09:10 | ES -1 | NQ +5 |
| 09:40 | ES 0.75 | NQ +12 |

(Half an hour after we Short, NQ is up a lot, and ES is also up, WATCH OUT).

| 10:10 | ES +5.75 | NQ +21 |

(Another half hour, ES is up and NQ is up a lot from +5 (at 09:10) to +21, STOP IMMEDIATELY).
   LOSS = -\$337.5
We are able to cut loss quickly and manage to lose only \$337.5 instead of \$500.
* An advance trader would have reversed the position to Long at 10:10 as NQ was up. Profit = \$575 at 15:00 close.*

Example (4) Long 6a – 2004/11/17 (-\$500.00)

1040422	1135	ES=	14.25	NQ=	34.00
1041117	835	ES=	6.25	NQ=	12.00
1041117	840	ES=	6.50	NQ=	11.00
1041117	845	ES=	5.25	NQ=	9.00
1041117	850	ES=	5.50	NQ=	10.00
1041117	855	ES=	5.75	NQ=	11.00
1041117	900	ES=	5.75	NQ=	10.50
1041117	905	ES=	7.00	NQ=	13.00
1041117	910	ES=	7.50	NQ=	14.50
1041117	915	ES=	8.25	NQ=	17.00
1041117	920	ES=	11.25	NQ=	23.00
1041117	925	ES=	10.50	NQ=	21.00
1041117	930	ES=	11.25	NQ=	23.00
1041117	935	ES=	9.50	NQ=	19.00
1041117	940	ES=	9.25	NQ=	19.50
1041117	945	ES=	9.75	NQ=	21.00
1041117	950	ES=	10.25	NQ=	22.50
1041117	955	ES=	9.75	NQ=	22.00
1041117	1000	ES=	9.50	NQ=	22.00
1041117	1005	ES=	9.25	NQ=	22.00
1041117	1010	ES=	10.25	NQ=	22.00
1041117	1015	ES=	9.75	NQ=	21.00
1041117	1020	ES=	10.75	NQ=	22.50
1041117	1025	ES=	10.75	NQ=	23.50
1041117	1030	ES=	11.50	NQ=	26.00
1041117	1035	ES=	11.50	NQ=	25.50

```
1041117 1040  ES=  11.25  NQ=  25.00
1041117 1045  ES=  11.25  NQ=  25.00
1041117 1050  ES=  11.25  NQ=  25.00
1041117 1055  ES=  11.25  NQ=  25.50
1041117 1100  ES=  11.25  NQ=  26.00
1041117 1105  ES=  11.00  NQ=  26.00
1041117 1110  ES=  10.75  NQ=  26.00
```

1041117 1115 ES= 11.50 NQ= 27.50 ← **RC 5 Long 6a**

```
1041117 1120  ES=  10.75  NQ=  26.00
1041117 1125  ES=  10.50  NQ=  25.50
1041117 1130  ES=  10.75  NQ=  26.00
1041117 1135  ES=  11.00  NQ=  26.00
1041117 1140  ES=  10.50  NQ=  25.00
1041117 1145  ES=  10.75  NQ=  24.00
1041117 1150  ES=  10.75  NQ=  24.50
1041117 1155  ES=  10.75  NQ=  25.00
1041117 1200  ES=  11.25  NQ=  26.00
1041117 1205  ES=  11.00  NQ=  25.50
1041117 1210  ES=  11.50  NQ=  25.50
```

1041117 1215 ES= 11.25 NQ= 26.50

```
1041117 1220  ES=  11.00  NQ=  26.50
1041117 1225  ES=  11.00  NQ=  26.00
1041117 1230  ES=  10.75  NQ=  26.00
1041117 1235  ES=  10.50  NQ=  25.00
1041117 1240  ES=   9.50  NQ=  23.00
```

1041117 1245 ES=   9.75 NQ= 22.50

```
1041117 1250  ES=   9.75  NQ=  22.50
1041117 1255  ES=   9.75  NQ=  22.00
1041117 1300  ES=   9.50  NQ=  22.00
1041117 1305  ES=   7.50  NQ=  18.50
1041117 1310  ES=   6.00  NQ=  13.50
```

1041117 1315 ES=   6.25 NQ= 16.00

```
1041117 1320  ES=   6.25  NQ=  16.00
1041117 1325  ES=   5.50  NQ=  14.00
1041117 1330  ES=   4.50  NQ=  14.50
```

```
1041117 1335  ES=   3.50  NQ=   11.00
1041117 1340  ES=   3.75  NQ=   12.50
1041117 1345  ES=   4.25  NQ=   13.50
1041117 1350  ES=   3.75  NQ=   12.00
1041117 1355  ES=   5.50  NQ=   16.50
1041117 1400  ES=   6.00  NQ=   17.50
1041117 1405  ES=   5.75  NQ=   18.00
1041117 1410  ES=   4.75  NQ=   15.50
1041117 1415  ES=   4.50  NQ=   15.50
1041117 1420  ES=   4.75  NQ=   16.00
1041117 1425  ES=   3.00  NQ=   13.00
1041117 1430  ES=   2.50  NQ=   12.00
```
1041117 1435 ES=   2.50 NQ=   12.00 ← **RC 5 Close**
```
1041117 1440  ES=   2.50  NQ=   12.00
1041117 1445  ES=   3.25  NQ=   15.00
1041117 1450  ES=   4.00  NQ=   14.50
1041117 1455  ES=   4.75  NQ=   16.50
1041117 1500  ES=   4.75  NQ=   17.50
1041117 1505  ES=   5.75  NQ=   18.50
1041117 1510  ES=   6.75  NQ=   20.00
1041117 1515  ES=   6.75  NQ=   20.00
```

Explanation:

| 11:15 | ES +11.5 | NQ +27.5 |
| 12:15 | ES +11.25 | NQ +26.5 |

(Not much change)

| 12:45 | ES +9.75 | NQ +22 |

(NQ down and leading ES down, WATCH OUT)

| 13:15 | ES +6.25 | NQ +16 |

(NQ is down over 10 points from 11:15 Long entry, CUT LOSS QUICKLY)

LOSS = -$262.5

We are able to cut loss quickly and manage to lose $262.5 instead of $500.

Example (5) Long 2b – 2002/6/12 (-$500.00)

1020612	835	ES=	-0.75	NQ=	-8.50
1020612	840	ES=	-3.00	NQ=	-12.50
1020612	845	ES=	1.25	NQ=	-3.00
1020612	850	ES=	-0.75	NQ=	-9.50
1020612	855	ES=	1.00	NQ=	-3.50
1020612	900	ES=	4.50	NQ=	5.00
1020612	905	ES=	3.50	NQ=	2.00
1020612	910	ES=	2.50	NQ=	-1.50
1020612	915	ES=	0.50	NQ=	-6.00
1020612	920	ES=	0.00	NQ=	-4.00
1020612	925	ES=	3.25	NQ=	4.00
1020612	930	ES=	4.00	NQ=	5.50
1020612	935	ES=	3.00	NQ=	5.50
1020612	940	ES=	3.00	NQ=	6.50
1020612	945	ES=	2.75	NQ=	3.00
1020612	950	ES=	2.50	NQ=	-0.50
1020612	955	ES=	2.00	NQ=	-3.00
1020612	1000	ES=	-1.75	NQ=	-10.00
1020612	1005	ES=	-4.25	NQ=	-11.50
1020612	1010	ES=	-0.50	NQ=	-6.00
1020612	1015	ES=	0.50	NQ=	-4.00
1020612	1020	ES=	0.50	NQ=	-6.00
1020612	1025	ES=	-0.75	NQ=	-8.00
1020612	1030	ES=	-0.25	NQ=	-4.00
1020612	1035	ES=	-2.25	NQ=	-7.50
1020612	1040	ES=	-3.75	NQ=	-11.00
1020612	1045	ES=	-4.75	NQ=	-12.00
1020612	1050	ES=	-8.50	NQ=	-18.50
1020612	1055	ES=	-8.75	NQ=	-19.00
1020612	1100	ES=	-9.75	NQ=	-22.50
1020612	1105	ES=	-10.25	NQ=	-20.00
1020612	1110	ES=	-8.25	NQ=	-15.50
1020612	1115	ES=	-7.75	NQ=	-16.00

```
1020612 1120  ES=  -7.75   NQ= -16.00
1020612 1125  ES=  -8.25   NQ= -17.00
1020612 1130  ES=  -7.25   NQ= -14.00
1020612 1135  ES=  -6.25   NQ= -11.00
1020612 1140  ES=  -8.75   NQ= -13.50
1020612 1145  ES=  -9.50   NQ= -17.50
1020612 1150  ES=  -8.75   NQ= -14.00
1020612 1155  ES=  -6.00   NQ=  -6.50
1020612 1200  ES=  -4.75   NQ=  -3.00
1020612 1205  ES=  -3.50   NQ=   3.00
1020612 1210  ES=  -3.00   NQ=   2.50
1020612 1215  ES=   1.50   NQ=  11.50
1020612 1220  ES=   1.75   NQ=  10.50
```
1020612 1225 ES=   5.00 NQ= 15.50 ← RC 5 Long 2b
```
1020612 1230  ES=   2.75   NQ=  10.50
1020612 1235  ES=   2.00   NQ=   8.00
1020612 1240  ES=   0.00   NQ=   6.50
```
1020612 1245 ES=   0.00 NQ=   5.00
```
1020612 1250  ES=   0.25   NQ=   7.00
1020612 1255  ES=   3.00   NQ=  11.00
1020612 1300  ES=   2.00   NQ=   8.50
1020612 1305  ES=   1.25   NQ=   3.00
1020612 1310  ES=  -0.25   NQ=  -1.50
1020612 1315  ES=   0.50   NQ=   2.50
1020612 1320  ES=  -3.50   NQ=  -7.50
1020612 1325  ES=  -3.25   NQ=  -6.00
```
1020612 1330 ES= -4.00 NQ= -5.50 ← RC 5 Close
```
1020612 1335  ES=  -0.75   NQ=   1.00
1020612 1340  ES=  -4.25   NQ=  -5.00
1020612 1345  ES=  -3.25   NQ=  -2.00
1020612 1350  ES=  -2.75   NQ=   0.50
1020612 1355  ES=  -1.00   NQ=   3.00
1020612 1400  ES=  -1.50   NQ=   2.50
1020612 1405  ES=  -1.50   NQ=   0.50
1020612 1410  ES=   1.25   NQ=   7.00
```

```
1020612 1415 ES=   0.00 NQ=   2.50
1020612 1420 ES=   1.25 NQ=   5.00
1020612 1425 ES=  -0.25 NQ=   3.00
1020612 1430 ES=   1.75 NQ=   7.00
1020612 1435 ES=   7.25 NQ=  18.50
1020612 1440 ES=   6.75 NQ=  16.50
1020612 1445 ES=   7.00 NQ=  16.50
1020612 1450 ES=   6.25 NQ=  14.00
1020612 1455 ES=   6.00 NQ=  15.50
1020612 1500 ES=   6.00 NQ=  19.00
1020612 1505 ES=   5.75 NQ=  17.00
1020612 1510 ES=   5.75 NQ=  16.50
1020612 1515 ES=   6.50 NQ=  16.50
```

Explanation:
    12:25   ES +5   NQ +15.5
    12:45   ES 0   NQ +5
(NQ is down 10 point in 20 minutes after we Long, so we CUT
LOSS QUICKLY)
    LOSS = -$250
We are able to cut loss quickly and lose $250 instead of $500.

Examples: Ride with Profit
Example (1) Short 3a – 2006/1/20 (+$662.5)
```
1060120  835 ES=  -1.00 NQ=  -0.50
1060120  840 ES=  -1.00 NQ=  -2.00
1060120  845 ES=  -1.50 NQ=  -2.50
1060120  850 ES=  -1.50 NQ=  -2.50
1060120  855 ES=  -1.25 NQ=  -2.50
1060120  900 ES=  -2.50 NQ=  -4.50
1060120  905 ES=  -2.50 NQ=  -7.00
1060120  910 ES=  -2.75 NQ=  -7.50
1060120  915 ES=  -4.75 NQ= -14.00
1060120  920 ES=  -4.00 NQ= -14.00
1060120  925 ES=  -3.75 NQ= -11.50
```

```
1060120   930  ES=   -4.50  NQ= -15.00
1060120   935  ES=   -5.75  NQ= -16.50
1060120   940  ES=   -5.00  NQ= -14.50
1060120   945  ES=   -7.25  NQ= -18.00
1060120   950  ES=   -7.00  NQ= -19.00
```
1060120   955 ES=   -9.00 NQ=-24.50 ← **RC 5 Short 3a**
```
1060120 1000  ES=   -8.75  NQ= -21.00
1060120 1005  ES=   -8.50  NQ= -20.00
1060120 1010  ES=  - 9.50  NQ= -21.50
1060120 1015  ES=   -8.50  NQ= -18.00
1060120 1020  ES=  -10.25  NQ= -23.00
1060120 1025  ES=  -10.25  NQ= -23.50
1060120 1030  ES=  -10.25  NQ= -20.00
1060120 1035  ES=  -10.75  NQ= -21.00
1060120 1040  ES=  -11.00  NQ= -22.00
1060120 1045  ES=  -12.00  NQ= -25.50
1060120 1050  ES=  -14.25  NQ= -28.00
```
1060120 1055 ES= -14.50 NQ=-30.00
```
1060120 1100  ES=  -14.50  NQ= -30.00
1060120 1105  ES=  -13.25  NQ= -29.00
1060120 1110  ES=  -13.25  NQ= -30.50
1060120 1115  ES=  -13.75  NQ= -32.50
1060120 1120  ES=  -13.75  NQ= -32.50
1060120 1125  ES=  -12.25  NQ= -29.50
1060120 1130  ES=  -12.00  NQ= -30.00
1060120 1135  ES=  -12.25  NQ= -30.50
1060120 1140  ES=  -12.75  NQ= -32.00
1060120 1145  ES=  -14.75  NQ= -35.50
1060120 1150  ES=  -14.25  NQ= -43.00
```
1060120 1155 ES= -14.00 NQ=-39.00
```
1060120 1200  ES=  -14.50  NQ= -40.00
1060120 1205  ES=  -17.00  NQ= -45.00
1060120 1210  ES=  -16.50  NQ= -44.50
1060120 1215  ES=  -16.00  NQ= -42.50
1060120 1220  ES=  -16.50  NQ= -42.50
```

```
1060120 1225  ES= -15.75  NQ= -40.50
1060120 1230  ES= -15.25  NQ= -37.50
1060120 1235  ES= -16.25  NQ= -41.00
1060120 1240  ES= -15.75  NQ= -40.00
1060120 1245  ES= -16.25  NQ= -40.50
1060120 1250  ES= -16.50  NQ= -41.00
1060120 1255  ES= -17.50  NQ= -42.50
1060120 1300  ES= -17.75  NQ= -44.50
1060120 1305  ES= -18.00  NQ= -44.50
1060120 1310  ES= -17.75  NQ= -43.00
1060120 1315  ES= -17.25  NQ= -43.00
1060120 1320  ES= -17.50  NQ= -43.50
1060120 1325  ES= -17.25  NQ= -43.00
1060120 1330  ES= -15.50  NQ= -38.50
1060120 1335  ES= -16.25  NQ= -40.00
1060120 1340  ES= -16.50  NQ= -39.50
1060120 1345  ES= -16.50  NQ= -39.50
1060120 1350  ES= -16.50  NQ= -39.50
1060120 1355  ES= -17.75  NQ= -42.50
1060120 1400  ES= -18.75  NQ= -45.50
1060120 1405  ES= -18.75  NQ= -44.50
1060120 1410  ES= -17.25  NQ= -40.00
1060120 1415  ES= -18.75  NQ= -43.50
1060120 1420  ES= -19.25  NQ= -45.00
1060120 1425  ES= -20.50  NQ= -46.50
1060120 1430  ES= -20.25  NQ= -46.50
1060120 1435  ES= -20.25  NQ= -47.50
1060120 1440  ES= -21.50  NQ= -53.50
1060120 1445  ES= -22.00  NQ= -52.00
1060120 1450  ES= -22.50  NQ= -51.50
1060120 1455  ES= -21.75  NQ= -48.50
```
<u>1060120 1500 ES= -22.25 NQ= -51.00</u> ← **RC 5 Close**
```
1060120 1505  ES= -23.00  NQ= -52.50
1060120 1510  ES= -23.25  NQ= -54.50
1060120 1515  ES= -23.75  NQ= -53.50
```

Explanation:

     09:55   ES -9   NQ -24.5
     10:55   ES -14.5   NQ -30

(One hour later, the trade goes well, NQ from -24.5 down further to -30. Please note -10, -20, -30 are difficult levels, each level is significant to the advance trader for adding more contracts).

          11:55   ES -14   NQ -39

(Trade goes even better, we Short more contracts and ride with profit till the market closes).

*Please note, you have to compute a new breakeven stop for all Short positions, and then move all stops to the new breakeven stop. So, if the market goes up, you can still breakeven, instead of turning a profit into a loss.

Example (2) Short 1a – 2002/1/29 (+$1700)

     1020129   835   ES=   0.00   NQ=   5.50
     1020129   840   ES= -0.75   NQ=   4.50
     1020129   845   ES=   0.25   NQ= 11.00
     1020129   850   ES=   0.25   NQ=   9.50
     1020129   855   ES=   1.75   NQ= 13.00
     1020129   900   ES= -0.50   NQ=   9.50
     1020129   905   ES=   0.00   NQ= 12.00
     1020129   910   ES= -2.00   NQ=   7.00 ← **RC 5 Short 1a**
     1020129   915   ES= -3.50   NQ=   1.00
     1020129   920   ES= -3.50   NQ=   2.00
     1020129   925   ES= -4.75   NQ= - 2.00
     1020129   930   ES= -6.00   NQ= -6.00
     1020129   935   ES= -6.50   NQ= -4.00
     1020129   940   ES= -7.25   NQ= -6.00
     1020129   945   ES= -6.75   NQ= -2.00
     1020129   950   ES= -6.75   NQ= -2.00
     1020129   955   ES= -6.50   NQ= -4.00
     1020129 1000   ES= -9.25   NQ= -12.50
     1020129 1005   ES= -10.00   NQ= -10.50
     1020129 1010   ES= -12.25   NQ= -16.50

```
1020129 1015  ES= -12.00   NQ= -15.50
1020129 1020  ES= -15.25   NQ= -21.50
1020129 1025  ES= -15.00   NQ= -20.00
1020129 1030  ES= -14.75   NQ= -17.50
1020129 1035  ES= -15.50   NQ= -20.50
1020129 1040  ES= -15.75   NQ= -21.00
1020129 1045  ES= -15.25   NQ= -18.50
1020129 1050  ES= -15.50   NQ= -17.50
1020129 1055  ES= -16.25   NQ= -18.50
1020129 1100  ES= -17.00   NQ= -24.00
1020129 1105  ES= -18.75   NQ= -30.50
1020129 1110  ES= -20.75   NQ= -34.00
1020129 1115  ES= -19.75   NQ= -30.00
1020129 1120  ES= -20.00   NQ= -30.50
1020129 1125  ES= -23.25   NQ= -39.00
1020129 1130  ES= -24.25   NQ= -42.50
1020129 1135  ES= -23.50   NQ= -39.50
1020129 1140  ES= -23.25   NQ= -38.00
1020129 1145  ES= -21.75   NQ= -34.00
1020129 1150  ES= -22.75   NQ= -37.50
1020129 1155  ES= -22.00   NQ= -36.00
1020129 1200  ES= -21.75   NQ= -34.00
1020129 1205  ES= -23.00   NQ= -37.00
1020129 1210  ES= -23.00   NQ= -38.00
1020129 1215  ES= -24.75   NQ= -40.50
1020129 1220  ES= -25.00   NQ= -41.00
1020129 1225  ES= -24.75   NQ= -40.50
1020129 1230  ES= -21.75   NQ= -33.50
1020129 1235  ES= -22.00   NQ= -34.00
1020129 1240  ES= -22.25   NQ= -34.00
1020129 1245  ES= -21.25   NQ= -27.00
1020129 1250  ES= -23.00   NQ= -30.50
1020129 1255  ES= -23.25   NQ= -32.00
1020129 1300  ES= -23.25   NQ= -34.00
1020129 1305  ES= -23.75   NQ= -34.50
```

1020129 1310 ES= -25.00   NQ= -38.00
1020129 1315 ES= -25.75   NQ= -41.50
1020129 1320 ES= -27.50   NQ= -44.00
1020129 1325 ES= -29.50   NQ= -46.00
1020129 1330 ES= -28.75   NQ= -43.50
1020129 1335 ES= -29.00   NQ= -45.50
1020129 1340 ES= -33.00   NQ= -55.00
1020129 1345 ES= -32.25   NQ= -52.50
1020129 1350 ES= -31.00   NQ= -49.50
1020129 1355 ES= -31.00   NQ= -50.00
1020129 1400 ES= -31.25   NQ= -50.00
1020129 1405 ES= -34.25   NQ= -54.50
1020129 1410 ES= -35.75   NQ= -58.50
1020129 1415 ES= -35.00   NQ= -57.00
1020129 1420 ES= -35.50   NQ= -55.50
1020129 1425 ES= -34.25   NQ= -50.00
1020129 1430 ES= -35.25   NQ= -53.50
1020129 1435 ES= -35.00   NQ= -53.00
1020129 1440 ES= -36.25   NQ= -56.00
1020129 1445 ES= -35.25   NQ= -51.00
1020129 1450 ES= -36.00   NQ= -49.50
1020129 1455 ES= -34.00   NQ= -46.50
1020129 1500 ES= -36.00 NQ=-48.00 ← **RC 5 Close**
1020129 1505 ES= -36.50   NQ= -45.50
1020129 1510 ES= -36.00   NQ= -44.50
1020129 1515 ES= -35.25   NQ= -42.50

Explanation:

    09:10   ES -2   NQ +7
    09:40   ES -7.25   NQ -6

(Trades go well, we Short and NQ goes from +ve to –ve, we can add more contracts and ride with profit. Remember to calculate and move to a new breakeven stop for the trade).

Example (3) Long 4a – 2003/3/17 (+$1025)

```
1030317   835  ES=  -7.75  NQ= -14.50
1030317   840  ES=  -5.75  NQ= -10.00
1030317   845  ES=  -7.50  NQ= -14.50
1030317   850  ES=  -4.50  NQ=  -9.50
1030317   855  ES=  -1.25  NQ=  -3.00
1030317   900  ES=   4.25  NQ=   6.00
1030317   905  ES=  -0.50  NQ=   1.50
1030317   910  ES=   0.25  NQ=   5.00
1030317   915  ES=   0.25  NQ=   5.50
```

1030317   920 ES=   7.00 NQ= 15.50 ← RC 5 Long 4a

```
1030317   925  ES=   5.75  NQ=  12.50
1030317   930  ES=   8.00  NQ=  15.00
1030317   935  ES=  11.75  NQ=  22.50
1030317   940  ES=  13.00  NQ=  23.50
1030317   945  ES=  15.00  NQ=  33.00
```

1030317   950 ES= 19.75 NQ= 40.50

```
1030317   955  ES=  15.50  NQ=  32.50
1030317  1000  ES=  16.50  NQ=  32.00
1030317  1005  ES=  19.00  NQ=  36.50
1030317  1010  ES=  20.00  NQ=  40.00
1030317  1015  ES=  21.50  NQ=  38.00
1030317  1020  ES=  18.25  NQ=  31.50
1030317  1025  ES=  16.75  NQ=  27.00
1030317  1030  ES=  16.75  NQ=  26.50
1030317  1035  ES=  16.75  NQ=  30.00
1030317  1040  ES=  15.50  NQ=  28.50
1030317  1045  ES=  16.50  NQ=  30.00
1030317  1050  ES=  16.50  NQ=  29.00
1030317  1055  ES=  19.00  NQ=  32.50
1030317  1100  ES=  18.25  NQ=  33.50
1030317  1105  ES=  17.00  NQ=  31.00
1030317  1110  ES=  17.50  NQ=  30.50
1030317  1115  ES=  17.75  NQ=  30.50
1030317  1120  ES=  19.00  NQ=  32.50
```

1030317 1125 ES= 20.00   NQ= 33.50
1030317 1130 ES= 20.75   NQ= 33.50
1030317 1135 ES= 20.75   NQ= 34.00
1030317 1140 ES= 20.75   NQ= 34.50
1030317 1145 ES= 21.00   NQ= 35.50
1030317 1150 ES= 20.50   NQ= 35.50
1030317 1155 ES= 19.50   NQ= 34.00
1030317 1200 ES= 20.50   NQ= 34.50
1030317 1205 ES= 19.50   NQ= 31.50
1030317 1210 ES= 17.50   NQ= 28.50
1030317 1215 ES= 18.00   NQ= 29.50
1030317 1220 ES= 18.50   NQ= 30.50
1030317 1225 ES= 19.50   NQ= 32.00
1030317 1230 ES= 18.50   NQ= 31.00
1030317 1235 ES= 19.00   NQ= 34.00
1030317 1240 ES= 19.75   NQ= 34.50
1030317 1245 ES= 19.25   NQ= 33.50
1030317 1250 ES= 20.00   NQ= 34.50
1030317 1255 ES= 19.25   NQ= 34.50
1030317 1300 ES= 18.50   NQ= 32.50
1030317 1305 ES= 20.00   NQ= 34.50
1030317 1310 ES= 19.75   NQ= 34.50
1030317 1315 ES= 21.75   NQ= 37.00
1030317 1320 ES= 22.25   NQ= 38.00
1030317 1325 ES= 22.50   NQ= 38.50
1030317 1330 ES= 23.25   NQ= 39.50
1030317 1335 ES= 24.50   NQ= 41.00
1030317 1340 ES= 22.75   NQ= 38.50
1030317 1345 ES= 23.00   NQ= 38.00
1030317 1350 ES= 22.50   NQ= 37.50
1030317 1355 ES= 22.00   NQ= 36.00
1030317 1400 ES= 24.25   NQ= 38.00
1030317 1405 ES= 23.50   NQ= 37.00
1030317 1410 ES= 23.50   NQ= 37.00
1030317 1415 ES= 23.50   NQ= 36.00

```
1030317 1420  ES=  26.50  NQ=  40.50
1030317 1425  ES=  25.25  NQ=  38.50
1030317 1430  ES=  24.50  NQ=  37.50
1030317 1435  ES=  24.25  NQ=  36.00
1030317 1440  ES=  25.50  NQ=  38.50
1030317 1445  ES=  27.25  NQ=  41.00
1030317 1450  ES=  27.50  NQ=  40.50
1030317 1455  ES=  28.00  NQ=  39.50
1030317 1500  ES=  27.50  NQ=  41.50
```
1030317 1505 ES= 26.50 NQ= 36.50 ← **RC 5 Close**
```
1030317 1510  ES=  26.00  NQ=  36.00
1030317 1515  ES=  26.75  NQ=  36.00
```

Explanation:

```
09:20    ES +7        NQ +15.5
09:50    ES +19.75    NQ +40.5
```
(Half hour after we Long, NQ is up 25 points and ES is up too. We can Long more contracts and ride with profit).

Example (4) Long 4a – 2006/1/3 (+$637.5)
```
1060103  835  ES=  7.00  NQ=  10.50
1060103  840  ES=  6.50  NQ=   7.50
1060103  845  ES=  7.25  NQ=  10.00
1060103  850  ES=  6.00  NQ=  10.00
1060103  855  ES=  5.00  NQ=   8.00
1060103  900  ES=  6.25  NQ=   9.00
1060103  905  ES=  4.75  NQ=   7.50
1060103  910  ES=  3.00  NQ=   4.00
1060103  915  ES=  2.75  NQ=  -0.50
1060103  920  ES=  3.25  NQ=   1.00
1060103  925  ES=  1.50  NQ=  -3.00
1060103  930  ES=  1.25  NQ=  -4.00
1060103  935  ES=  0.50  NQ=  -4.00
1060103  940  ES= -0.75  NQ=  -7.50
1060103  945  ES=  0.75  NQ=  -3.50
```

1060103	950	ES=	1.25	NQ=	-2.00
1060103	955	ES=	1.25	NQ=	-1.50
1060103	1000	ES=	1.50	NQ=	-1.00
1060103	1005	ES=	1.25	NQ=	-1.00
1060103	1010	ES=	1.75	NQ=	0.00
1060103	1015	ES=	1.75	NQ=	-0.50
1060103	1020	ES=	2.50	NQ=	1.00
1060103	1025	ES=	2.50	NQ=	0.50
1060103	1030	ES=	2.50	NQ=	1.00
1060103	1035	ES=	3.00	NQ=	1.50
1060103	1040	ES=	3.50	NQ=	4.50
1060103	1045	ES=	3.75	NQ=	4.50
1060103	1050	ES=	3.25	NQ=	4.00
1060103	1055	ES=	3.25	NQ=	4.00
1060103	1100	ES=	4.75	NQ=	7.50
1060103	1105	ES=	3.75	NQ=	6.50
1060103	1110	ES=	5.25	NQ=	10.00
1060103	1115	ES=	5.00	NQ=	9.00
1060103	1120	ES=	4.00	NQ=	7.50
1060103	1125	ES=	4.00	NQ=	8.50
1060103	1130	ES=	3.75	NQ=	7.50
1060103	1135	ES=	3.50	NQ=	8.00
1060103	1140	ES=	3.75	NQ=	7.50
1060103	1145	ES=	3.50	NQ=	6.50
1060103	1150	ES=	5.25	NQ=	8.50
1060103	1155	ES=	4.75	NQ=	8.50
1060103	1200	ES=	4.50	NQ=	7.50
1060103	1205	ES=	4.75	NQ=	8.00
1060103	1210	ES=	4.75	NQ=	8.00
1060103	1215	ES=	4.00	NQ=	6.00
1060103	1220	ES=	4.25	NQ=	6.50
1060103	1225	ES=	3.50	NQ=	5.50
1060103	1230	ES=	4.00	NQ=	6.00
1060103	1235	ES=	3.75	NQ=	5.50
1060103	1240	ES=	4.25	NQ=	6.50

```
1060103  1245  ES=   4.75  NQ=    7.50
1060103  1250  ES=   5.00  NQ=    8.50
1060103  1255  ES=   5.00  NQ=    7.50
1060103  1300  ES=   4.50  NQ=    7.50
```
1060103 1305 ES=   8.50 NQ= 14.00 ← **RC 5 Long 4a**
```
1060103  1310  ES=  10.00  NQ=  18.00
1060103  1315  ES=  10.50  NQ=  20.50
1060103  1320  ES=  12.00  NQ=  22.50
1060103  1325  ES=  11.00  NQ=  21.50
1060103  1330  ES=  12.25  NQ=  24.00
1060103  1335  ES=  14.75  NQ=  28.50
```
1060103 1340 ES= 15.00 NQ= 30.00
```
1060103  1345  ES=  16.00  NQ=  31.50
1060103  1350  ES=  16.25  NQ=  30.00
1060103  1355  ES=  16.00  NQ=  31.00
1060103  1400  ES=  16.50  NQ=  31.00
1060103  1405  ES=  20.25  NQ=  39.50
1060103  1410  ES=  21.25  NQ=  41.00
1060103  1415  ES=  21.50  NQ=  42.00
1060103  1420  ES=  21.00  NQ=  41.00
1060103  1425  ES=  21.00  NQ=  41.50
1060103  1430  ES=  21.50  NQ=  42.50
1060103  1435  ES=  23.50  NQ=  44.50
1060103  1440  ES=  23.25  NQ=  42.50
1060103  1445  ES=  23.00  NQ=  42.50
1060103  1450  ES=  22.25  NQ=  40.00
1060103  1455  ES=  21.50  NQ=  38.50
```
1060103 1500 ES= 22.75 NQ= 38.50 ← **RC 5 Close**
```
1060103  1505  ES=  23.25  NQ=  37.50
1060103  1510  ES=  23.50  NQ=  39.50
1060103  1515  ES=  22.00  NQ=  40.50
```

Explanation:

13:05	ES +8.50	NQ +14
13:40	ES +15	NQ +30

(Thirty Five minutes after Long, NQ is up more than 10 points, Long more contracts and ride with profit).

Example (5) Short 4b – 2002/6/3 (+$1625)

1020603	835	ES=	2.75	NQ=	-1.50	
1020603	840	ES=	2.75	NQ=	-1.50	
1020603	845	ES=	2.00	NQ=	-3.00	
1020603	850	ES=	2.75	NQ=	-3.50	
1020603	855	ES=	3.00	NQ=	-3.00	
1020603	900	ES=	2.75	NQ=	-5.00	
1020603	905	ES=	6.50	NQ=	5.50	
1020603	**910**	**ES=**	**5.75**	**NQ=**	**2.00**	← RC 5 Short 4b
1020603	915	ES=	0.50	NQ=	-8.50	
1020603	**920**	**ES=**	**-1.75**	**NQ=**	**-13.50**	
1020603	925	ES=	-2.50	NQ=	-15.00	
1020603	930	ES=	-2.25	NQ=	-15.50	
1020603	935	ES=	-3.00	NQ=	-18.50	
1020603	940	ES=	-5.75	NQ=	-21.50	
1020603	945	ES=	-6.50	NQ=	-26.50	
1020603	950	ES=	-6.00	NQ=	-22.50	
1020603	955	ES=	-5.75	NQ=	-21.50	
1020603	1000	ES=	-8.00	NQ=	-25.00	
1020603	1005	ES=	-9.25	NQ=	-27.50	
1020603	1010	ES=	-8.75	NQ=	-26.50	
1020603	1015	ES=	-7.50	NQ=	-25.50	
1020603	1020	ES=	-8.00	NQ=	-24.50	
1020603	1025	ES=	-6.75	NQ=	-23.00	
1020603	1030	ES=	-7.25	NQ=	-24.00	
1020603	1035	ES=	-7.50	NQ=	-25.50	
1020603	1040	ES=	-7.50	NQ=	-24.50	
1020603	1045	ES=	-7.75	NQ=	-25.00	
1020603	1050	ES=	-8.25	NQ=	-26.00	
1020603	1055	ES=	-10.00	NQ=	-28.50	
1020603	1100	ES=	-9.00	NQ=	-26.00	
1020603	1105	ES=	-10.25	NQ=	-26.00	

```
1020603 1110  ES= -12.75  NQ= -30.50
1020603 1115  ES= -12.50  NQ= -29.50
1020603 1120  ES= -11.25  NQ= -28.50
1020603 1125  ES= -12.25  NQ= -32.50
1020603 1130  ES= -11.25  NQ= -32.00
1020603 1135  ES= -10.00  NQ= -29.00
1020603 1140  ES= -10.50  NQ= -29.50
1020603 1145  ES=  -8.50  NQ= -27.00
1020603 1150  ES=  -8.75  NQ= -27.50
1020603 1155  ES=  -9.25  NQ= -28.00
1020603 1200  ES=  -9.50  NQ= -26.50
1020603 1205  ES=  -8.00  NQ= -24.00
1020603 1210  ES=  -9.25  NQ= -26.00
1020603 1215  ES=  -9.00  NQ= -24.50
1020603 1220  ES=  -9.50  NQ= -26.00
1020603 1225  ES= -11.25  NQ= -29.50
1020603 1230  ES= -11.25  NQ= -29.00
1020603 1235  ES= -13.00  NQ= -33.00
1020603 1240  ES= -12.25  NQ= -32.00
1020603 1245  ES= -10.50  NQ= -29.00
1020603 1250  ES= -10.00  NQ= -28.50
1020603 1255  ES=  -9.00  NQ= -24.50
1020603 1300  ES=  -9.25  NQ= -26.50
1020603 1305  ES=  -9.25  NQ= -26.50
1020603 1310  ES=  -9.00  NQ= -27.00
1020603 1315  ES= -10.00  NQ= -29.00
1020603 1320  ES=  -9.00  NQ= -27.00
1020603 1325  ES=  -9.75  NQ= -27.00
1020603 1330  ES=  -9.00  NQ= -26.50
1020603 1335  ES=  -8.50  NQ= -25.00
1020603 1340  ES=  -8.75  NQ= -26.00
1020603 1345  ES=  -7.75  NQ= -22.50
1020603 1350  ES=  -8.25  NQ= -24.50
1020603 1355  ES= -10.00  NQ= -28.00
1020603 1400  ES= -10.75  NQ= -30.50
```

```
1020603 1405  ES= -11.00  NQ= -31.50
1020603 1410  ES=  -9.50  NQ= -30.00
1020603 1415  ES= -10.00  NQ= -30.00
1020603 1420  ES= -11.00  NQ= -33.00
1020603 1425  ES= -11.25  NQ= -35.00
1020603 1430  ES= -12.75  NQ= -36.50
1020603 1435  ES= -13.25  NQ= -36.00
1020603 1440  ES= -16.75  NQ= -39.50
1020603 1445  ES= -19.00  NQ= -42.00
1020603 1450  ES= -21.50  NQ= -44.50
1020603 1455  ES= -24.50  NQ= -49.00
```
1020603 1500 ES= -26.75 NQ=-48.00 ← **RC 5 Close**
```
1020603 1505  ES= -26.25  NQ= -45.00
1020603 1510  ES= -26.75  NQ= -43.50
1020603 1515  ES= -25.50  NQ= -44.50
```

Explanation:

09:10	ES +5.75	NQ +2
09:20	ES -1.75	NQ -13.5

(Just 10 minutes after the Short entry, NQ is down over 10 points and from +ve to -ve. Short more contracts and ride with profits). These examples illustrate how to master the NQ indicator during trading and learn to cut loss quickly, to ride with profit or to average up and add more contracts. Practice a lot and you do would better than RC 5.

16

What is Trading?

I f the positioning of this topic suggests that it is a result of a typesetting error, let me clarify: the positioning is deliberate.

Allow me to explain.

Your approach to trading should not be any different from the approach of a diligent participant in a business, profession or sports. If you were a businessman, you would like to run a profitable business. If you were a professional, you would like to learn continuously and do a good job of the work at hand, right? If you were a sportsman, you would practice relentlessly and keep improving to win. Trading is no different. Play a good game, never mind the result, and you will have no regrets. Just do your best and enjoy the process of doing it.

I trade with passion and perseverance. I just want to give it my best shot. If I succeed, I will be happy. If not, I will not have regrets since I have done my best.

Now, to answer the question: what is trading? We are not looking for a definition here. Trading is both interesting and challenging. Otherwise, I would not have written this book and you would not be reading this. But remember, though trading is part of life, life is much more than just trading. All of us have short lives and have too much to do. Enjoy your family and friends when they are around. Someday they will be gone. If you live each day as if it is your last day, you would be consistently doing only what is really meaningful and would not touch superficialities. Before we are gone, let's do our best to make it a better world.

Having said that, when you trade, remember the three cardinal rules which we have tried to drill into your mind.

A) **Follow the trend** and countertrend (by using your trading edge indicators).

B) **Cut loss quickly** with a protective stop (by using your trading edge indicators).

C) **Ride with profit** (with your trading edge indicators to guide you).

To be a consistent trader, find your trading edge and practice hard. Trade with confidence and a relaxed mindset.

Also, just because you cannot put down this book, that doesn't mean you should jump into trading tomorrow. Trading is not for everyone. One can find other interesting things and challenges to take on. Maybe if you indulge in hobbies that help you achieve a relaxed mindset, you could prove to be a better trader. I read poems, which reflect the thoughts of ancient times, to keep my mind relaxed. You might be interested in something else. It doesn't matter, as long as it is a passion and you are pursuing it actively. It will help you trade better.

Anyone who has read this book would know how NQ (symbol of Nasdaq futures) works as one of the key indicators for trading in ES futures. Those who know my systems know how I have a set of parameters besides ES and NQ, which is unique for the RC system. The parameters I use in RC systems are @ ES.D, @ NQ.D, $ ADVQ, $ DECLQ, $ DJI and $ IVX. The first four symbols are very important. $ ADVQ and $ DECLQ point to the number of advancing and declining shares of Nasdaq. Many traders use $ ADV or $ DEC (advancing and declining ES shares). Some may even use the advancing or declining shares of NYSE (New York Stock Exchange shares).

Some dishonest traders claim that *they* have discovered certain unique features used in the RC system. I am least worried as imitations will never succeed over originals. Anyone can be a successful trader or succeed in any endeavor, if he is honest and if he works hard. My advice to you: whatever you want to do in trading, do some original research and homework. Don't ever give up on hard work and honesty. They will take you very far. Good luck.

Appendix 1
How to Set up TradeStation and Workspace for RC 5 System

1) Select "Programs" from the Windows "Start" menu, and click "TradeStation 8.1".
2) The operation screen appears.
3) Enter the "User Name" and "Password" and click "Logon" if you want to work online (Figure 1.1A.)
4) Click "Work offline" if you want to work offline.

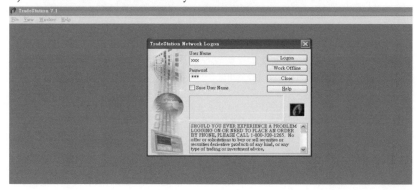

Figure 1.1A.

Setting up a "Chart Analysis"

1) Click the "Chart Analysis" icon in the shortcut bar. (Figure 1.2A.)

Figure 1.2A.

A chart will be displayed afterwards. (Figure 1.3A.)

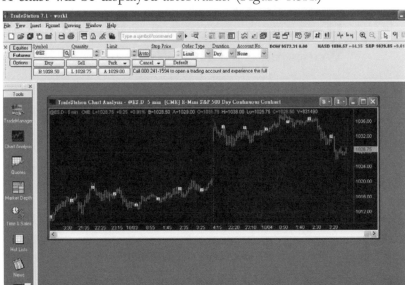

Figure 1.3A.

2) Click "Format" in the menu bar. A list will be displayed.

3) Choose "Symbol" from the list. (Figure 1.4A.)

Figure 1.4A.

4) A "Format Symbol" window will be displayed. Enter the information as follows:
   a. Symbol: **@ES.D**
   b. Select interval: **Intra-day**
   c. Interval setting: **5 Minute Bar**
   d. For volume, use: **Trade Vol**
   e. For bar building: **Session Hour**
   f. Last date: **click the red box (with today's date next to it) at the bottom of the combo box**
   g. Enter **1** and choose "**year back**" in the combo box
   h. Subgraph: **One**
   i. Time Zone: **Local**
   j. Click OK

A chart showing the @ES.D data will be displayed.

5) Click "Insert" in the menu bar. A list will be displayed.
6) Choose "Symbol" from the list.
7) Enter "**$DJI**" in the "Insert symbol" window and click "Plot".

Figure 1.5A.

8) Click "Format" in the menu bar and choose "Symbol" from the list displayed.
9) Click the row of "**$DJI**" and click "Format".
10) In the "Format symbol", click the combo box of Sub-graph and choose "**Hidden**". Click OK.
11) Repeat step 8 – 11 with symbol "**$IVX**".
12) Repeat step 8 – 11 with symbol "**@NQ.D**".

A chart with all the necessary data will be displayed.

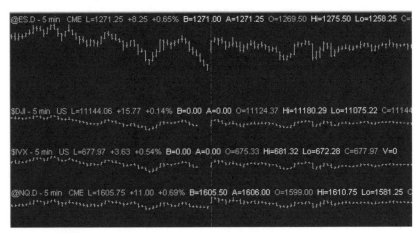

Figure 1.6A.

Importing EasyLanguage Document

1) Click "File" in the menu bar.
2) Choose "Import/Export EasyLanguage ..." from the list displayed. (Figure 1.7A.)

Figure 1.7A.

3) An "Import/Export Wizard" window will be displayed.

4) Choose "Import EasyLanguage File (ELD, ELS/ELA)" and click "Next". (Figure 1.8A.)

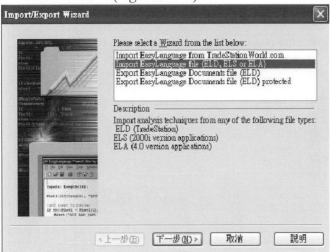

Figure 1.8A.

5) Click "Browse…". (Figure 1.9A.)

Figure 1.9A.

6) Go to the directory containing the EasyLanguage document hat you wanted to import and click the document.
7) Click "Open".
8) Click "Next".

9) Click "Next" when the Import Wizard shows the analysis types contained in the importing file. (Figure 1.10A.)

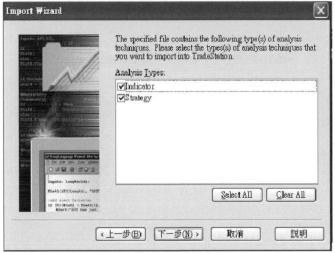

Figure 1.10A.

10) Click "Next" when the Import Wizard shows the analysis techniques contained in the importing file.
11) Click "Finish".

Inserting Strategy to the Chart

1) Click "Insert" in the menu bar.
2) Choose "Strategy ..." from the list displayed.
3) A list of available strategies is displayed. Click the one you want to insert to your chart and click "OK". (Figure 1.11A.)

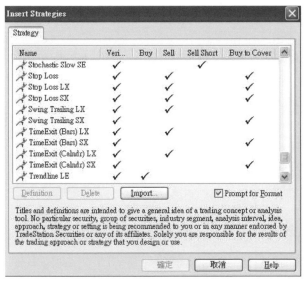

Figure 1.11A.

4) "Calculating Analysis Techniques and/or Strategies ..." will appear on the chart. (Figure 1.12A.)

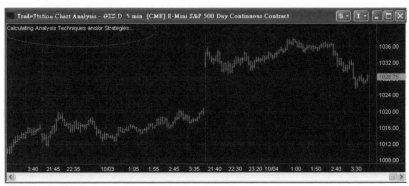

Figure 1.12A.

5) When these words no longer appear on the chart, you can view the performance report of the applied strategy.

Viewing the performance report of a strategy

1) Click "View" in the menu bar.
2) Choose "Strategy Performance Report" from the list displayed. (Figure 1.13A.)

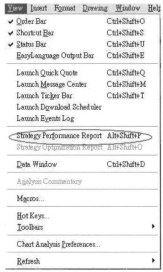

Figure 1.13A.

3) A strategy performance report will be shown a while later.

Save a Workspace

1) Click "File" in the menu bar.
2) Click "Save workspace as".
3) Enter the name you want the workspace to have.
4) Click "OK".

Exit TradeStation

1) Click the "Cross" at the top-right corner of TradeStation. (Figure 1.14A.)

Figure 1.14A

Open Print Log

1. Click "View" in the menu bar.
2. Choose "EasyLanguage Output Bar" from the list displayed.
3. You should see the following appear in the screen. Click "Print Log". (Figure 1.15A)

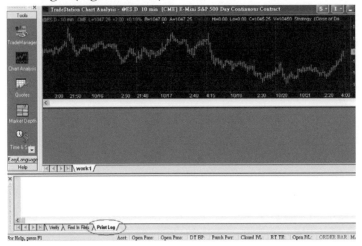

Figure 1.15A.

Source: Created by TradeStation

In order to guarantee all the settings are done correctly, please do the following. If you get the exact result as listed in the table below, this indicates that your setting is correct. Remember, the following steps are only for checking if your settings are correct or not.

1) Click "Format" in the menu bar and choose "Symbol" from the list displayed.
2) Click the row of "**@ES.D**" and click "Format".
3) A "Format Symbol" window will be displayed. Change the information to the following:

   a. Last Date: (today's date)

   b. Enter **1** and choose "**years back**" in the combo box

   c. Click OK

4) Repeat step 1–3 with symbol **$DJI.**
5) Repeat step 1–3 with symbol **$IVX.**
6) Repeat step 1–3 with symbol **@NQ.D.**

Appendix 2
How to Set up Autotrade
in TradeStation

In order to perform autotrade, the symbol used for data 1, i.e. @ES.D for continuous contract shown in appendix A, should be changed according to the month of trade, e.g. ESM06.D implies trade for the month of June 2006 (Figure 2.1A to 2.3A). Finally, choose "Close" (Figure 2.4A). The new chart would be shown. If the trade is performed in June, 2007, the symbol should be ESM07.D. Please consult TradeStation for more details.

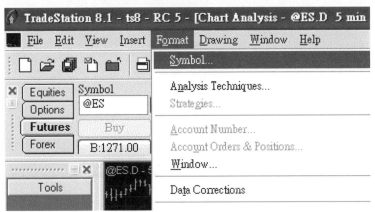

Figure 2.1A.

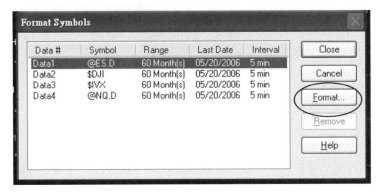

Figure 2.2A.

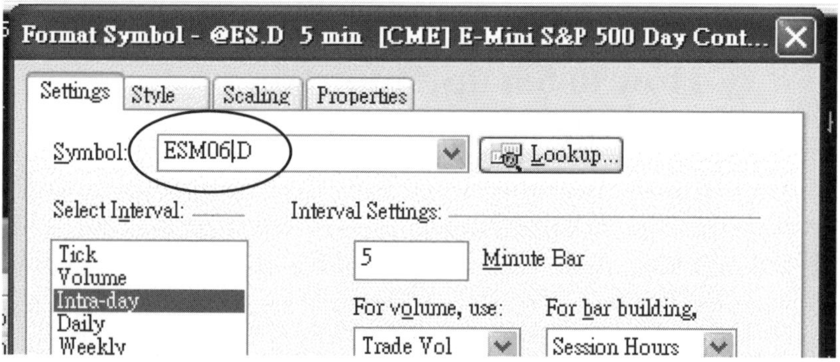

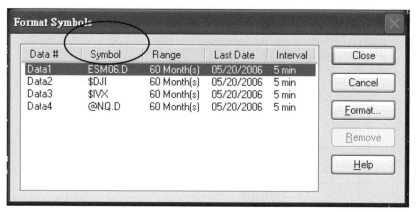

Figure 2.3A.

Figure 2.4A.

To view your account status, show view the order as shown in Figure 2.5A. After you open the accounts with TradeStation (TS) the account numbers should appear on every workspace in the location marked as (a) in Figure 2.6A. If no account is visible, you should contact TS to activate the accounts.

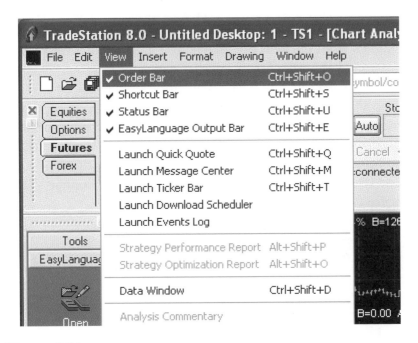

Figure 2.5A.

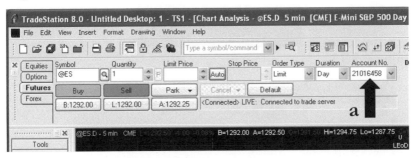

Figure 2.6A.

Set up the workspace and insert your trading strategy (see Figure 2.7A.). While the workspace is opened, click "Format" then "Strategies" (see Figure 2.8A.). When the "Format Analysis Techniques & Strategies" window opens, click on the "Strategies" tab (see item b in Figure 2.9A.). At the bottom of the window check "Generate strategy order for display in TradeManager's Strategy Order tab" (see item c in Figure 2.9A.). Also check

"Automate execution using" and select one of your account numbers from the next box (see item d in Figure 2.9A.). When a pop-up box appears, click "I agree". Change the next box "Account with confirmation", to "Off" (see item e in Figure 2.9A.). When a pop-up box appears, click "I agree". Next click on "Properties" (see item f in Figure 2.10A.) and a window will pop up titled, "Strategies Properties for all Strategies on this chart". Click on the "General" tab. On the bottom right box enter the number of contracts you want to trade under "Fixed Shares/Contracts" (see Figure 2.11A.). Click OK.

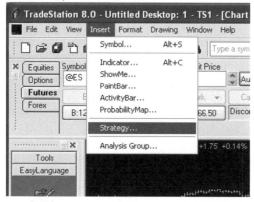

Figure 2.7A.

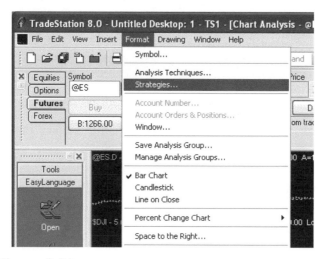

Figure 2.8A.

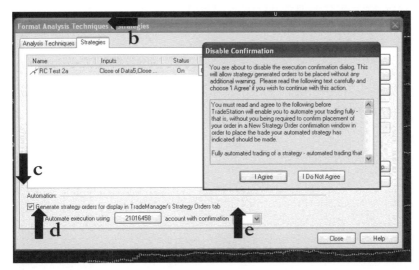

Figure 2.9A.

Figure 2.10A.

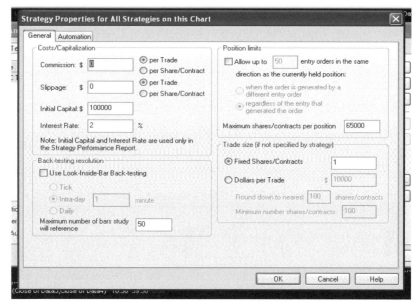

Figure 2.11A.

Source: Created by TradeStation

Finally click "Close" on the window "Format Analysis Techniques & Strategies". If you have done everything correctly and you are using TradeStation 8.1, a little "SA" will appear on the top left corner of the workspace. When you put the mouse on top of the "SA" it will show a message "Strategy automation. Automate execution using account (your account number) with confirmation OFF".

Index